P9-DLZ-110

BY
THOMAS STERLING

STANLEY'S WAY

Thomas Sterling

STANLEY'S WAY

A Sentimental Journey
Through
Central Africa

NEW YORK ATHENEUM PUBLISHERS

1960

Copyright © 1960 by Thomas Sterling
All rights reserved
Library of Congress catalog card number 60-7780
Printed in the United States of America by
The Murray Printing Company, Forge Village, Massachusetts
Bound by H. Wolff, New York
First American Edition

A portion of this book originally appeared in
The New Yorker, in different form

TO

P. M. STERLING

IN BELATED GRATITUDE FOR HER SUPPORT AND NURTURE

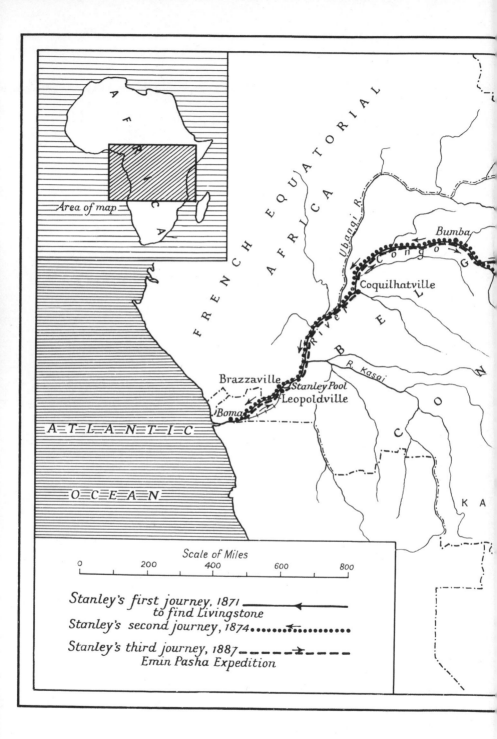

Area of map

F R E N C H   E Q U A T O R I A L   A F R I C A

Ubangi R.

Congo

Bumba

Coquilhatville

River

R. Kasai

B E L G I A N   C O N G O

Brazzaville

Stanley Pool

Leopoldville

Boma

A T L A N T I C

O C E A N

K A

Scale of Miles

0   200   400   600   800

Stanley's first journey, 1871
to find Livingstone

Stanley's second journey, 1874 ••••••••

Stanley's third journey, 1887 – – – – →
Emin Pasha Expedition

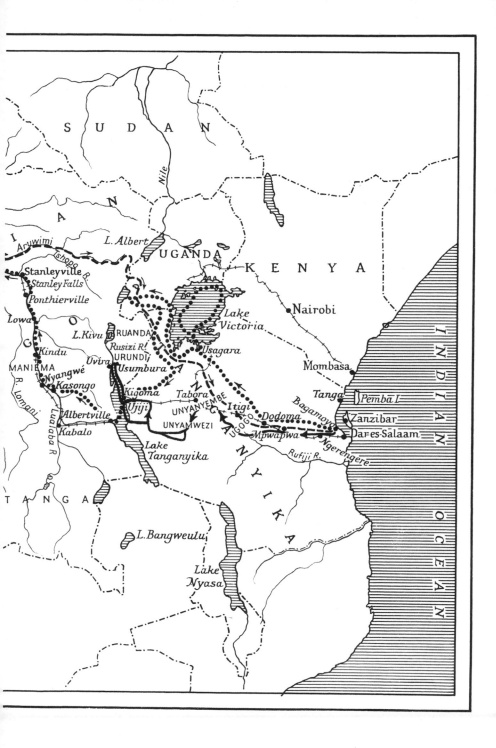

STANLEY'S WAY

"Good-bye, good-bye! Come again soon. Come
any time. And please, please, don't write a book
about us!"

*A group of Africans in Uganda saying farewell
to a European friend*

INTRODUCTION

WESTERN America in the 1920s was ruled by the standards of the previous century, in which it was born. So that for me, as a child, finding Henry Stanley's works on the bookshelf was as much in the pattern of things as watching, through tears, my grandmother scrubbing my feet in the kitchen sink with a stiff brush, or listening to my mother's stories of Wyoming.

Those books furnished austere dreams of romance and adventure which I did not then suspect were hopelessly anachronistic. The world was no longer divided between the savage and the civilized, as it was in Stanley's time. We were destined to be one or the other together.

Then in Rome, thirty years later, I came across a copy of *How I Found Livingstone* and all the old nostalgia came back, nearly ruined by the certain knowledge that it was ridiculous. I had already been to Africa once and I knew that one often met people a good deal more cultivated than oneself. Adventure, in the patronizing sense that I had intended as a child, was out of the question. Of course there is still a great wilderness in Africa but in these days it seems chiefly inhabited by White Hunters on safari—great leathery boys who mean no harm to anyone. The real jungle is all around us and there is no reason to go looking for it on other continents or even on other streets.

But I thought it would be interesting to tell the story of this young American explorer again, just because it takes us back to our beginnings. I thought, also, that it would be more amusing if it were told against the background of the places

9

Stanley originally saw and the people he met—as these have changed enormously. So I left Italy a few months later and followed his route through the dark continent from East to West. I wasn't looking for savages and, with two exceptions, both European, found none.

Unless otherwise specified, all amounts of money mentioned historically here have their original values. If you wish to transpose these, the dollar from 1870 to the turn of the century was worth about three times what it is now, the pound about five times. These are conservative estimates and often misleading, which is the chief reason I have not transposed them myself. Clothing was relatively much more expensive than it is now, food less. A man could be rich on a few hundred pounds or even dollars a year, simply because there were so many people who were very poor.

CHAPTER ONE

HE wore walking shoes, high stockings, a pair of khaki shorts which he claimed to have got in North Africa during the war, a shirt to match, and a slouch American hat with an unobtrusive but genuine flamingo feather in the band. He picked off the hat at the doorway and came into the dining-room, peering through shadows until he saw me. The room was silent beneath discreet luncheon noises as the merciless sun banged against the shutters. He put his hat and the *Tanganyika Standard* on an extra chair and sat down, smiling like a death's head. He asked if I had got my kit together, using that word, and I said that I had managed to find a few things in Nairobi and would get more here, in Dar-es-Salaam. He nodded and summoned a waiter, from whom he ordered courses by their number on the menu, so as not to tax the man's English. I found it hard to remember that he was a British Journalist and not a seasoned White Hunter; he was so carefully threadbare and had the unshakeable poise of a man who has been sitting on verandas in bare knees for years. Of course he had been to Africa before, three or four times.

"You know," he said, leaning forward. "You don't have to get wool or cotton stockings. For a few shillings more you can buy nylon. Stay up by themselves, too. No garters."

It was for things like this that I valued his growing friend-ship. He had helped me get a room in the hotel and had done several other little favours which were the sort no one feels obliged to do.

We discussed a map, which he had brought from London and was going to lend me. It traced the journeys of Burton and Speke, Speke and Grant, Livingstone, Stanley, and Cameron. He was worried that his Burton and Speke line was off in one particular. As he was writing a history of early explorations in East Africa this was important. He knew that I was interested in Stanley and thought I might know something about the other routes. Suddenly, I looked to him, across a plate of dead English vegetables, and asked if he weren't pleased to be back in Africa.

"Oh my God, yes. I feel so free."

He went on, then, to speak of other things but the word 'free' was repeated several times, even when another might have served as well or better, and I could see that it preoccupied him. He may have been celebrating his escape from the small quarrels of European life, or simply from troubles at home. In any case it was clear that being here was almost a physical pleasure for him—the muscular release of an animal turned out of a cage.

"Of course," he said, at last, "I wouldn't live here. I don't see how I could. But . . ." He ordered number 6, the diced mangoes, instead of number 5, the pudding.

I, too, was glad to be in Africa, but not for the same reason. I'd been here before, in the Sudan, and something—the tremendous sky, the great distances or the clear light—had caught me. As Miss Dinesen said, ". . . everything you see is made for greatness and freedom and unequalled nobility." It was much like falling in love, in the beginning an unreasonable attachment which is all the stronger for being so.

Also, in Central Africa, one may step back in time. Not a great distance, it is true; fifty years, usually, seventy-five or eighty at the most (from October 1958). Every now and then one may see the nineteenth century caught in a gesture or a word, life-like, as a fly in amber. Sometimes it is like going through a drawer of old family photographs—those enduring portraits printed on cardboard, frayed at the corners and

12

smelling of must. Here are the Norcrosses and the Stanleys and Mapeses, rigid, determined figures, a bit suspicious of the camera, vigorous and self-assured. The colour of the skin and the clothing is different, but the expression is the same.

Here, in a sense, our own grandparents are reliving their lives in the midst of outrageous contradiction and social change. I mean *our* grandparents, for there is something peculiarly American about these people. They are undergoing the revolution—not always political—which changed the face of the United States just after the Civil War in the period now called Victorian. Before that, our land was a wilderness; afterwards . . . We know what came after, but seeing it all again in Central Africa is like reading a historical novel whose last chapters are known. The characters haven't yet gone through the triumphs and disasters, marriages and divorces, which the plot has in store for them. And there is also just a chance—not a very good one—that it isn't the book we know at all but a sequel . . . something with a happier ending.

Here are the skilled craftsmen, the ward bosses, the labour leaders, the women fighting for emancipation—even to list them sounds like a line of Whitman's; and, more important, here is a great mass of people stirring of its own accord, gathering in cities, going to schools, holding meetings, asserting its independence in every way and shrugging off the hand of custom. This is not always wise; sometimes it is very stupid. It may all lead to disaster. But you can't help feeling, watching people who seem to have stepped out of oleographs, that you are in better company than you are used to. They are a bit more than life-sized and their gestures are grander.

And so I was glad to be back. Also, though it is really part of the same thing, I had always been interested in Henry M. Stanley and was now half-committed to follow his firm, Victorian steps across the continent for a news-feature syndicate.

He would not recognize the Central Africa of today, but it would recognize him.

My new friend was speaking of Stanley's journey with Livingstone on Lake Tanganyika, which they had called a picnic. We rose and went to the veranda to take coffee, and when I envied his hat he said that he thought, if all went well, that he might get a snake-skin band for it. He was wonderfully bronzed and sinewy and I think I was the only one there who knew that he had got that weathered look sitting on the top deck of a Lloyd Triestino cruise ship all the way down from Venice, drinking gin and tonic. He left his map with me and I promised to drop it off at the desk. That was the last I saw of him for a number of months.

In these days, people who are not fond of cruises enter Africa by air. From Khartoum on down—in spite of ruddy, puffing Englishmen en route to Nairobi, and their martial wives whose uniform is the print dress and whose pack is the regulation blonde vanity case—the continent is still primitive. The tiny shadow of the plane darts over vast lands where Nature is absolute sovereign. To the right is a lake, which might take days to row across, lying in what appears to be a larger lake of mud, surrounded by rolling scrub hills and hundreds of miles of forests and raw, eroded earth.

At Nairobi itself Nature is temporarily put in her place when one learns in an airport waiting-room that there are European-type gentlemen and non European-type gentlemen. And in town no amount of flowering jacaranda can dispel the gloom that racial tension creates. So it is a genuine relief to take to the air again and, crossing the equator, to look down on the green velvet land, sequined here and there with rivers and pools, looking as though it had been mauled by a kitten. And it is a joy to land at last by the crystal sea, in the thoroughly unreal world of Zanzibar.

CHAPTER TWO

W HEN Stanley first came to this island in 1871, leading the
New York Herald Expedition to rescue Livingstone, he
expected to find little more than a sandbar in the Indian Ocean,
pestilent, hot and ugly. What he found was the very prototype
of a languorous, garlanded, tropical island; and that is more
or less what it is now. Here are lovely courtyards lined with
bougainvillaea, like jewel boxes, and shady rooms hidden
behind blue and green shutters. Here are lissom Indian girls
spitting betel-juice, bearded Oman and black, clean-shaven
mainland Arabs in white cotton kanzus. The air is thick with
the smell of cloves, of which Zanzibar and its neighbouring
island, Pemba, are the world's major producers. The warm,
green sea laves a powdery shore and at night hundreds of
thousands of flowers cast their scent on the breeze.

At times, when it is night and there is a swollen moon in
the sky, the streets are bathed in an exotic light which may
almost never be seen outside of the precious isles and enclaves
that shelter the characters of Ronald Firbank. One half expects
to find Mrs Yajnavalkya and Queen Thleeanouhee of the Land
of Dates gossiping before the Blue Jesus. And somewhere,
surely, Lady Parvula de Panzoust is wending her erotic way.
It is hard to walk through Zanzibar without remembering
Firbank's phrase about Mohamadanism being fine if only it
didn't *sprawl* so, and it becomes alarmingly clear that he wrote
with far less imagination and more documentation than anyone
supposed.

In Stanley's time the island was a good deal less neat and
museum-like. The streets were filled with filth, bodies of

slaves were cast away on the beach and there were regular epidemics of cholera. But the sudden blight of Zanzibar's most important crop—human beings—fixed it as a period of physical splendour. The Arab architecture remains, and cool halls and courts now dream behind heavy, carved, brass-studded doors—which nevertheless look a bit self-conscious from being mentioned so often in guide books. The great wooden chests are still brought over on dhows from India on the north-east monsoon (December to March) and if they are more flimsily constructed now, that is due to a revolution in India, not in Zanzibar.

These same dhows return during the summer on the south-west monsoon carrying cloves and copra and other produce of the islands, nostalgic for the old days when a cargo of slaves and ivory would have brought a fortune. What remains most unchanged here is the population itself. There are the eternally middle-class Indians, squatting on the floors of their shops, investing their capital, and guarding their children like precious vases. Then the Arabs, some of whose ancestors have been here since the thirteenth century. Most of them are now more African than Asian, as they were in Stanley's time. They stand around in the streets fondling their walking-sticks, talking politics and drinking ginger-flavoured coffee. And finally there are the Africans, or Afro-Shirazis as the political majority call themselves. They claim descent from the Persians in the dim past—but very dim. They do most of the island's labour.

It was from among these last that Stanley chose the first members of his expedition as guides and soldiers. Six of them were veterans of a former expedition of Speke's and one, a big man named Bombay, had had his front teeth knocked out in a fight with his employer in Uganda. Stanley made him Sergeant-Major. He also appointed two ex-sailors named Shaw and Farquhar as his assistants, a boy from Jerusalem called Selim as his valet, and Omar, a Turkish dog, to watch over his effects. Stanley was offered quarters by the American consul until he collected his supplies and, what is in these days astonishing, a guarantee of credit. With this he managed to cash drafts on the *New York Herald* with the local Indian merchants at a rate of seventy-five cents on the dollar.

It was one thing to have money for supplies and another to know what to buy. No one in Zanzibar among the European colony had the faintest idea what one had to take into the continent. Only four white men had gone there before and they had left no notes. At last he went to an Arab merchant engaged in the ivory trade, who sent him on to other merchants.

It was, he found, just as fatal to take too many goods as it was to take too few. Forty yards of trading-cloth a day would feed one hundred men but, of that, a little less than two-thirds had to be American sheeting (Merikani). The rest was to consist of Kaniki (Indian blue jeans) and such coloured cloths as Barsati, Sohari and Kunguru-Cutch, blue and pink. Thus, Stanley calculated, two years' travel would require 16,000 yards of American sheeting, 8,000 yards of Kaniki, and 5,200 yards of mixed coloured cloths. Then he had to take beads, and not all of the same kind. In Unyamwezi he could only use red (*sami-sami*) beads. Black (*bubu*) beads were currency in Ugogo, *sungomazzi* in Ujiji and white Merikani beads in Usagara. There were as many systems of exchange as there are in modern Europe.

In addition, he was required to take three hundred and fifty pounds of wire, for, as Stanley said, if beads were like copper in trading; cloth was like silver and pure copper wire was gold. Then came the ordinary provisions of an expedition, cooking utensils, rope, tents, needles, bedding, ammunition and tea, of which he drank about twenty cups a day. He also purchased twenty-two donkeys. Altogether he had six tons of material, including such diverse supplies as Liebig's meat-extract, a dog-whip, Collis Browne's Chlorodyne, field-glasses and a sextant, quinine, and a bottle of Elixir Végétal de la Grande Chartreuse.

Before he left for Bagamoyo, directly opposite Zanzibar on the coast, where he was to pick up porters, he sought out Sir John Kirk who was the acting British consul at Zanzibar. He wanted to ask him about Livingstone, particularly as Kirk had served with him on the Zambesi explorations a decade before.

One of Stanley's chief difficulties on this first expedition of his was to hide from everyone, including himself, his real objective. He had been told to find Livingstone and no one but his editor considered the man exactly lost. It was known that the Doctor had gone into the heart of the continent in 1866. From time to time he had communicated with the outside world, and he was generally believed to have his base at Ujiji, on Lake Tanganyika. Stanley had really been sent to get a sensational story and get it any way he could. The *New York Herald* was then the most flamboyant newspaper in the English-speaking world and James Gordon Bennett, Jr.—whose idea this was—was the most ardently unscrupulous editor of an era that equated sensationalism with sensualism.

But Stanley had that kind of literal, inner sincerity which turns the most devious plot to stalwart legend. In his own mind, before his journey was over, Livingstone really was lost and he had come to save him. What was more, fate agreed with Stanley—as it usually did—and by the time he arrived at Ujiji the old Doctor, who had not been in need before, was.

This sincerity did not keep the young newspaperman from being circumspect. He had let it be known in Zanzibar that he had come to explore the Rufiji River, but as his expedition eventually cost well over forty thousand dollars and Stanley had been spending money recklessly in Zanzibar for a month, people did not believe him.

When he met Kirk he was so ponderously sly (' "Ah yes, Doctor Kirk," I asked, carelessly. "About Livingstone, where is he do you think, now?" ') that the consul grew suspicious and told him that he thought the Doctor didn't want to see anybody and that he would probably run away if Stanley were to 'stumble on him,' as the young man had suggested he might do. As it turned out, this is more or less the way he *did* come on Livingstone. But, as I have said, no matter how elephantine Stanley ever managed to be, fate came on with even heavier steps.

Henry M. Stanley, like many great men, moved so grandly on the world stage because he was following an intense personal drama which had little or nothing to do with the big show. While everyone else saw his journey as a heroic attempt to save the man who had, almost alone, thrown the light of European civilization on the dark continent, Stanley's view was a great deal simpler. He was looking for his father.

Henry Stanley had little patience with symbols or abstractions, but he would have admitted to any close friend that all of his life he had been looking for his father and, for that matter, any other member of his family on whom he could lavish his frozen love. He speaks of it many times in his writings, his longing to cling to any family—any mother, any brother, any sister and most of all any father who will have him. The two most important events of his life were a direct result of that search.

He was born in Wales in 1841. During his early youth he was called John Rowland, after the man who begot him. The boy never saw him and hardly ever saw his mother who was a domestic worker in London. She left him in the country with her parents as soon as possible and went back to work.

At the age of six, his grandfather having died, he was

marched to a workhouse under the impression that he was going to visit his aunt Mary. When the door closed behind him and he found himself with a strange man he broke into tears. As he said later, 'It took me some time to learn the unimportance of tears in a workhouse.'

The place was known as St Asaph's and was the very model of those Dickensian institutions where sadistic assaults are made on the heroic natures of little children. Here was a one-handed schoolmaster, unqualified as a teacher in any way, who savagely beat his charges for the least infraction of the rules. The workhouse was also the unofficial home of the pimps, drunks and prostitutes of the parish whose influence on the children was all the stronger because they were under no other.

The Board of Governors had refused to supply slates and maps, as they considered knowledge of arithmetic and geography unnecessary, and lessons were based on the Catechism, the Scriptures and Doctor Mavor's Spelling Primer. The children slept two to a bed, an older with a younger, and no doubt this led them to practise what they saw practised so frequently around them. It is hard to see how one could consciously design a school more apt to teach its pupils to despise the society around it.

One day, a boy whom Stanley described as 'king of the school for beauty and amiability,' died under peculiar circumstances. Stanley sneaked into the room where he was laid out, lifted the sheet and discovered that he was covered with welts and bruises. His description of this scene has a Tom Sawyerish quality which robs it of what must have been its true horror. This frequently happens in Stanley's books and it is strange to reflect that one of the world's great reporters was so nearly inarticulate. Florence Nightingale called his *How I Found Livingstone* 'the very worst book on the very best subject I ever saw in all my life.'

The brutal schoolmaster's name was John Francis, and when John Rowland was fifteen years old, in perfect Victorian tradition he knocked the bully down and beat him senseless with his own birch. Then he climbed the workhouse wall and ran away to a world that he was shortly to conquer. Also true to tradition, John Francis went insane some time later and was dragged off to a madhouse, where the poor man died in conditions which were probably more inhuman than any he had created at St Asaph's.

After this, young John Rowland went to live with his aunt Mary, the woman he had thought he was going to see nine years before. She was an unpleasant person, but she was fair and even generous, and the boy was comparatively happy, working as a shepherd. All he lacked, as he said, was a bit of love. A few years later he went to live with an uncle and an aunt in Liverpool, where he got a job as an errand boy. In these flights to aunts and uncles one can sense his need of a family and his heart-broken disappointment at not being accepted.

Years later, when his mother died, she had a brass plate put on her coffin saying that she had borne 'Henry M. Stanley, African explorer,' and if her son ever saw her grave it must have taken a great deal of strength not to feel bitter. But he might have been moved simply to pity, especially if he knew then that his illegitimate half-sister, Emma, who had been some years with him at St Asaph's, had quietly taken the name Stanley.

He stayed with the family in Liverpool for a few months but he was continually treated as a poor relation and at last took a job as a cabin boy on a ship to America. 'If my discontent had not been so great,' he wrote, 'I had clung to them like a limpet on a rock.'

The ship proved an even greater hell than the workhouse

and when he arrived in New Orleans he deserted. While wandering around, he allowed another boy to take him to a brothel but was so horrified by what he saw that he ran out. This would have been a very normal reaction in any boy, but aside from the fact that Stanley was not a person who had exactly normal reactions, his nine years in St Asaph's must surely have taught him something of these matters.

This, plus the fact that he had nothing more to do with any woman until he was married at the age of forty-nine, tends to confirm rumours, years after, that he was homosexual. Stanley's emotions were probably a great deal more complex than that. It seems clear that he had withdrawn them almost entirely from areas that are considered normal, but he did not necessarily express them abnormally. His longings were in the direction of a family and anything that fell short of one failed to move him. This indifference to either a healthy or an unhealthy sex life worked to his enormous advantage later in Africa.

One morning in mid-February 1859, about a week after he discovered that his room-mate, whom he called Dick, was an English girl named Alice Heaton who had run off to sea in breeches, John was walking down Tchapitoulas street when he saw a man reading a newspaper. He walked up to him and said, perfectly in character,

"As you are the first gentleman I have seen, I thought I would apply to you for work, or ask you for advice as to how to get it."

"So," the man ejaculated [and one imagines that in those days people really did ejaculate and asseverate], tilting his chair back again, "you are friendless in a strange land, eh, and want to work to begin making your fortune, eh? Well, what work can you do? Can you read? What book is that in your pocket?"

"It is my Bible, a present from our bishop. Oh yes, sir, I can read."

"Let me see your Bible . . . Can you write well?"

"Yes, sir, a good round-hand, as I have been told."

The man's name was Henry Morton Stanley. He was a former minister, still ordained, but now a wealthy merchant. As it happened, young Rowland *was* deeply religious, believing in God, as he said, 'as a very real personage,' and in the 'immediate presence of angels,' good and bad. It is not surprising that both of the men who took the place of a father in his life should have been God's official representatives.

Mr Stanley brought John into his family, where young Mrs Stanley was 'the first lady I ever conversed with.' Stricken by his own lack of culture he began to read *Paradise Lost*, the *Decline and Fall* and Pope's *Homer*—in fact all the books which would enable him in later years to pass as a gentleman and which had such a lamentable effect on his prose style.

During one of the absences of his patron, who had gone upriver on business, Mrs Stanley fell gravely ill and John left his job with Speake and McCreary, commission merchants, to nurse her. She died, however, and one half of the boy's new family was gone. When Mr Stanley returned he was so touched by the young man's devotion to his late wife that he gave him his name and promised to care for him. This was the first show of affection John had received in his life.

He wrote: Before I could quite grasp all that this declaration meant for me, he had risen, taken me by the hand, and folded me in a gentle embrace. My senses seemed to whirl about for a few half-minutes, and finally I broke down, sobbing from extreme emotion. It was the only tender action I had ever known, and, what no amount of cruelty could have forced from me, tears poured in a torrent under the influence of the simple embrace.

He travelled with his new father for several years, learning his business. The boy was very quick and had an astonishing memory. He could learn a page of figures by glancing at them. It seems, however, though Stanley doesn't mention it, that something went wrong between them and the older man never did legally adopt him.

At last the merchant was called to Havana to visit a sick brother and left young Henry in the care of a friend in Arkansas. In Cuba he died, though Stanley did not learn of this for several years. From this time he was again without a parent.

People whose natures are essentially extravagant and grand, as Stanley's was in spite of its surface propriety, seem to be involved by accident in a series of momentous events which sweep them up and deposit them far from their beginnings. In less than ten years Stanley joined the rebel army during the American Civil War (he said, because someone sent him a negress's petticoat), joined the northern army after he was captured in the battle of Shiloh, joined the U.S. Navy as ship's writer after he was discharged from the army, deserted the Navy and went to Turkey, was shipwrecked off the coast of Spain, covered the Indian wars with Generals Hancock and Sherman for the *Missouri Democrat* and, finally, scored a three-week beat on General Napier's Abyssinian campaign for the *New York Herald* and became its star reporter.

During this time he also made two visits to members of his family in England, including his mother. His welcome grew warmer in direct proportion to his affluence.

In 1869 he was earning two thousand dollars a year—not much, by our standards, for a famous foreign correspondent, though he did have an unlimited expense account and was shortly to use it as no other journalist has dared since. He had begun to indulge a taste for luxuries he hadn't even known existed ten years before. When collecting his supplies for the Livingstone expedition, for instance, he included a bottle of Sillery, a rare champagne from the neighbourhood of Rheims, made only of white grapes and much lighter and dryer than ordinary champagne. On his eight-and-a-half-month journey

24

to Ujiji he brought, as personal effects, a bearskin, a Persian carpet, a bath, silver eating-utensils, a silver teapot and two silver goblets to drink his champagne with Livingstone. He also carried, loyally, bundles of back numbers of the *New York Herald.*

On the sixteenth of October he was in Madrid, having just covered the battle of Valencia, when he received a telegram from James Gordon Bennett, summoning him to his suite at the Grand Hotel in Paris.

Bennett had already shown an interest in Livingstone and, the year before, had sent Stanley to Suez to check on rumours that he was coming out of Africa by way of the Nile. At that time David Livingstone was one of the heroes of the world—especially of the wealthy and arrogant part of it which spoke English. He was a doctor, a missionary and an explorer and so, at one stroke, satisfied the longings of the Victorian era for science, faith and adventure. His paternal figure loomed in the day-dreams of red-blooded young men and guided, with gentle firmness, the tightly corseted judgment of their sisters. What was more important, Livingstone had devoted his life to the abolition of slavery, and the anti-slavery movement was one of the most explosive forces of the nine-teenth century, to its eternal credit. As this man hadn't been heard of for several years Bennett felt that a story was building up, and he was perfectly right.

"Where do you think Livingstone is?" Bennett said to Stanley.

"I really do not know, sir."

"Do you think he is alive?"

"He may be and he may not be."

"Well, I think he is alive, and that he can be found, and I am going to send you to find him . . . Draw a thousand pounds now, and when you have gone through that, draw another thousand, and when that is spent, draw another thousand, and when you have finished that, draw another thousand, and so on; but FIND LIVINGSTONE." Bennett was going to regret that 'and so on.'

But this was all perfectly in the tradition of adventure-journalism, and the astonishing thing about the entire story is that, from beginning to end, not one person forgets his part. The weaklings are weak and the strong are strong. The rich and capricious have the courage of their impulses and the poor show such patently false humility that—in the wink of an eye —they themselves become rich and capricious. A man may be a wastrel or he may have a will of iron; he is not fond of half-measures.

Before Stanley went after Livingstone, Bennett, a practical man for all his caprice, suggested that he go to the inauguration of the Suez Canal, proceed up the Nile to learn about Sir Samuel Baker's expedition into Upper Egypt; go to Jerusalem and look into the discoveries of a certain Captain Warren; visit Constantinople and find out about the trouble between the Khedive and the Sultan; visit the Crimea and the old English battle-grounds, go across the Caucasus to the Caspian Sea, go through Persia to India and write an 'interesting letter from Persepolis,' drop in on Bagdad and 'write up something about the Euphrates Valley Railway.' Then, after India, he could go for Livingstone.

"Good night, and God be with you."

"Good night, sir. What it is in the power of human nature to do I will do; and on such an errand as I go upon, God will be with me."

Bennett was no doubt certain that this strange little man with black hair and a red, fat face with hypnotic grey eyes and a chest like a gorilla, was equal to the tasks he had given him. But he might have been doubtful had he known that Stanley was going to strike into the centre of Africa, to Ujiji, where only three Europeans had been before. One was Livingstone himself and two others were army officers, rigorously trained in the tropics.

In fact, two years later, when he first received Stanley's enormous drafts to equip his expedition, he refused to honour them. He changed his mind, however, when it became evident that the young man might succeed. He had no way of knowing that Stanley was on another single-minded and fanatic quest for his lost parent.

CHAPTER THREE

WHEN Seyyid Said bin Sultan, the Imam of Oman, transferred his capital to Zanzibar in 1832, he began to promote commerce—primarily in slaves and ivory—with the interior of Africa. The island was therefore the staging-ground of most of the early Arab expeditions, and the principal trade route was that leading to Tabora and on to Ujiji, which Burton reports the first Arabs reached in 1840.

With certain deviations this is the line of the present railway crossing Tanganyika. The coastal terminus has moved a few miles south to Dar-es-Salaam, the capital of the territory. Bagamoyo, which saw hundreds of thousands of slaves embark for the markets of Zanzibar and the Middle East, is now chiefly noted for its seaside country club.

As a measure of slavery's defeat the Universities Mission church in Zanzibar was built on the site of the old slave market, with its altar raised over the whipping-post. For all their commemorative zeal, the missionaries produced a very ordinary church, and though built of coral stone it is otherwise like thousands of others in the Anglo-Saxon world.

When I visited it on a Thursday afternoon at the end of October no one was there. It seemed to have just recovered from a prayer meeting. Forlorn Swahili hymnals were scattered on the pews and there was an odour of grained wood and of propriety. It was all so painfully sincere and so anti-climatic. On the lectern, across which must have been delivered some of the dullest and most heart-felt sermons on earth, were two long-playing records of Chopin's *Nocturnes*.

This persistent and faintly antiseptic English character permeates Zanzibar and wars with its luxuriant nature. One has the sensation of drinking chartreuse out of a tooth-glass. On the Residency Road, for instance, stands a stone column with a sign beside it reading, 'Visitors are asked to refrain from scribbling on the milestone.' On the face of the column are carved the names of several towns, Dar-es-Salaam, Tanga, Mombasa, etc., with their distances. And at the very top it reads, 'LONDON—8064 miles.' In the post office one must learn that '*Tofadhalini sunameni kua mistari*' means 'please queue up.'

The Zanzibar hotel, where I stayed, was also triumphantly British. It had a pleasant lobby lined with deep chairs suggesting comfort without being particularly comfortable, a small bar that kept English drinking hours and a busy reception desk above which were optimistic slogans reading, 'You don't have to be crazy to be in this business but it helps,' and, 'The impossible we try to do at once, a miracle takes a little longer.' And on the Jubilee Wharf, in front of Bargash bin Said's old palace, which now houses the Government offices, rickshaw men doze in their own rickshaws, gossip and drink fruit-juice in their unmanned carriages throughout the somnolent afternoons. Here I left a note for Mr Robertson, administrative officer of the island, asking for an appointment.

That night at the hotel, after an English boarding-house dinner, served with almost satirical care, I had coffee and brandy in the lobby with the hotel receptionist, a voluble girl with straw-coloured hair and painfully sunburnt arms.

"Have you been to the Pigalle? Here in Zanzibar, I mean. It's the only hotel for food, not that I want to run down my own place." She leaned forward and put her glass down. "Two real Frenchwomen run it."

29

Others were coming in from dinner, among them an old Indian woman, wearing a gauze-silk sari and a diamond in a wing of her nose, whose every movement and hulking gesture proclaimed her to be some miserable girl's mother-in-law.

"You see him? He's an assistant District Commissioner but he'll never be promoted."

I glanced across the room and saw a large, dejected-looking man sucking a pipe. A couple entered and sat at my right. She was brisk and horsy; he had blue shoebutton eyes and brindle moustaches.

". . . always thought Zanzibar was full of humming-gales and all those blue things," my companion continued.

Brindle mumbled something.

"Don't be ridiculous, Nigel—if they go out to the reserve in the afternoon they won't see anything. You know perfectly well the lions don't get up till tea-time."

The assistant District Commissioner had grown conscious of his hands. "Why won't he be promoted?" I said.

". . . can go boating every day and I might not quit if I could *just* get a tan. After all, I'm practically the only girl on the island—only *girl* that is."

The assistant District Commissioner got up and walked out, staring into the bowl of his pipe. His shorts bagged badly behind.

The following morning at breakfast I had word that I could see Mr Robertson. Meeting British officials is always an intimidating experience, not because they are unfriendly as a rule but because they represent a nation which insists on having plates warmed when the temperature is over ninety in the shade, and has arrogantly decreed that its only two edible meals—breakfast and tea—shall be those which most other people in the world never touch.

The inside of Bargash's palace, where Mr Robertson had his offices, looked like an old-fashioned department store—sold out. It rose in galleries supported on slender wooden pillars and was open in the centre to the roof. This was levered up and extended over the four walls so that there was space for air to circulate. Everything was sparely and delicately constructed, though the doors to the rooms off the galleries were thickly carved and the banisters were cut to lacy patterns—different on each floor—and painted white.

In this building Mr Robertson was wonderfully at home. He wore a perfectly cut white suit and shirt, a tie that seemed to have grown to his neck, and a smile that comforted one with understanding. He sat down at his desk, indicated my chair, and tented his immaculate fingers while I explained my visit. He was extremely handsome, running a bit to flesh—no more than a pound or two—and had the complexion of a gardenia petal. He was probably athletic in a few chosen sports. Whatever the assistant District Commissioner had done to lose his promotion, it was obvious that his greatest fault was in falling so far short of this splendid ideal.

This was the only sort of man who could frighten Henry Stanley. He was sure that any *real* gentleman would snub him. That was why he took such a strong dislike to Sir John Kirk when he arrived on this island. He thought the man despised him, which may have been true. But it did not occur to Stanley —such was his innocent conceit—that he could be despised for any other reason than his birth. He never forgot the cornet in the Scinde Horse in General Napier's campaign, who, on being approached, drew back as though bitten and said, "Whom have I the honour to address?"

Mr Robertson was very kind and helpful, though actually not too informative. As he sketched the history of the island there were even several important events of which he seemed to be unaware. But he was personally such a magnificent expression of government that it was difficult to believe that he had not feigned his ignorance for some critical reason of state.

Until recent years the history of Zanzibar and its neighbouring island, Pemba, is the history of the sultanate. Of the ten rulers only the first three had any degree of autonomy. These were Said bin Sultan, who established Zanzibar as his capital in 1832 and his two sons, Majid bin Said (Sultan 1856-70) and Bargash bin Said (Sultan 1870-88). From that time the Sultans' power was largely curtailed by the British. The present one, His Highness Seyyid Sir Khalifa bin Harub, GCMG, CBE (whom God preserve) acceded on 9 December 1911, and has held his title longer than any other ruler on earth by agreeing with the Colonial Office that he is not wholly competent to administer his realm.

Recently there has been agitation among the Arabs for a larger voice in the Government. In 1957 they managed to force elections for half of the Legislative Council, which might have been a great victory for them if they had remembered that they, as well as the British, were a minority on the island. The Africans, who used to be more tractable, treacherously organized a party of their own and won the election . . .

But politics become mercifully unreal in a place like Zanzibar, and it is really impossible to remember how many students Nasser invited to Cairo or whether or not there are any Communists here or how the Indians voted in 1957 . . . One wanders off into Ngambo, the African quarter, where sticks of trading beads are still sold and one may see violently coloured women's brassieres in the shops with alternating green and red breasts. Duller matters fade from the mind when one discovers that a woman who assumes that an ivory button

32

in her upper lip is attractive, or at least tantalizing, is perfectly right.

As a child I used to read those huge books of Stanley's with marbled covers—filled with wonderful, stiff woodcuts in which drama was primarily a matter of posture. One of those illustrations—all yellow and with its page flaked at the edges —showed a young girl being marked out by cannibals for butchering. As she was naked this scene was especially fascinating.

Those books, now lost, had been in my mother's family since she was a girl and I had been told by an aunt, who kept track of such things, that Mr Stanley was my kinsman, being related to grandmother Stanley. When I learned the truth about his birth I never dared tell her because she was very proud of her Stanley connections and had given one of her children that name.

But before I left Zanzibar I saw the girl in the woodcut again. I had gone swimming. On the beach the clove-spiced air mingled with the tang of the sea until the bay seemed to be a great bath, faintly clouded with Cologne. The African sky stretched for hundreds of miles and held blue heavens and black storms as casually as a hand may hold a few patches of coloured stuff.

After swimming in the honeyed water I fell asleep on the sands and woke in the presence of a beautiful little girl, as dark as sleep, wearing a bright green dress which hung on her thin shoulders as on a hanger, and carrying a long piece of black seaweed. She stared at me with the remarkable concentration that children achieve while being merely interested. Her shaved head was perfectly elliptical and her lovely teeth showed through a half-smile. Still smiling, she turned and walked to the water and began to beat it mercilessly with her seaweed whip.

She was, in fact, a young version of Epis, who lives fifteen hundred miles farther on, in the Congo. Of course, at that time I had not met Epis, but there are certain people in the world who are nearly perfect, within the limitations they have set, and one is always heading away from one and towards another, like landmarks on a road.

So now this child, who wore pretty black moccasins completely run down on the sides, tramped through the tide proudly ruining her shoes, glancing from time to time at me and whipping the sea. At last I got up and walked over to her, while she stood still. I pointed to her, trying to ask her name, but she thought I was asking her to button the top of her dress and did so.

We stood together, then, and looked out towards the sea at a bobbing sailboat, while tiny, translucent crabs crawled from homes in the sand and fled the incoming waves. In the distance we could hear someone hammering. The girl didn't move, and with adult impatience I asked her name again. She spanked the water in embarrassment and at last looked up. Her eyes were full of trust—not of me, she didn't exactly trust me—but of the world itself. It seemed, on the surface, absurd that anything so frail shouldn't be frightened. But she wasn't. And then she turned and went, walking up the strand dragging her whip, never looking back, as a breeze ruffled her green dress like a flag.

From those books of Stanley's, also, another character strayed into the dreams of my childhood. His name was Tippu Tib and his home is preserved in Zanzibar as a historical monument. It has a stiff and almost prim look which curiously befits the former residence of a mass-murderer. This man was half-

African, and when he died in 1905 he left his mother's land with a hatred and fear of slavery which, all things considered, is a valuable legacy.

No other continent on earth has been so systematically pillaged and none was so poverty-stricken to begin with. Its living creatures—elephants and men—were its only wealth. Literally millions of men were torn from their homes and sold on the markets of the world. And for every one of them, at least one more person was killed in slave raids in which human beings were deliberately slaughtered as a means of creating panic. Furthermore, in a land where food was scarce, it was a great temptation to consider slaves as cattle; hundreds of thousands were butchered simply for meat, and a traveller could buy a person to take along with him and eat on the way.

The raiders completely destroyed the villages and plantations they attacked, leaving the few survivors to die of starvation. Possibly a hundred million people were sold or murdered. It is not surprising, then, that this remains the central memory of Africa and that the word 'freedom' may on occasion have an almost hysterical significance.

Not that these raids came entirely from outside. They were generally led by Arabs—especially from the east and from the north—but many of these, like Tippu Tib, were themselves partially African. In addition, the staunchest allies of the slave hunters in Central Africa were the people of the Maniema country on the eastern approaches to the Congo basin. By the time Stanley returned on his second expedition in 1874 to 'complete Livingstone's work' Tippu Tib had already penetrated far west of Lake Tanganyika to Nyangwé. He had been stopped short there, however, and did not go farther until Stanley himself blazed the way.

That was hardly what Livingstone would have called completing his work. The old man had thought that if Africa were opened to normal trade, slavery would disappear. This eventually happened, but in the beginning the only practical result of these explorations was to make more of the continent accessible to the slavers.

Years later, while leading an expedition to rescue Emin Pasha, Stanley found Tippu Tib entrenched deep in the Congo at Stanley Falls. He bought the slaver's co-operation by making him governor of that station and proceeded through the great forest to Lake Albert. It was typical of Stanley to keep his eyes on the main chance and to sacrifice everything to it, including his convictions. But if Livingstone had been alive then it is likely that the two men would have stopped speaking.

The old missionary cared for nothing but his convictions. For him, tolerance of human slavery was an unforgivable sin.

David Livingstone was among the last of the Abolitionists. In common with many of his predecessors he expressed a revolutionary belief in the Rights of Man with the unmistakable accent of the London Missionary Society. The Abolitionist movement had swept England in the eighteenth and nineteenth centuries and even as early as 1689 Locke could say: "Slavery is so vile and miserable an estate of man, and so directly opposite to the generous temper and courage of our nation, that it is hardly to be conceived that an Englishman, much less a gentleman, should plead for it."

Later, the Quakers began their active opposition to it and in 1774 they decreed that any Friend who had anything to do with the slave trade should be expelled from the Society. By 1808 the trade had been abolished in England, and twenty-five years later slavery itself was outlawed, while West Indian slave owners were given an indemnity of twenty million pounds.

William Wilberforce, then one of the leaders of the Abolitionist movement, lay dying as this particular bill was being debated in Parliament and—more accustomed than we to think of slaves as property which could be purchased, even to relinquish title—he said: "Thank God that I should have lived to witness a day in which England is willing to give twenty millions for the Abolition of slavery."

England was also pumping that money into a badly crippled industry and, at the same time, doing away with a system of labour which was proving uneconomic. It was not the Abolitionist campaign to eat East Indian instead of West Indian sugar that doomed slavery in the Caribbean but the simple fact that eastern sugar, produced by free labour, cost less. Backed by these practical interests the Abolitionists suddenly became powerful.

This is not to say that England took the lead in the anti-slavery movement simply because it was more practical to do so. Throughout Europe and America there was a growing acceptance of the principle that men are born equal, before God, and when Adam Smith said in 1776, "It appears from the experience of all ages and nations that the work done by free-men comes cheaper in the end than that performed by slaves," he didn't mean that if slavery were less expensive he would be in favour of it.

It is also hard to find the profit motive—though there may have been one—in the British offer to Portugal in 1815 to remit four hundred and fifty thousand pounds debt and to make an outright gift of three hundred thousand pounds on the condition that she would confine her trade in slaves to transport from south of the Equator to her own possessions across the Atlantic—meaning that only Angola and Mozambique could export and only Brazil could import. What was more, British naval patrols to enforce the abolition of the slave trade employed about one-sixth of the fleet and cost the English taxpayers seven hundred and fifty thousand pounds a year.

In spite of these measures, during the height of the Abolitionist movement in 1840 the slave trade flourished as never before. Britain had been pressing countries with which it had anti-slavery treaties for the right of reciprocal search of their ships, to check slave smuggling. As the United States was one of the last countries to accept such search most slavers flew the American flag, whether they were American or not.

America's position on slavery was naturally a delicate one. There were many Abolitionists in the North who would have been delighted to have American ships searched in such a cause. From the beginning there had been strong anti-slavery feeling in the United States and in the first draft of the Constitution Jefferson, a slave owner, tried to include a condemnation of slavery, but the clause was struck out on the objections of South Carolina and Georgia. And one of the reasons why England herself had so little difficulty getting out from under the commercially and morally deadening weight of slavery was that the successful American Revolution had stripped her of the largest of her slave territories, and therefore of those colonists most likely to object to Abolition. As in Africa today, European settlers violently opposed changes which their home governments practically took for granted.

Quite naturally, human suffering on slaveships intensified as slaving persisted beyond the law. Sometimes half the cargo would die in conditions which were no longer even nominally regulated. And when there was danger of being overtaken and searched the cargo would often be jettisoned.

For this reason Abolitionist circles felt that the only way finally to abolish slavery was to open up Africa itself to nineteenth-century trade and colonization. In this, also, one can

38

see self-interest not too carefully hidden. But that hardly dims the fame of a man like Livingstone who devoted his life to this 'positive policy' for abolishing human slavery.

To make Africa known to the world he performed a series of remarkable explorations. While serving as a medical missionary in Bechuanaland he crossed the Kalahari desert and reached Lake Ngami in 1849, when Stanley was eight years old and at St Asaph's. In 1851 he discovered the Zambesi River. Between 1853 and 1856 he made his way on foot with inadequate supplies from Linyanti on the upper Zambesi to S. Paolo de Loanda on the coast of Angola. Then he came back across the continent to Quilimane on the coast of Mozambique, thus becoming the first European known to cross the continent. An Arab named Said bin Habib bin Salim Lafifi possibly did it a few months before.

Between 1855 and 1863, while Stanley was establishing himself in America, he explored the Zambesi region.

Having thoroughly proved his qualifications, moral as well as physical, Livingstone was chosen by the Royal Geographical Society in 1865 to go west of Tanganyika, into what is now the Congo. There is no doubt that a good deal of his support—including a grant of money from the Government—came from British trading interests who felt that Arab slavers were ruining legitimate business in Africa, as no doubt they were. But his own passionate opposition to slavery was entirely ideological.

His description of the human market in Zanzibar shows his feelings. 'All who have grown up seem ashamed at being hawked about for sale. The teeth are examined, the cloth lifted up to examine the lower limbs, and a stick is thrown for the slave to bring and thus examine his paces . . .'

He started on his last journey in March 1866, five years before Stanley set out to rescue him. Everywhere he went he found occasion to complain of the slave trade, even declaring that it was responsible for inflation in some areas so that he hadn't cloth enough to buy food. His loathing of slavery extended to the slaves themselves. He said that they never became men again.

During the trip he read the Bible four times over, by oil light. He was obsessed with the idea of finding some literal proof of the Old Testament in order to confound the Evolutionists. He felt that the followers of Darwin and the new sciences were trying to prove that some societies of men are historically more evolved than others. He was worried that this view, however mistaken, would make backward peoples eligible for slavery of one sort or another, especially as the term 'backward' is used only by those who consider themselves forward.

He hoped to discover Meroe, which, according to legend, Moses had founded in honour of Pharaoh's daughter Merr. Also, he believed that there were four fountains rising in Katanga (from which vast quantities of copper and uranium ore now flow), thus confirming Herodotus and perhaps Genesis. If he could find these, he said, then the ulcers on his feet, which were often so bad they ate to the bone, 'would only be discipline.'

A far more severe discipline for him would have been the knowledge that the rising class in England that supported his religious, anti-slavery views was also coming out on the side of the damned Evolutionists and the scientists who questioned the authority of the Word. The contradiction was less Livingstone's than the world's for, like Stanley, he had a boyish simplicity which rose above such things. He solemnly referred to the Governor of Bombay as 'a brick' for offering to help in his anti-slavery work; and when he began his final journey he wrote:

40

The effect of travel on a man whose heart is in the right place is that the mind is made more self-reliant . . . The countenance is bronzed and there is no dyspepsia . . . No doubt much toil is involved and fatigue . . . but the sweat of one's brow is no longer a curse when one works for God . . . actually a blessing.

In the seven years that remained of his life he was to see only one other European. And to that man this bigoted old humanist entrusted his mission.

CHAPTER FOUR

WHEN Stanley had collected his supplies in Zanzibar he moved across to Bagamoyo on the mainland where he finished recruiting. Here, for about twelve dollars apiece, he found porters willing to go on to the trading-post of Tabora, three-quarters of the way to Ujiji. As the journey lasted three months that was only a few cents a day for each.

A porter was expected to carry, on his head, a seventy pound load across mountains, swamps, forests and deserted savannah, subsisting on the barest rations and risking his life at the hands of hostile tribes. At Tabora, if he were lucky and still sound, he could hire out to a caravan returning to the coast. The other members of the expedition were paid by the year. The soldiers got thirty-six dollars, Stanley's sergeant-major, Bombay, eighty dollars, and the white men, Farquhar and Shaw, each three hundred dollars, which they never lived to collect.

Stanley—'the vanguard, the reporter, the thinker, and leader of the expedition,' as he called himself—had decided to send his column in five contingents to disguise its size and reduce the amount of tribute that would have to be paid to tribes along the way.

On 18 February 1871, the first party left for the interior under the leadership of one of the sergeants who was also a tribal headman. Another followed on the 21st and a third, under Farquhar, on the 25th. Two weeks later the fourth and largest caravan left under two native chiefs, and on March 21 the last party, carrying two boats, boxes of ammunition and personal effects, filed up a narrow lane shaded by two parallel hedges of mimosas, chanting "Forward!" which Stanley had chosen as its '*mot du guet*,' and proudly displaying the American flag.

Sporting a Hawkes patent cork solar topee, a white flannel tunic and size-eight Wellington boots, Stanley rode at the head of this caravan on a big bay horse. Shaw brought up the rear on a donkey, wearing sea-boots and a topee that looked like a canoe. The expedition numbered 192 souls, two horses, twenty-seven donkeys, some goats and Omar the dog. The reporter and thinker mentions that they left Bagamoyo with a good deal of *éclat*, which is certainly understandable when one realizes that his expense account was already twenty thousand dollars, was destined to go to more than twice that, and that probably nothing comparable has come into the accounting office of the *New York Herald* or its successor since.

Few of the people who watched Stanley depart ever thought to see him again. In those days Americans were looked upon with almost as much condescension as Africans are now. It was inconceivable that this graceless young man should venture into an unknown land which had strained the resources of Burton, Speke and Grant, and Livingstone himself.

Even now, in British East Africa, one feels that there has been a conspiracy to forget as much as possible about Stanley. He wasn't really the right sort; there was something ignoble about him. He was, of course, an egomaniac, but that wouldn't necessarily disqualify him as a British hero. Any account of his adventures is just a little embarrassing because he longed not for power or fame or even wealth, but merely success and respectability. During his first months in the interior he was undoubtedly more frightened of making a fool of himself than of losing his life. At the same time he was absolutely determined to accomplish his mission and was prepared to go all the way across the continent to the Atlantic Ocean if necessary, keeping a careful account of expenses along the way.

He was, in short, a typical American of his time, suffering from an immense sense of inferiority and endowed with the boundless energy and genius of the European poor. The pride he took in being an American was the pride of a man who sees his way open, at last, to the top. Only after his position was secured, many years later, would he admit to anyone that he had been born in Wales or that his name had ever been John Rowland.

The odds were very much against his ever reaching Ujiji. The three other white men who had done it were carefully chosen for their experience in the tropics. They also had the support of the Royal Geographical Society, an organization as august as its Queen and probably richer. All Stanley had was the quirky backing of an unscrupulous editor and his own high sense of destiny. He plunged into the heart of Africa to find his parent and his fortune, which were confused in his mind because they had so little external reality. His one other advantage, which may have been decisive, was that he had been born and had lived the first eighteen years of his life in the teeming jungles of lower-class England. There were few beasts in Africa more savage than those he had already fought.

For a number of days the party travelled through park land, occasionally fording a stream and getting along very comfortably. At the Kingani River Stanley amused himself by taking pot-shots at hippopotami, trying first a Winchester ·44 (no effect) and then his trusty No. 12 smooth-bore. He also went hunting in a jungle dressed in flannel pyjamas and sneakers and got badly torn and cut and bruised, so that he said, with customary heavy humour, 'I mentally vowed that the penetralia of an African jungle should not be visited by me again, save under most urgent necessity.'

44

Notwithstanding his 'epidermal wounds' he finds the country lovely, not at all what he had been led to expect by Burton's *The Lake Regions of Central Africa*. He had pictured hundreds of miles of swamp choked with 'crocodiles, alligators, lizards, tortoises and toads,' with a 'miasma rising from this vast cataclysm of mud, corruption, and putrescence, as thick and sorely depressing as the gloomy and suicidal fog of London.' But instead of foul beasts and warring adjectives he found a sweet country of meadow and intermittent jungle. He obviously felt it was cut to his measure and his high spirits are entirely appropriate to a young man just turned thirty, setting out on the greatest adventure of his life.

However, troubles begin as he overtakes his dilatory fourth caravan and passes into tsetse-fly country. Because Sir John Kirk in Zanzibar had warned him that this fly would sooner or later be fatal to all his animals Stanley would never admit, out of dislike for the man, that this was the cause of their death.

Livingstone had already described the insect in his book on South Africa, stating that this particular species (*glossina morsitans*) destroys most domestic animals but does no harm, except to cause pain, to men or wild beasts. In the interest of science Stanley permitted one to alight on his flannel pyjamas, of which he evidently had several pairs. Its sting, he said, was like the deep thrust of a fine needle. But he was so determined not to believe John Kirk that he was barely concerned when he saw the horses and donkeys streaming with blood and rearing in pain.

From this point the animals began to die and Stanley spent a great deal of time and patience on autopsies to prove that the flies hadn't killed them.

The absence of any pack animals but human beings was one of the main reasons for the isolation of interior Africa.

Deprived by the tsetse fly of both transport and nourishment, most tribes became comparatively immobile, changing territory only in slow migrations.

This situation persisted until the beginning of our own century, and even now there are huge tracts of land which cannot be visited except on foot, where a hundred miles is equivalent to a thousand. In 1871, however, this isolation was sometimes a blessing as it kept out the Arabs, who were a good deal more dangerous than fly. Until Stanley penetrated beyond Nyangwé into the Congo five years later the inaccessibility and utter poverty of the vast central basin of Africa had protected the inhabitants from every savagery but their own.

It is difficult for people from indolent northern climates to picture the poverty of that region, where any food at all is considered something of a wonder. Our minds reject the thought that a land so nearly primeval is not also generous. We think of Nature as an abundant mother whom we have betrayed by becoming civilized and to whom we must return to be renewed. This is the final luxury, like enjoying a blizzard through a picture window, or admiring the fluid beauty of a caged tigress.

In fact, this country is often so spare and implacable that it may become as barren as arctic tundra. Like the American plains before they were domesticated, it has no respect for human life and food is grown and stored with the greatest difficulty. Wheat and white potatoes and apples may be raised at high altitudes, but they are generally too exotic to be produced on a large scale. Many things are grown, when the rains come on time and if they last long enough, and some of them can be stored. Central Africa is nothing like so poor as it was a few hundred years ago.

It is hard to see how anyone could have lived there then. Nearly all the victuals now consumed have been brought in from the outside. Manioc, corn, sweet potato and tomato came from America; banana, sugar-cane, rice, sorghum, citrus, mango and breadfruit from Asia. Practically nothing is native. There has always been game, but it is not easy to kill creatures your own size or larger who are hungry themselves. The pigmies, who are the only certainly indigenous people here, are —with the Eskimos—also the world's last great hunters.

The distance between the coast and Tabora was five hundred and twenty-five miles. Between those points there were no settlements which were even remotely civilized except for two native townships called Simbamwenni and Mpwapwa, the first a hundred and nineteen miles from Bagamoyo and the second sixty-eight miles beyond that. Here, they could rest and find adequate supplies of food and water.

The first of these towns took nearly a month to reach, as the caravan pushed across the maritime plain. Stanley had caught up with his fourth contingent several times and had been considerably delayed by it. His men were also beginning to be plagued by a sickness they called Mukunguru, which the leader subsequently caught himself. As a cure he used an old Arkansas remedy, a purge and fifteen grains of quinine, with excellent results.

But Stanley's greatest accomplishment during this first month was to keep his people going ahead. Arab caravans made this trip continually, but they had a great deal more experience than he had. Henry Stanley's success must be weighed against the great probability of his failure. The animals were dying, the rainy season had begun, there were desertions and thefts and the men suffered from rheumatism, sore throats, weakness of the loins, bilious fever and diarrhœa.

At sunrise this energetic and officious little American would rush out of his tent, which was tall and square like a bathing-hut, and run around the camp in his pyjamas banging a tin pan

47

with an iron ladle. There is no doubt that he was thoroughly loathed by everyone, but he was also beginning to inspire trust. At least, as they came farther and farther from the coast they were constrained to depend on his will to go forward, simply because there was no place else to go.

He, too, sensed his growing power as civilization disappeared behind them, and his account of the journey acquires a lumpish good humour. He describes 'the belles of Kisemo, of gigantic posterioral proportions' grinding corn with mortar and pestle.

Swaying with the pestle as it rises and falls the pectoral and posterioral exuberances alternate to her strokes in the very drollest rhythm; so strongly marked that I feared for the walls of the hut before which I saw the corn-pounding going on.

It is no doubt this style which a London critic later referred to when he spoke of 'the racy, sub-erotic flavour of the *New York Herald*.'

At Kisemo an Arab caravan delivered a file of late *Heralds* to Stanley, sent by the American Consul at Zanzibar. Among them he found a description of President Grant's second levee, written by a colleague named Jenkins whom Stanley didn't like. He accuses him of laboured verbosity and contrasts the grand toilets of the ladies—the lavender ostrich plume, the diamonds, the overskirt with ruchings of crimson satin—with the simple attire of the plump black girls of Kisemo who were at that moment peering through the door of his tent.

Apart from the fact that Jenkins couldn't really help what Washington ladies were wearing (and laboured verbosity was hardly a safe charge for the author of *How I Found Livingstone* to fling at anyone) Stanley had no right to accuse his paper's White House correspondent of being adulatory because he spoke of a Republican President's deep manly voice and searching grey eyes.

48

The *Heralds* must have made him homesick, however, for shortly afterwards he professes to see in the country beyond Kisemo the very likeness of Central Park.

Take away the gravelled paths, the lakes and ponds, the museums within, the trellised arbors, the kiosk, the uniformed policemen and well-dressed visitors . . . and Central Park thus denuded, with only its refreshing lawns, gentle hollows, and grove-clad ridges, would present, to those who could imagine the New York park in this state, a not unfaithful image of the country which opened before us.

Stanley rested five days at Simbamwenni, a fortified town of about four thousand inhabitants ruled by a Sultana. He sent the fourth caravan on ahead again. It was raining heavily—'a real London rain'—and their camp was infested with red, white and black ants, centipedes, worms, wasps and beetles as large as mice. On the morning of April 23 there was a bit of sun and they forded a swollen river and struck out towards Mpwapwa.

Stanley had heard from passing Arabs that Farquhar's caravan, ahead, was in a pitiful state. While down with fever at the beginning of May he had Shaw write the following note:

Dear Farquhar—at the request of Mr Stanley I write you to asertain all your misfortunes, what quanterty of clorth you have expened and how much you have left, how many donkeys is dead, and, in fact, all the perticlurs . . . What is the matter with you. What is the matter with Jacko, and what was the matter with the donkeys that dide . . . In two days we shall be up with you.

They were up with him in five days and found him in a state of complete hysteria. His body was bloated with elephantiasis and he had spent almost all of the supplies of his caravan satisfying what Stanley called his 'lust for goatmeat, eggs and poultry.'

Nine of his ten donkeys were dead and he had so abused his men that they were terrified of him and he had to offer them large bribes to serve him. He was continually crying like a sick

49

baby for half a dozen people to wait on him, and flew into rages when they did not understand his English. He had become, in short, a moral weakling—obeying the inexorable Victorian law that a man must sound whatever depths he has. Shaw also was beginning to disintegrate, and at Simbamwenni had started whining and complaining of overwork and threatening to quit.

The two men together resolved on mutiny. On May 15, at breakfast time, when Stanley invited them to have a roast quarter of goat, stewed liver, half a dozen sweet potatoes, hot pancakes and coffee, Shaw—who had apparently rehearsed the wrong line—said, "What dog's meat is this?" and after a brief argument with his employer, in which he was reminded of his position, he measured his length on the ground.

That night, when Stanley had gone to bed, a shot was fired and a bullet tore through his tent. He went at once to Shaw and found him pretending to sleep, with a warm revolver beside his pillow. With this token rebellion the conspiracy collapsed.

Both Farquhar and Shaw had now become blubbering wrecks and the leader grew each day more like a heroic statue of himself. He never spoke again of the incident until he met Doctor Livingstone, a fellow statue. The tale, by then, must have acquired an epic childishness, for the Doctor listened sternly, then replied, "He intended murder!"

The third and fifth caravans arrived in Mpwapwa on May 17. Stanley's watch-dog, Omar, had died a few days before, just on the threshold of the Ugogo country where, as his master pitilessly reminded him, he might have been of some use. They rested three days in this place, filling their stomachs with milk and mutton and bullock hump, and when they pushed on, the otiose Farquhar stayed behind with six months' supplies. He died several weeks later, but the news didn't reach the caravans until the middle of August when they had all gathered in

Tabora. Stanley, by that time, had Shaw so terrified that when he told him the news he added, "There is one of us gone, Shaw my boy, who will be the next?" Probably each was certain that it would be Shaw, as it was.

Both of these unfortunate victims of Stanley's triumph come very much alive in his book, and their escape from oblivion may console them for a miserable end. But the African members of the expedition are seldom more than black faces, showing now and then some animation and then disappearing. Before crossing the Kakata swamp, for example, Bombay loses the property tent, an American axe and a pistol, and is demoted by Stanley for being irresponsible and lazy. A man named Uledi is also relieved of his post as second captain for the same reason. But it is apparently this same Uledi who, five years later, repeatedly saves Stanley's Congo expedition from disaster.

On leaving Zanzibar I intended to go straight to Bagamoyo and follow Stanley's route in a Land Rover. But when I began to check the possible roads and assailable dirt tracks I saw that they deviated from his route far more than the present rail line does. I felt foolish riding on to Tabora in a train, even a slow train, but consoled myself with the thought that a good many other people would be coming along.

I was mostly worried about Stanley—or rather his ghost. Then I remembered that he had said, "I live at railway celerity." Surely no one *else* could have said a thing like that and it seemed to settle the matter. As soon as I arrived at Dar-es-Salaam, a few miles down the coast from Bagamoyo, I went to buy a ticket.

CHAPTER FIVE

THE young railway clerk asked if I had any objection to sharing a compartment with an Asian; there were no other second-class seats for Europeans. As he wore a large, blue Sikh turban his impassivity was remarkable. Actually, I think he was tired of the whole subject. There is always the danger that the burning issues of one generation will become simply boring to another. Already the idea of white supremacy has a certain fustiness which, in the course of thirty years' fashion, could make it a charming anachronism, like a fringed lampshade in a rocket ship. As the train left twice a week I would have several days' wait.

Dar-es-Salaam was originally planned by Bargash's older brother, Majid bin Said. Its name means Port-of-Peace and many people now simply call it Dar. The newcomer must beware of this, however, for old residents will grow pedantic and their 'Darislaam' becomes a reproach. Majid died before his new capital was complete, and work was only begun again in the 'eighties under the Germans. Many of the buildings of that period achieve a Bavarian-tropical effect which is very pleasant.

Along Azania Front, on the harbour, one frequently sees these great, peaked, wooden boxes with inviting porches. Many of them have been used as government offices, but they are gradually being torn down in favour of structures more suitably banal. My hotel was also German-built and was wonderfully comfortable.

The city has about a hundred thousand inhabitants, and every morning a radio programme called 'Jambo!' wakes them with a song:

"Jambo! happy meeting you
Jambo! means how do you do."

This is a standard greeting all over East Africa and it soon becomes natural to use it, though not necessarily at dawn. The European section is bounded at each end of the harbour by the government offices and the railway station, and in asking directions one is oriented by the Askari Monument at the centre of town, where there are a number of good shops besieged—in early November—by Christmas shoppers.

Unlike Nairobi, there is very little feeling of race tension here, and people of all colours come and go pretty much as they please. The city is well furnished with churches, banks, mosques, temples, hospitals, picture palaces and schools.

There is also a Yacht Club, which was founded in 1933. An official publication, striking a faintly archæological note, mentions that 'there is evidence that another yacht club existed in 1922 but apparently failed for lack of boats and people keen enough to race regularly.' As the British only took the city over in 1919, at the conclusion of peace with Germany, this feeble response may be forgiven. Even now, the sporting activities of the community are sometimes curtailed by hippo bobbing in the harbour and an occasional leopard patrolling the suburbs, perhaps attracted by the RSPCA drinking-pans before public buildings.

As I had time, I arranged with the Government Information Office to see a representative of the Tanganyika African National Union, a political organization headed by Mr Julius Nyerere. TANU has control over all of the elective seats in the Legislative Council and is vigorously preparing to form its own government when the British leave. There is naturally some argument about when that will be, some of it bitter. But TANU will probably have its way in a few years.

Mr Nyerere was visiting in Uganda, at Makerere University, and I was put in the hands of an ebullient young man named Crabbe who acted as a sort of liaison between the government and African movements it otherwise held at arm's length. Perhaps this was more a question of delicacy than disdain, particularly in the case of Mr Nyerere's party, which, though anti-British, is as parliamentarian as Britain's Labour Party, which some people also believe to be anti-British.

Getting too chummy with the opposition would have been a little like opening its mail. Of course many Africans did not understand this and—as has happened in other lands—they mistook complicated British rules of behaviour for outright dislike, which they very much resemble.

Mr Crabbe, who had the blond, resolute look of a scout leader, took me into a district called Kariakoo, north-west of the railway station. The roads were lined with casuarina and frangipani trees, and it was so hot my body left a print in the seat of the car when I got out of it. There had been a sudden shower that morning, a full, direct fall as though a tub had been emptied overhead and now the air was heavy with moisture.

I was taken to TANU headquarters on New Street, a parallel of Livingstone Street, bisected by Stanley Street. There I was introduced to Mr Isak M. Bhoke Munanka, treasurer of the Union. Before I had a chance to look around, Mr Crabbe was edging to the door. He spoke heartily of some unnecessary errand. Mr Munanka and I both urged him to stay. "Oh no," he said, glancing desperately towards the street. "You two will want to be alone." His ears had gone red.

"But won't you have something to drink," Mr Munanka said. "A cup of tea?"

"No—no. Thanks awfully. Have to get on. Terribly late now, really. Good heavens! Half-past three." He backed into

54

the blazing street and jumped into his car. We followed him out. "Good, then—one hour suit you?" I nodded, noticing an Arab Music Club across the street which harmoniously displayed the portraits of Nasser and Queen Elizabeth. Crabbe drove off, and Mr Munanka led me back into the mud building which was his office.

It was little more than a square hut, built contiguous with a small garden. It had corrugated iron roofing, but most of the houses on the unpaved street were thatched. The walls were of mud, plastered over entwined sticks. The garden had a thatched roof over the part nearest the hut and was partially shaded by several trees. There was no natural shade anywhere else, and anything metallic left in the sun for more than a few minutes literally burnt one's fingers.

Mr Munanka was fat, with the deep-set grace of a man who was born to it. He had a shrewd, ugly face, all convex so that his features formed one continuous curve from his forehead to his chin, like a scimitar. I asked if it were true, as I had heard, that TANU accepted no members who weren't African.

"That is correct, we are an organization of Africans."

I pointed out that in a country where ninety-eight per cent of the people are African and where TANU controlled the elections this would eventually have the effect of disenfranchising the Asians and Europeans—it amounted to race discrimination.

Mr Munanka smiled. "Probably. We didn't really begin it here, you know—discrimination, I mean."

I asked if they had any way of determining who was an African and who was not.

"Oh yes. Indeed we have."

"How?"

"You are an African if both of your mother's parents were African." He shifted his weight in his chair and called a boy to the doorway, then said to me, "I'm sorry. Would you like a

Coca-Cola? I'm afraid it's a bit hot for you. Just before the rains, you know."

I wiped my forehead and nodded. He sent the boy racing out in the infernal heat. I asked if there were any religious differences in TANU, between Arabs and Christians, for instance.

"Not at all. Mr Nyerere is a Roman Catholic, as you may know. I myself am a Lutheran. Some of us are Arabs and some have no religion. Our basis for organization is nationality, not religion. That is why in the last elections we . . ."

He began to discuss politics with the total absorption of a professional, hardly noticing that I wasn't taking it all in.

". . . Legislative Council with thirty-four official and thirty-three unofficial members . . ." He paused, significantly.

"Hmmm," I said.

". . . of the unofficial, ten Asians, ten Africans and ten Europeans representing the ten constituencies and the other three . . ."

Mr Munanka's nose was very sharp at the ridge, and looked like a pruning knife. I wondered if, in spite of Lutheran connections, he might not be partly Arab.

". . . first elections last month . . . fifteen unofficial members . . . three from each of five constituencies . . ." He proceeded to give me detailed results of the election, and at last the boy came back with the Cokes, which were hot.

What did he think of the British? I said, taking advantage of Crabbe's absence, after all. Did he *like* them?

For the first time Mr Munanka frowned. It was clearly a question he had pondered before. He said "yyyyesss," at last. "I believe they mean well. Really I do," he added hastily, and with determined emphasis. "The Government, that is. It's the white settlers who're bad. Fortunately, we don't have too many of *them*. Nothing like Kenya or the Rhodesias. They're the ones causing all the trouble."

"But you *do* think they mean well—the Government."

"Welllll, yes. I think so."

"That's something, isn't it? After all, you wouldn't say that about some other governments, I suppose."

"No, I suppose not." Mr Munanka paused, then looked straight at me, for the first time displaying uncertainty. "Are they *very* much worse?"

Then, after a long silence, he called into the next room, in Swahili. In a moment a ragged young man came in with some mimeographed sheets stapled together. The light inner surfaces of his hands were stained with ink and he wore a nobly fanatic expression which can only be found in religious revivals and progressive political movements.

In the background I heard the clicking of the mimeograph machine, without which no liberal organization can function. Munanka explained that this was the approved constitution of still another society dedicated to the overthrow of the well-meaning British. It was called the Pan-African Freedom Movement of East and Central Africa and was known, predictably, as PAFMECA. He happened to be the Secretary.

Glancing down at the papers I saw the words, 'White racialism ... black chauvinism ... so-called trusteeship ... foreign self-seekers,' and looked up at Mr Munanka. He was sipping his Coke benignly. The mimeograph clicked.

To assist in the establishment and organization of united nationalist movements in African territories through periodic conferences [God yes, periodic conferences] ... press for full industrialization and the enhancement of cooperative methods and for the control of the major means of production ...

Mr Munanka broke in. "As you are going on to Tabora, I thought you would like to meet some of our people there."

I thanked him and said that I would.

"Good. I'm having letters of introduction typed for you."

57

He stood up. "And now, I would like you to come into the yard with me to visit our day school. The British *say* they are giving us enough educational facilities, but why should we set up our own schools if they were?" He stood aside as I preceded him out the door into the stifling yard. Behind us the mimeograph machine ground out endless smudgy messages of hope.

Shortly after, with my letters safely put away, I was picked up by Mr Crabbe. We drove past some labour unions on Livingstone Street and stopped at his office, which was a small, nearly empty store, where people were encouraged to congregate. Here, Mr Crabbe practised a kind of rough-and-ready public relations by democratically distributing pictures of the Queen, which were much admired. He also tried to help people get work and to represent their legitimate interests to the Government.

He spoke now to a group of children outside the office and they dissolved in giggles. His Swahili was headlong and fluent and perhaps not very accurate. He was obviously well-liked in the neighbourhood, though I believe it was in spite and not because of his frantic cordiality. I noticed a sign in his window and asked him to translate it.

"Follow the bees and find the honey!" He beamed. "Our motto."

Behind him a little girl wickedly dangled a dead mouse down her sister's back. Another lowered her tightly braided head and charged at a small boy's stomach like a goat.

"You see what that means?" Mr Crabbe said, cheerily. "It's an old Swahili saying."

"No, I don't see," I said, dodging the goat-girl.

"It means, associate with educated people and some of it wears off on you."

"Some of what?"

"Education."

"You're sure that's what it means in Swahili?"

"Positive. Come, I'll take you back to the hotel. Have a good talk? Nice chap, Munanka. Bit hot, isn't it?"

On the day my train was to leave for Tabora there was another quick shower, and I was thoroughly wet. In addition, I had been hit on the head by a falling mango, not very ripe and therefore hard, and by the time I found my compartment I had a headache and was much dispirited. I felt, however, that Mr Stanley would not have been pleased with the way I was meeting the hazards of African travel and resolved to take heart and so ordered a bottle of beer. After all this talk about Asians I was to be alone, and as this was a long trip I settled back to enjoy the pleasures of segregation.

The carriage was about forty years old, built in the heroic age of railroads, with stiff views of Tanganyika on its oak walls and uncompromising instructions from the East African Railways Corporation framed by the door. As we began to cross the plain we passed some native huts and, about four miles out of Dar-es-Salaam, a graveyard for old automobiles. It began to rain again, but the people who stood along the track waving to us seemed not to notice. At an improvised stop some boys came up and performed liquid dances on the siding.

In the first-class cars of this train one generally saw Europeans and rich Indians, in second-class were thrifty and probably even richer Indians, Arabs and myself. Africans, with some well-dressed exceptions, were confined to the third-class. For the most part, the division seemed to be financial rather than racial, though this amounted to practically the same thing.

The Africans were poor, and they lived in their carriages much as poor Europeans do—as though hiding out in bomb shelters or charity hospitals. They came on board loaded with food and drink and kerosene lanterns and children and many mysterious packages. Once inside, the women and children spread, the men sprawled, and bits of food began to pile up beneath the wooden seats and in the aisles. There was continuous lively confusion and heads and arms stuck out the windows like unbound stuffing.

Only a pure, unStanley-like fear of sitting more than twenty-four hours on a hard wooden bench, trying to provide for myself without a word of Swahili and making everyone uncomfortable in the process kept me from travelling third class.

What is more, travelling in third can be extremely expensive unless one knows how to bargain. At each station, as in Southern Europe, merchants passed under the windows selling food. Here, it was coconuts, mangoes, bananas, pineapple and paw-paws in beautifully woven palm baskets. At one stop I managed to keep from paying three dollars for a coconut only by leaning perilously out the window and cancelling the exchange with a grab and a toss. A bunch of bananas normally cost about five cents, a mango one cent, a large pineapple about eight cents and a coconut from one to three cents. This seems very cheap, but if you earn eight or nine dollars a month it is not. If you earn even less, or nothing, it is disastrous—except when a mango falls on your head.

An hour and a half from the coast we were more or less in Stanley's own tracks, and the underbrush was so thick one would have had to tunnel through it with an axe. As we gained altitude a little later the growth thinned out.

The ground was somewhat sandy and, in spite of a few palm trees and some vaguely tropical plants like eucalyptus, the country resembled those rare, undeveloped portions of New Jersey and Rockland County after a long, dry summer. The enormous sky was spotted with rain clouds and the sun streaked through them like fresh dye.

Now and then the land was planted with paw-paws, corn and squash. Squalls of rain swept across the fields, but the ground soaked it up as fast as it fell. The uncultivated plains were black from grass fires which had been set deliberately to avoid accidents. All of the unforested stretches of tropical Africa, which during the rainy season run to ten and twelve foot grass that dries to parchment in the sun, are threatened by flash fires. Here and there were small villages, some with solid stone houses and rich enclosures of frangipani growing around.

At sunset we arrived at the first sizeable town west of the coast, a place called Ngerengere. A few people got out of the third-class coaches, among whom I noticed a young woman of about twenty-three or twenty-four carrying a bundle on her head, a three-legged stool in one hand and a small paper suitcase bound with twine in the other. She approached a young man who was standing on the platform waiting for her.

When she had come up to him she put down the stool and the suitcase and, with an especially graceful gesture, lifted the bundle from her head and set it on the stool. Only then did she reach out her hand to touch his. Though neither smiled or clung to the other for more than a moment one could see—as one always can—that they lived intimately with each other. That was the first time I had noticed this strangely detached and undemonstrative greeting—which may also be a leave-taking. Afterwards I saw it many times and even performed it myself. Africans seem to be less volatile about these things than we are. They consciously refrain from kissing and embracing and other displays of emotion, but they are not less warm for that.

We rode on as night fell. The rain had washed out the stars and a blunt moon to the west shone through ragged clouds. The dark beyond the window was so intense one longed to push a finger through it. In America the nights are sometimes this black but, even there, one hasn't quite the feeling of unlimited space, splendidly invisible. My window was partly open and breezes pushed gently in, smelling of cooling fields and damp earth. In the next compartment a child with croup gasped for air as its mother tried to soothe it. A waiter came through the car playing savage rhythms on a dinner-gong while, outside, disembodied voices of children cried to us and a drum chattered.

The territory of Tanganyika lies just south of the Equator, and is bounded by Lakes Victoria, Tanganyika, Nyasa and the Indian Ocean. It is seven hundred and forty miles long and about as broad. It was first inhabited by men of a stone-age culture in the Pleistocene period. During this time it was also the home of the largest land animal known to have existed, as well as a giraffe with antlers and an elephant which had tusks like a walrus. Much later, during historic times, the littoral was visited by the Chinese, who didn't like it, by the Persians, who colonized it, and by the Arabs, who conquered it and developed the Swahili language and culture. The interior was visited by practically nobody until a century ago.

During the modern era, after a brief period of British influence, Tanganyika became part of German East Africa. This was brought about largely by the activities of a man named Carl Peters, who in 1884 and again in 1888 invaded Africa with fire and sword and treaty forms and lined up a great many petty chiefs under German protection in country which had been more or less controlled by the Sultan of Zanzibar. This was no more than the French, Belgians and British were doing in various other parts of Africa, but Peters distinguished himself by developing a policy he called *Schrecklichkeit* (frightfulness). At one point, in Ugogo, when the local ruler sued for peace, he replied: "It shall be the eternal peace. I will show the Gogo what the Germans are." He did this so efficiently that

Hitler was moved to admiration fifty years later, called him 'a model, if stern, administrator,' and had him made a colonial hero.

Tanganyika was subsequently ruled so conscientiously by these model administrators that barely two hundred thousand people were killed in mistaken rebellions, and many outmoded tribal organizations were destroyed. Probably Count von Götzen was right when he described these rebellions as the last fling of paganism against the Christian culture of Germany, for when the British took over in 1919 they largely ceased and the dictum of a famous Prussian general that it was 'impossible in Africa to get along without cruelty' was modified.

At present, Tanganyika is under United Kingdom trustee-ship, by agreement with the United Nations. Because of this special international status, and because the disintegration of tribal culture had tended to create genuine nationalist senti-ment, as demonstrated by TANU, this might well be the first country to attain independence in East Africa.

At sunrise we stopped in a place with the splendid name of Humwaw Halt. A chill breeze blew through a desolate stone block village which was built around the station. A man in an undershirt and a sarong stood on a rock with a tea kettle in one hand, brushing his teeth, while children walked stiffly across the station house gravel and brightly shawled women withdrew in doorways from the cold.

The sun was already gleaming in the tree-tops and the sky was pink at the horizon. We were some distance past Mpwapwa and had travelled in eighteen hours as far as Stanley had gone in two months.

I felt him getting angry again and rang for a pot of tea, remembering that he and Livingstone used to drink it by the pint (the old man shared Stanley's passion for it) and talk about food. "You will think of me," the Doctor said, speaking of the banquets at the Royal Geographical Society, "when you taste those marrow bones at the Geographical, and the Devonshire Cream." I had bought two large and rather bitter bananas the evening before and made a breakfast on them and the tea which, in East African Railway carriages, flows like water from six in the morning on.

Shortly afterwards we came into Dodoma, which is the largest rail and road centre east of Tabora. We stopped in a railway yard next to some Shell and Caltex storage tanks. Though it was quite early there were many people wandering around the station. One man, wearing nothing but a pair of saffron corduroy pants, led a group of women with rings on their ankles and bundles on their heads on to the train. A small fellow, nearly a pigmy and almost naked, followed a tall policeman to the ticket office, holding his hand—or being held.

Here, also, were willowy warriors, carrying spear-shafts and umbrellas, and wearing patches of rubber tread tied to their feet. Most of the women, even the very young ones, had babies strapped to their backs under their shawls. One girl suddenly clapped her hand on her child's backside and raced for the lavatories.

It was the women who were most impressive here, as they seemed to be all across Africa. The men succumb easily to the stresses of modern life and, as with us, step from full tribal regalia into business suits and rimless glasses with very little difficulty or even shame. But the women are passively and stubbornly consistent.

Enveloped by their shawls, which they are always hitching up at the waist and which lie loose across the breast so that the baby may be shifted around to suck without breaking a stride, they harbour dignity and tradition, oblivious of the world of men.

64

This does not mean they have decided that a woman's place is in the hut, and that they must give up all idea of running off to be literary agents or advertising executives or senators. (A large number of women were leaders of TANU, as I later learned.) Their secret seems to be that they haven't decided *anything*, and they walk around without that strange double emotion towards the other sex which so much bothers us. When they flirt they do it most openly and, it seems, with every intention of immediate fulfilment. They do not appear to have had their respect for their own sex placed even temporarily in doubt.

The train moved on across a plateau of acacia scrub and short, umbrella-shaped trees. There were mountains to the south, and the air was full of the smell of burning grass. In a dry country such as this a railway exerts the same fascination as a river, and at each little village people ran from their huts to dance and wave and wish they were somewhere else.

At the outskirts of one village a hunter leaned desolately on his spear, shaft in the ploughed earth, blade in his hand. At a distance behind him some great brown and white birds, three or four feet tall, suddenly rose into the air and, circling, flew away. The hunter turned and walked eastward along the tracks.

We were several hours beyond Dodoma and human dwellings were becoming less and less frequent. The last we had seen was a complex of mud huts and sheds and thatched roofs supported on poles, evidently the communal buildings of one large family or small tribe, the men of which all seemed to carry neatly folded umbrellas and were otherwise fairly naked.

Then, in the bush, I saw a large animal bound from view and a moment later we passed a pack of baboons in a clearing who appeared to be arguing. I felt, as a cousin, that they should be warned about the large animal, though perhaps they already knew and were indifferent, as I had heard that they were fierce. But all of a sudden this innocent bush country, which a moment before had appeared to me to be properly in the hands of lightly clothed men carrying umbrellas, showed itself in its true light. It was just not safe—that ant hill might be a crouching lion, that tree a buffalo—and to one who is used to safety this comes as a shock.

All that day we travelled across the central plateau of Tanganyika, which rises to well over four thousand feet and may become quite cold at night. We reached Itigi at noon, vivid with light and dark orange flamboyant trees, poinsettia, cosmos, pink roses and great, plain geraniums. Here, children dragged blocks of wood tied to fibre strings behind them, pretending that they were railway cars or maybe animals. Here, also, above a land which would have made the south Italian coast look drab, was an infinite sky dotted with puffs of clouds greying together in the distance. The young men of Itigi, I noticed, tended to wear imitation leopard jackets and vests.

At lunch, the dining-car was crowded with Europeans. Other races either couldn't afford the meal or were forbidden it by wise dietary laws. The English, who understood the properties of the food, sensibly buried it in salt; but a very fat Belgian couple, who had grown in domestic harmony together until they could no longer lift each other, chewed methodically down the menu.

Next to them a grizzled District Commissioner, who hadn't noticed what he was eating in years, was giving gratuitous advice to an Indian landowner. ". . . can't understand why they don't grow cotton up there. Same land in Uganda gives the best cotton in Africa." The landowner politely nibbled some fruit. "Been to Meru lately? They've opened up there. Round in back of the mountains, you know. Interesting. That whole country's being opened up. You want a steady rain the whole year around, though. Can't raise anything without it. Steady."

There was also a woman I had seen several times on the station platforms, a great, deep-chested English garden lady. Opposite her sat a pale young man with bitten finger-nails, who may have been her son. He was reading Paul Bowles, and the D.C. would have said that he wanted to get out in the open more.

That evening, as it grew dark, we came into Tabora, having made the whole trip in a little more than thirty hours. It took Stanley from 21 March to 23 June, 1871, to cover the same ground eighty-seven years four months and eleven days ahead of me.

CHAPTER SIX

W HEN Henry Morton Stanley arrived in Unyanyembe—of which Tabora was the main Arab compound—he was received with the honour and deference due to a veteran traveller and a rich man. The first, second and fourth parties of the *New York Herald* Expedition had arrived safely ahead of him, confirming his fame and affluence.

He was warmly greeted by Mkasiwa, ruler of Unyanyembe, and by the Arab Governor of the district, Sayd bin Salim, who presented him with a comfortable house an hour's walk from Tabora. And just as he was getting settled a troop of slaves arrived from the other Arabs, bearing gifts of food and live-stock. As he had paid off his porters, his people were now reduced to twenty-five and he ordered a bullock slaughtered to celebrate this 'prodigal plenitude.'

Stanley said that he considered himself to be on classic ground and, as usual, one must take him almost literally. Unyanyembe had been hallowed by the presence of Burton, Speke, Grant and Livingstone, and in the young explorer's incorruptibly child-like mind these were mythical names. He could not have been more awed if he had been following in the footsteps of Hector or Achilles or Paris, or if he had been sent to bring comfort to a lost Agamemnon.

By now he firmly believed that if he and his companions lived to complete their task they would become 'immortals.' He was not far from the truth. Stanley's dreams were made of such solid stuff that he was assured of nearly eternal fame less than five months later, if only for one of his pompous phrases.

With over five thousand inhabitants, Tabora was the largest

68

Arab settlement in Central Africa. Though they were so nearly isolated, here at the edge of the unknown, the important traders nevertheless received stores of luxuries regularly from the coast. Moreover, the settlement itself possessed large herds of cattle and goats, and the fertile land provided all the grains, fruits and vegetables that could be found in Zanzibar.

Most of the Arab establishments were furnished with Persian carpets, sybaritic bedding, precious dinner services and harems. Stanley strongly disapproved of Mohammedan sensualism and scorned the Arabs not only for 'gratifying the pruriency of their animal natures' but for

... lingering wantonly over the inharmonious and heavy curves of a negroid form, and looking lovingly on the broad, unintellectual face, and into jet eyes that never flash with the dazzling lovelight that makes poor humanity beautiful.

In all of his books on Africa, Stanley accepts the idea of white supremacy as thoroughly as he does every other Victorian convention, frequently in the face of overwhelming contrary evidence. He does this, one feels, less from malice than loneliness. He tries so hard, always, to belong to someone and he takes a genuine pleasure in being—for want of any other family—a *bona fide* member of the white race.

A few days later, the Arabs invited him to a feast at the *tembe* of Sheikh Khamis bin Abdullah, whom Stanley describes as 'the noblest Trojan amongst the Arab population.' When he arrived he found a number of Arabs in white gowns and caps in heated discussion. 'I was in time for a council of war they were having,' he says. As Stanley had in his possession a great many arms, more modern than could be found anywhere in Tabora, it is probable that he would have been in time for this council of war if he had come a day, or even a week, late.

He was asked to join in and did so, highly flattered. He

learned that a native called Mirambo, who had formerly been a porter for one of the Arabs, had gathered a band around him and, some years ago, had succeeded by force to the chieftainship of a near-by tribe. From these beginnings he had extended his power over a great area and had lately blocked an Arab caravan bound for Ujiji. They had been sent back to Tabora with the alarming news that passage to the lake by the direct route through Mirambo's country could only be made over his dead body. This was a severe financial blow, for in Ujiji a slave could be bought for a little more than a pound that would bring five times as much in Zanzibar.

"This is the status of affairs," said Khamis bin Abdullah. "Mirambo says: that for years he has been engaged in war against the neighbouring Washensi and has come out of it victorious, he says this is a great year with him; that he is going to fight the Arabs, and the Wanyamwezi of Unyanyembe, and that he shall not stop until every Arab is driven from Unyanyembe, and he rules over this country in place of Mkasiwa. Children of Oman, shall it be so?"

Then the children of Oman, with one or two cautious exceptions, made impassioned speeches swearing that it should not be so, while the child of Park Row listened excitedly. After all, he thought, if the war were over quickly—at most within fifteen days, as the Arabs had promised—why not? He had to get to Ujiji somehow and this was the shortest route. Stanley rose and, glowing with martial ardour, volunteered to join the war party.

'The Arabs were sanguine of victory,' he wrote, 'and I partook of their enthusiasm.' This healthy optimism was not justified. Not only was that year a great year for Mirambo but so were the following twelve, and when he died of natural causes in 1884 he had carved out an empire for himself nearly the size of France and controlled all routes to **Lakes Tan-** ganyika and Victoria.

James Gordon Bennett would have been appalled to learn that his special correspondent was blithely preparing to risk his expedition in a fight that had nothing whatever to do with the *New York Herald*, or Livingstone. The young warrior himself awoke to his responsibilities in a few days, but by that time it was too late to try to make any sort of deal with Mirambo, as he was known to have supported the Arabs.

After that he had no choice but to strike out on another route of his own, if he was still determined to find Livingstone. The whole blunder must be laid to high spirits—and what stout-hearted young man wouldn't have joined the fiery sheiks of Tabora against an ignorant marauder?

The trouble was that most of the sheiks were really great cowards and Mirambo was far from ignorant. As this savage chieftain later wrote to the British Consul in Zanzibar:

Is it expected that if my power is destroyed the petty chiefs of this country would make it . . . more open to traders, more peaceful? . . . I can only say that this country is a hundred times more prosperous . . . a thousandfold more safe than it ever was before I became chief of it. I wish to open it up . . . to learn of Europeans . . . to trade honestly with my neighbours.

When the council of war broke up, Khamis bin Abdullah caused to be served a great dishful of rice and curry, in which almonds, citron, raisins, and currants were mixed. The guest was also brought

platters of roast chicken, kabobs, crullers, cakes, sweetbread, fruit, glasses of sherbet and lemonade, dishes of gum-drops and Muscat sweetmeats, dry raisins, prunes and nuts.

Stanley always lovingly described his food. Eating was one of the few means he had of gratifying the pruriency of *his* animal nature and when he was with Livingstone he liked to fix special dishes for the old man, which the two would consume while drinking several quarts of tea and speaking about their digestions.

After the banquet Stanley was taken around Tabora and shown the homes of the best people. He also visited the site of Burton and Speke's house, as a shrine, and returned to his own *tembe* towards evening with more gifts of food and no sense at all of having been taken.

Preparations for war took up the first days of July, but on the seventh Stanley fell ill with fever. Malaria is particularly virulent around Tabora, even now. While delirious the scenes of his life passed in review before him:

> ... a young life's battles and hard struggles came surging into the mind in quick succession; events of boyhood, of youth, and manhood; perils, travels, scenes, joys, and sorrows ... The loveliest feature of all to me was the form of a noble, and true man, who called me son ... And I remembered how one day, after we had come to live near the Mississippi, I floated down, down, hundreds of miles, with a wild fraternity of knurly giants, the boatmen of the Mississippi, and how a dear old man welcomed me back as from the grave ... I remembered also my travels on foot through sunny Spain, and France, with numberless adventures in Asia Minor, among Kurdish nomads ... I remembered the shock it gave me to hear after my return ... of the calamity that had overtaken the fond man whom I called father, and the hot fitful life that followed it.

Perhaps because of his constant attacks of delirium, Stanley was beginning to look upon his expedition as divinely accredited, or at least backed by a higher power than the *New York Herald*. Prodded by faith in his cause he began to wonder if his friends the Arabs weren't trying to keep him from Livingstone and use him in their fight against Mirambo.

In an extract from his diary, written one night after a bout of fever, he says:

If they think so, they are much mistaken, for I have taken a solemn, enduring oath . . . No living man, or living men shall stop me, only death can prevent me. But death—not even this; I shall not die, I will not die, I cannot die! And something tells me, I do not know what it is . . . something tells me tonight I shall find him, and—write it larger—FIND HIM! FIND HIM! Even the words are inspiring. I feel more happy. Have I uttered a prayer? I shall sleep calmly tonight.

In a week Stanley had recovered; Shaw and his Arab valet Selim had nursed him. Then it was Shaw's turn, and afterwards Selim's. By July 29 Stanley had fifty men loaded with bales, beads and wire for Ujiji.

It was his plan to accompany the Arabs on their journey to Mirambo's stronghold, leave his baggage in the rear and attack with them. They marched out of Tabora singing and letting the American flag snap in a stiff wind. They thought this banner might terrify the enemy.

On the third day out they came to a town called Mfuto, where Stanley proposed to leave his supplies while they went and thrashed Mirambo. Here Shaw lay down and declared that he was dying and Stanley gave him a glass of port, a bowl of gruel and put him to bed.

On August 3 the combined forces marched against Mirambo. They didn't reach the first of his fortresses until noon of the 5th, by which time Stanley was again down with fever and had to be carried in a hammock. This fortress was invested and, from there, parties sallied out against other enemy positions, leaving the two Europeans behind, delirious.

On the sixth, however, news came of a crushing Arab defeat and by the morning of the seventh everyone was talking of retreat. Stanley strongly advised the Governor against this as it would only draw Mirambo on Tabora itself, but in the afternoon of that day Selim roused him from his sick-bed and told him that everyone was running away, even Khamis bin Abdullah, the noblest Trojan.

He staggered out and found Shaw stealing the saddle off his donkey. Only seven of the original fifty men who had left Tabora could be found, among whom were Bombay and Mabruki Speke. They struck out on the road for Mfuto, glancing over their shoulders. Shaw kept falling off his donkey and finally Stanley had him held in place by men walking on either side of the animal. He, too, was very sick and was ready to lie down and die, but he was supported by thoughts of his high mission.

Fortunately for Stanley, Mirambo didn't press his counter-attack and he was able to get all his supplies out of Mfuto and back to Tabora. Here he retired to his *tembe*, cut loopholes in the walls for guns, and refused to have anything more to do with the Arabs who had left him, he claimed, to die on the field of battle. They denied this and said that they thought he had already gone, but relations between them continued strained.

Stanley now had not only to defend himself but to hire a whole new set of porters; the ones who had gone to Mfuto would only agree to travel by the regular road and he was proposing a southern détour.

On August 14, a week after the retreat, Shaw again fell ill, this time seriously. On examining him Stanley decided that he was suffering from a 'venereal affliction.' He gave two soldiers a hundred and fifty dollars apiece to go to Zanzibar to get some medicine for him, as he had not thought to bring along anything for such a disease. This was surprisingly prudish—even for Stanley—as spirochaete and gonococcus were as common in Central Africa as white ants. The leader was beginning to have doubts about bringing his assistant along on the second stage of the journey. Shaw, by this time, had become practically fungoid.

74

On August 22 Tabora was attacked. Khamis bin Abdullah, atoning for his previous retreat by a show of bravery, marched out to meet the enemy together with some of the younger Arabs and eighty slaves. Mirambo drew them into a trap, drove off the slaves and surrounded Khamis and four of the Arabs. These his men killed, and cut off the skin of their foreheads, their beards, the skin of the lower parts of their faces, the fore parts of their noses, the fat over their stomachs and abdomens, their genital organs and a bit from each heel. From such assorted bits of flesh they made a powerful medicine which, like all weapons of war, was intended to insure that the same thing wouldn't be done to them.

Stanley spent the next two days reinforcing his house, determined to sell himself dearly. He had heard that Mirambo and his principal officer carried umbrellas and he planned to make a gold bullet to pick the chief off with. In the meantime he kept the American flag flying over his *tembe*, hoping that this would shatter the nerves of the superstitious savages.

In the end the attack fizzled out, though Tabora was partially sacked and burnt. Mirambo retreated with a large quantity of booty and the Arabs made a show of chasing him away. Stanley returned to his plans to reach Ujiji by a southern détour. Shaw began to improve but seemed incapable of any work and looked on listlessly as everyone scurried about.

To hearten him, Stanley took him aside and revealed that they had not really come to map the country, as he had always told him, but to FIND LIVINGSTONE. This news had very little effect on the sick man and probably wouldn't have moved him much if he were well. He was just terribly sorry he had come, though he could never hope to make his employer understand this.

On another day, knowing Stanley well by now, and knowing what would impress him, he said that his father had been a captain in Her Majesty's Navy and that he had been present at four levees of Victoria. Stanley took this news gravely. It would have been a great blow to him if it had been true. But, as he said in his diary,

this can hardly be as I cannot imagine a naval captain's son being so ignorant of penmanship as scarcely to be able to write his own name, nor can I see how it is possible that he could have been presented to the Queen, for I have always understood that the Court of St James's is the most aristocratic in Europe.

It was only after the former John Rowland had himself been presented to the Queen—who gave him a gold snuff-box—that he began to feel free of the incubus of his vile birth, and socially at ease. Though it would have hurt him, he might not in his heart have disagreed with the Queen's description of him in a letter to the Princess Royal in Berlin: 'I have this evng. seen Mr. Stanley, who discovered Livingstone, a determined, ugly little Man—with a strong American twang.'

During their last days in Tabora Stanley was even sicker than his assistant and Shaw began to perk up. He went around the camp saying that if anything happened to the leader—if he should 'die like a donkey,' for example—*he* would head back to the coast and to hell with Livingstone. To Stanley this seemed heresy, but to a man who believed his life depended upon it—as Shaw's did—this was a purely reasonable attitude. Once, a bit maliciously, he came to his employer's bedside at the height of one of his fevers and asked to whom he should write in case of death. "Even the strongest of us die," he added, perhaps remembering Stanley's heartiness when they had heard of Farquhar's lonely end.

On September 20, amidst 'considerable shouting, and laughing, and negroidal fanfaronnade,' Stanley marched out of Tabora towards the south with a caravan of fifty-four men, most of whom he had hired at treble pay to take this uncharted route. He had also lightened the porter's loads to fifty pounds, leaving the bulk of his supplies behind, so that he could make longer marches.

The *New York Herald* Expedition had been three months in Tabora—almost as long as it had taken to get there from the coast. Stanley would have been the first to criticize this waywardness in another man, though he didn't seem to think that he himself had been at fault in joining the campaign against Mirambo.

And, as usual, luck was squarely on his side. If he had left Tabora a few weeks after he arrived at the end of June, he probably would never have found Livingstone. Since March 1871 the old man had been deep in Central Africa, at Nyangwé, trying to get boats to go down the Lualaba and, thence, down the great river that Stanley later proved to be the Congo. But before the rescue caravan left Tabora the Doctor turned back, sick and weary. He arrived at Ujiji in October—less than a month before Stanley found him—in time to save that ruthless young man from oblivion.

Though Stanley was still very ill when he started he wanted to put a distance between himself and Tabora so that his men wouldn't run back to see their women friends. They hadn't gone an hour, however, before Shaw—whose moment of triumph was over—fell off his donkey. He never was a very good rider. At his screams, everyone ran up. "What is it, my dear fellow?" Stanley asked. "Are you hurt?"

"Oh dear, oh dear! Let me go back, please, Mr Stanley."

"Why? Because you have had a fall from a donkey? Come, pluck up courage, man . . ." The leader then delivered the kind of lecture that had been so deeply depressing his assistant all these months. A few days later Mr Shaw's foot missed a stirrup and he fell flat on his face. Stanley refused to allow him

77

to be picked up and let him lie for an hour in the sun. When he spoke to him at last the unfortunate man burst into tears.

"Do you wish to go back, Mr Shaw?"

"If you please, I do not believe I can go any farther; and if you would only be kind enough, I should like to return very much."

"Well, Mr Shaw, I have come to the conclusion that it is best you should return. My patience is worn out. I have endeavoured faithfully to lift you above these petty miseries which you nourish so devotedly. You are simply suffering from hypochondria . . . Mark my words—to return to Unyanyembe, is to DIE! . . . Once again, I repeat, if you return, you DIE!"

But with this question settled—and it seems likely that the poor fellow deliberately chose death to Mr Stanley's further endeavours to lift him above his petty miseries—the two men became friends. The evening before they parted Shaw played some nostalgic tunes on his accordion, among which was *Home, Sweet Home.* Stanley said that he fancied that they had softened towards each other, but no one ever heard Shaw's side of the story. He was sent back with a leg of kid and a canteen of cold tea to Tabora, where he died a short while later.

CHAPTER SEVEN

Tabora of the present day has expanded considerably beyond its old boundaries, not so much because there has been a great increase in population but because the Germans, who gave the town its form at the close of the century, expected it to become the capital of Tanganyika. It was possibly laid out in Berlin by someone who had never been here, and walking through it now is like walking on a great, empty blueprint. The roads are straight as rulers and cross each other at regular intervals, leaving huge meadows which were meant to be filled with buildings.

The main highways all lead to the Boma, or Government offices, and are so broad and unobstructed that they may easily be raked with machine-gun fire. If things had gone according to plan it would have been one of the most disciplined cities in the world. But in spite of the fact that Tabora's weather is far superior to Dar-es-Salaam's and that it lies in the very centre of the country, when the British took over they preferred to remain at the coast in the friendly shade of their warships.

I went first to see Mr B. J. A. Dudbridge, who was the political counsellor of the district, not so much because I was interested in politics but because I had his name. To reach his office I had to walk down several miles of undeviating roads bordered by empty fields, made green here and there by clumps of mango trees. Once in a while there was a house, surrounded with palms and dark red frangipani and flowering thorn.

The yards of many of these dwellings were neat and undeniably English. Some of the others, less neat but with more essential order, grew delicate Indian children, guarded by

79

African nurses. There was a constant wind, which Stanley had mentioned, and it seemed a perfect country for kites.

Mr Dudbridge was a tall man with a stern manner which hid a pleasant, actuarial nature. He liked to be precise about things and to make sure that his listener understood him. His office was trim and designed for three hundred honest days' work a year. He had a habit, when speaking sincerely, of slipping his little finger towards one nostril and then trailing it guiltily to the corner of his mouth. This seemed to have been acquired at some over-strict public school.

Mr Dudbridge had devoted many years of his life to the British Government and to the people of Tanganyika and was a thorough and thoughtful civil servant. I showed him the names on the two envelopes that the Dar-es-Salaam TANU chapter had given me. One, Chief Fundikira, he approved of strongly. The other, a man named Maswanya, he was less enthusiastic about. "Former Warrant Officer," he said, indicating by his tone the sort of person that might be. "Of course I can't *stop* you from seeing him," he continued, defining the position of his Government more than his own wishes.

People in this part of the country, I gathered, were sensitive about questions from strangers. On several occasions they had been criticized by the United Nations Trusteeship Committee for their administration of the Territory, and they felt that they had been treated unfairly, as they may have been.

I asked—possibly at the wrong moment—about the status of Africans and the discrimination against them by Indians and Europeans. "If there *is* any discrimination," Mr Dudbridge said, with marked restraint, "it is all to the African's advantage." He proceeded to remind me of the various laws in force to protect African work and property rights, and of the tax system biased in their favour.

I persisted, saying that, after all, one did feel it here—though not as strongly as in Kenya. "Oh, if you're talking about *feelings*," he said, leaning back in his chair, obviously relieved.

"Yes," I said, "I guess that's what I was talking about."

Mr Dudbridge shrugged. "You know, we regret that very much. But what do you suggest we do about it? There is, after all, a certain *cultural* discrimination we can't help."

I asked what he meant.

He smiled. "May I know what your father did?"

"He was a business man."

Mr Dudbridge nodded. His little finger, which had been lightly touching his jaw, crept gently upward. "That's what I was expecting you to say."

I watched, fascinated. "What do you mean?"

"Well—would your father have invited his typists home with him?" The finger reached the nostril and shied away.

By coincidence, my *mother* had been a typist, so that I had an excellent opportunity to score a point on his own analogy, but the finger was creeping upwards again and the moment for attack passed.

"You see what I mean?"

"Well . . ."

"Well what?"

"Well," I finished lamely, "in *French* Africa there isn't very much cultural discrimination, as you call it."

Mr Dudbridge dropped his hand from his face and leaned forward. He spoke with simple, disarming pride. "Yes, but my dear fellow, I am an Englishman. I can't change that!"

Before I left he kindly called the Educational Officer, Mr Kingdom-Hawkins, and asked him to see me. In this he showed considerable judgment. As I later learned, there were two sorts of Europeans in Tabora—the bridge people and the hi-fi people. I was taped as hi-fi and sent over to Education. He, obviously, was bridge.

Before seeing Kingdom-Hawkins, I dropped in on Chief Fundikira. The family is an old one and there was a chief by this name ruling the Wanyamwezi (people of the moon) during the days of Said bin Sultan, over a hundred years ago. They have survived several scandals, including a nasty case of embezzlement and suicide. The present Chief is a plump young man with a good education, five official wives and a cream-coloured Chevrolet. He had lately been elected to the Legislative Council with the help of TANU, being sensitive to the changing patterns of rule.

I took a taxi in the direction of Stanley's old *tembe*, though I hadn't yet had time to see it. Fundikira's compound was built in the native style, with mud buildings and thatched roofs, but it was on a very much larger scale.

At the entrance to the grounds, baked hard by the sun and packed by naked feet, there were a number of great drums suspended from a ridge-pole. I tried hitting one and it rumbled like thunder. Some young men came around the corner of the house and looked at me. I covered my embarrassment by asking where I could find the chief, but before they understood the question he came wandering across the yard in slacks and an open white shirt.

We went inside out of the sun, and his followers, who normally sit on the floor outside of his office, rose and clapped their hands twice. Fundikira nodded, in an abstract and distant manner, suggesting dignity, and led me into a room dominated by an executive desk, with the usual appurtenances, including a telephone.

This was the first African chief I had ever met, and, inevitably, the experience was disappointing. Not that I expected feathers and bones, but a member of the first elected legislature should have been a little less ordinary, a little less like an *American* politician. He dutifully mouthed all the current slogans and repeated catch-words like 'reactionary' and 'imperialistic' and even 'liberty' as though they were signs of office.

Of course, a Congressman would have had other words and slogans but the effect was much the same. Fundikira then spoke warmly of the poverty of his people, which was evident enough in the waiting-room outside his office, and said that he hoped the Western world would remember its responsibilities towards them. He said nothing of his own, and one had the feeling that it would come as a sharp surprise to him one day to discover that there were any.

The chief was otherwise such a model of caution that he managed to seem practically mute. He criticized the English, of course, but that was the style these days. At all events he was never so far out on a limb that he couldn't crawl back.

Before lunch I dropped into the headquarters of TANU, on Usagara Street, off the market. The block here was formed of strong, mud-walled houses, connected along the length of the unpaved street with rush fences. In small gardens behind these, families contended.

TANU had a great mango tree before its door and a number of people were gathered in its shade. Mr Maswanya, District Chairman for Tabora, could only spare me a minute this morning but promised to come and see me the next day and take me around to the local offices of his organization.

Maswanya's office had a tattered old carpet, an oil-can cut in half for a waste-basket, pictures of Nkruma and Nyerere on the walls, splintered office furniture, torn folders in a makeshift file; on his desk there were some ink-smeared rubber stamps, a telephone and a pair of 'in' and 'out' baskets.

He was tall and muscular, possibly thirty-five years old, with a habitually impassive face. Though he was neither as well educated nor as well thought-of as Fundikira, *he* had got the chief elected and he meant to see that no one forgot it. In this, at least, he was the more sophisticated of the two men—a sort of elementary Tammany leader, doing his best with the material at hand.

On leaving, I asked why he had quit his job as a Warrant Officer in the Government security forces. He smiled and there was a faintly mocking light in his eyes. "Well, I just got tired of teaching young Englishmen my own job and finding that they had been made my superiors at my next station." He paused and then continued, still smiling, "And then I didn't honestly like being a policeman." In everyday Swahili there is probably a word for 'cop.'

The hotel in Tabora was originally built as a hunting-lodge for the Kaiser, though he never saw Africa. It caters now to commercial travellers, transient government people and an occasional Indian merchant.

After lunch, which included sauté potatoes, carrots maître d'hôtel and beans aux fines herbes, which turned out to be chips, boiled carrots and parsley-and-beans in white sauce, I was browsing through the books in the hotel office—where *Larousse Gastronomique, Good Housekeeping Cookery Book, Gourmet Cookery Book, Constance Spry Cookery Book* and *Cooking of All Nations* glare all day in silent reproach at their director—when Kingdom-Hawkins dropped by for me. He was going to visit the Tabora boys' secondary school and asked if I would like to come along.

Although distinctly hi-fi, he was every bit as efficient and dedicated as Mr Dudbridge. He had a dark, Scottish face and though he was of a humorous and permissive nature he was probably subject to black moods. He drove very fast, talking volubly and well. I had the impression that in his present job he didn't get a chance to do either as much as he liked.

We swerved out into the main road. "Notice all those

84

mangoes around here?" Kingdom-Hawkins said, pushing the little Peugeot into top gear. "All brought in by the Arabs and the Germans. Also a lot of wattle and gum from Australia. Changed the face of the country. As a matter of fact, the most common name for East Africa is 'the place of foreign trees.' "

He turned out of the path of a meandering bicycle. "Never teach *any*one to stay on his own side of the road . . . Terribly funny about the mangoes. If you buy them on the land—the trees themselves, I mean—they cost sixteen shillings; they just grow by themselves, you know, and the tree is full of fruit. There're thousands around here. But in the market the fruit costs twopence apiece."

He turned sharp left. "Sweet little car. We've been awfully pleased with it. I picked it up second hand and never had a bit of trouble. American cars used to be very popular out here but they've rather outpriced and outstyled themselves now. Can't get over a bump in the road with them and there's too much power going to waste." He slowed for a crossing. "That can be important. On the road to Pemba there's a sign. It says: stop, have you food and water, petrol and oil, have you checked your motor? That sort of thing. *You have been warned* it says. Great big skull and cross-bones. And it's really like that, you know. Hundreds of miles with nothing at all but the road. If you break down you're stranded for weeks, if you live."

I stared down at his knees. In East Africa these are often a man's most extrusive feature. "Rather interesting school out here, *I* think. Of course the boys you're going to see are a good deal older than they would be in European or American schools. They start later. That's why we don't have co-education. Anyway, the girls get married when they're fifteen or sixteen so they're hard to educate. And you can't really expect more than two years' work out of a woman teacher—but I suppose she goes off and teaches her own family."

85

I said that I had noticed a number of other schools around Tabora and asked what they were and how they differed from this one. "Well, this is mostly a school for Africans. Oh yes, there's quite a strong colour feeling in the schools. Not just among the whites. The Indian half-castes as well, Goans and people like that. They all want to stay with their own." I learned, however, that the Catholic church was soon to establish an inter-racial school.

Kingdom-Hawkins turned to me. "Not too much wind on you, is there? The weather *is* marvellous out here. That's the best part about it. This is just as hot as it gets. It can even be very bracing—but of course there is the wind. Up that road is the Livingstone *tembe*, where Stanley stayed." I reminded him that it was the Stanley *tembe*, where Livingstone stayed.

"Really? We'll drop by afterwards if you care to. I hear they have it all fixed up. I don't know that I've seen it. All these things are great frauds if you ask me—never learn history that way. Now right down the road there is the tsetse-fly barrier. They'll let you out all right but they won't let you in without checking. The fly doesn't travel by itself, you see, it has to catch a ride."

"Tabora itself is quite healthy, but it's just an island. There's plenty of bilharzia and yaws and trachoma out there. The Africans lose about fifty or sixty per cent of their children . . . here we are. We turn in here."

We were greeted by the superintendent, who showed us around. The school spread over a large area and was composed of long, rectangular buildings stuck together like dominoes.

A new section had just been added and was not entirely finished; its windows were purposely made small, for in Africa even a crack in the door will flood a room with light. Otherwise the school was depressingly like every other one in the world;

the dormitories smelled of old sneakers, the Chem labs displayed neat files of bunsen burners and test-tubes, and on the blackboard of one classroom, temporarily deserted, someone had been trying to divide

$$x^3 + 2x^2 + kx + 10 \text{ by } x^2 - 3x + 2.$$

In still another room one of the teachers had asked his pupils how the British colonial dependencies in tropical Africa were progressing towards self-government and how far they had been successful. This seemed a rather dangerous subject, but the truly noble British capacity for sticking out their own necks and teaching others the art of beheading was even better displayed in a corollary question which asked the students to describe the activities of the leaders of the French Revolution and to say how much they sympathized with them. Many of the teachers at the school were African and most of the lessons were given in Swahili.

"Our real trouble here," the superintendent said, "is to keep our boys from studying too hard. They would just burn themselves out if we let them. We had a student for a while from your country, I think it was California, but he didn't last very long. Things got too tough for him," he added, with a touch of satisfaction. "Of course you understand that most of the boys here *are* picked. That probably explains it. We'll have some failures when we have more schools," he said, confidently. The superintendent was also trying to say that American schools weren't very good and he was probably right.

I asked what sort of work the students did and he gave me a number of papers for an examination they had just taken. Among other things they had been asked to write down the expansion by the binomial theorem of $\left(3x - \dfrac{y}{2}\right)^4$, and simplify the coefficients; to prove that the ratio of the areas of similar triangles is equal to the ratio of the squares on corresponding sides; to show how the slave trade was organized *either* in East *or* in West Africa and how Europe became aware of its evils; and to reduce two hundred and eighty-seven English words to one hundred. There were also the usual questions, designed to restrain eager spirits with a dead academic hand. This was probably all for the best, for without having to illustrate Chaucer's delight in detail by reference to *three* of the following, and without having to write on Tennyson's use of simile and metaphor *or* the vividness of his descriptive passages by reference to suitable poems, these young men in spotless white shorts would soon have out-stripped their masters and then it wouldn't only have been the boy from California who found the going too tough.

When we were let out of school we went over to Stanley's *tembe* and found it hopelessly forlorn as any souvenir. Kingdom-Hawkins raced me through the little museum, past Stanley's room and Bombay's room, as though he were afraid someone would catch him. He was suffering the embarrassment that afflicts people in Rome and New York when they take visitors to the Vatican and the Empire State Building. I suggested that we go, and he joyfully shoved me into the Peugeot and sped off, past the tsetse-fly barrier.

We were going some distance from town to visit a school that was being constructed on the land of a Catholic church. As the Government contributes a fixed share of the expenses of the religious schools it was part of Kingdom-Hawkins' job to inspect the work.

"From here on out you can expect fly," he said, closing the windows of the car. "Always travel closed up like this, no matter what the temperature."

I said I thought the *glossina morsitans* only affected domestic animals.

88

"Not necessarily. You can catch sleeping sickness any time, though it can be easily cured unless it gets into your spinal fluid. But they bite like needles, you know, especially in the bright sunlight. When we were driving up North last year I had to put water in the radiator and we waited for an hour in the sun for a cloud to pass overhead . . . It was in the sky, a little patch, then bigger and bigger, but it wouldn't come. You see, when they hitch a ride with your car you can't get rid of them unless a bigger car comes by—a truck or something. They they go off with it. Unfaithful creatures, thank God."

When we arrived, Kingdom-Hawkins ran off to look at his buildings and I wandered towards the church. Its peaked, thatched roof dominated a small settlement. Beyond this was nothing but empty fields and bush, but there must have been several villages near by or the church would never have been built here. It looked like a great native hut; very large inside, really cathedral size, with the highest point of the roof reaching up forty or fifty feet.

Birds had made their nests there in the open thatch, and the vast room, unobstructed except for low, hand-carved wooden benches, echoed their Franciscan voices. There were several little chapels with hideous porcelain statues set before charming paintings. One of these was of Mary, and beneath it was a phrase in Swahili.

A voice behind me spoke: "It says, 'I will cleanse you of original sin.' " I turned and found a small, dried priest, very black and very old. Behind him was another priest, a bit younger. "Where do you come from?" the old one said, humming his words at the back of his throat, as one might after a lifetime of liturgy.

I mentioned Kingdom-Hawkins but they shook their heads. They wanted to know where I *lived*. I said that for the present

I lived in Rome, and they nodded wisely. Perhaps Kingdom-Hawkins had already told them.

"Then you are a priest," said the youngest, with assurance. I said I was not. "But you must be. Why do you live in Rome?" Nothing could persuade them that I wasn't at least some kind of priest, and when they mentioned a bishop who had been educated in Rome they were astonished that I didn't know him.

Their voices became more confiding and professional and the old man slipped so far into liturgy that it was almost impossible to understand him. I was crowded into the vestry to see their yellow, green and black vestments, their personal chalices and the sacred host. They kept me there, showing off their innocent gaudery, until Kingdom-Hawkins came looking for us.

Though it has witnessed savage perversions of its mission, the Christian Church, Protestant and Catholic, seems to feel more at home in Africa than in Europe. Here, with the roots of its faith bared, it may take up a natural function that it has almost forgotten elsewhere. It moves among the people, at times, as though it were again at its origins and is unexpectedly refreshed by the necessary mechanics of charity and compassion.

The prevalent notion of a missionary as a tight-lipped fugitive from deep analysis is not accurate. Many of the white priests and pastors who come to work in Africa—especially in the interior where there are few European settlers—are either radically different from their colleagues at home or they grow different with their work. In the presence of a real need for their secular services, and sometimes even for their religious ones, they lose the injured, Christian Democratic look they are likely to have when they leave Europe or America. The black clerics also seem to share this sense of fulfilment and they have not yet quite formed a separate class—a sort of spiritual bourgeoisie—like so many of their white brothers.

In heavily settled areas, relations between the Church and indigenous peoples aren't so idyllic. It has often fallen under the influence of the white colonists who have made it a sop for the Africans and tried even to use it against each other in national quarrels.

The establishment of Protestant missions in Tanganyika, for instance, was frequently interrupted by the tribal wars of the British and the Germans, who turned religious orders against each other and sometimes against the ideals of Christianity. At the outbreak of the Second World War a portrait of Adolf Hitler, painted by a clerical admirer, was found behind the altar of a German mission near Dar-es-Salaam. This did not dispose the members of an inferior race to worship, especially at such an impermanent shrine.

All considered, it is only natural that the more international, Roman Church which had been working these vineyards with fewer interruptions for nearly a century, should have made great gains. By now, the majority of Christians in Tanganyika are Catholic.

Among the Roman Orders now at work are the White Fathers to whom Pope Leo XII in 1878 entrusted the evangelization of the regions of the Central African lakes. These men are pleasant, tolerant Hollanders with traces of cigar ash on their white robes and good beer on their breaths, but there would be no further reason to remark them if not for the fact that they seem to be the instruments of a new Church policy in Africa.

As one of their main stations is at Tabora, which is the rail hub for lines which go to Lakes Victoria and Tanganyika, I asked Kingdom-Hawkins to drop me off to see Archbishop Bronsvelt, to whom I had a cautious introduction from the Superior General in Rome. Before Kingdom-Hawkins left he invited me to dinner to meet his wife.

The Bishop was an urbane, comfortable man who had devoted his life to teaching. Though his own position was conservative, he seemed to confirm what I had heard about the Order—that they were firmly on the side of TANU and were actively supporting the independence movement. The Bishop disapproved of some of Nyerere's speeches (a few were unnecessarily inflammatory, he said, and were only made to keep his following), and he was surely not anti-British; but he obviously intended to keep the White Fathers here long after the English had gone and he believed this was the way to do it.

So far, everything was going well, with the leader of TANU itself a communicant. "Mr Nyerere has a good, big, Catholic family," the Bishop said, with immense satisfaction. But this alone was not enough. Leaders may be deposed.

The White Fathers at Kipalapala, just outside Tabora, own and operate one of the largest and most versatile printing plants in East and Central Africa. They do a good deal of government work—also for the Rhodesias—many bibles in odd Sudanese and Bantu dialects, prayer books, religious calendars, a Swahili translation of *Pinocchio*, etc. They also, as though by chance, edit and publish the most fiercely nationalist and anti-imperialist newspaper in all of British Africa. It is almost wholly written by a small, pallid, indignant Dutchman called Father Van Dam, whose proudest boast is that few people who read the paper know he isn't black.

Both Bishop Bronsvelt and Father Van Dam would object to this description of *Kiongosi*, a name which I believe means Guide or Herald. The Bishop would have said that I have exaggerated the intentions of a religious publication, written in Swahili and of little interest to anyone but Africans. Father Van Dam, on the contrary, would feel that these intentions *were* strongly political. As it was, he suspected me of pro-imperialist sympathies and accused me of not seeing enough Africans.

His conception of *Kiongosi* was probably accurate. It made token passes at moderation but it owed its enormous success to the fact that it took the African side in political as well as in social matters. Mr Maswanya, for instance, thought very highly of it.

Considering that each copy was read by at least five people and often aloud to whole villages, its 24,000 circulation in Tanganyika was the equivalent of the combined weekly editions of *Time* and *Life* in the United States and, in concord with them, it viewed the Church of Rome benevolently.

I saw Father Van Dam towards dusk, all in a lovely garden at Kipalapala behind the busy printing plant. The Father had a pimple on his nose and spoke long and earnestly over a bottle of beer. His views were classically liberal. Reactionary forces were battling progress in their old blind, stupid way, unwilling to see their own salvation being held out to them. There would come a time when the extremists would take over and then . . .

"If they would only *realize*," he said, leaning forward in his wicker chair, his ascetic head set off in a background of hibiscus flowers, "that these people are . . ." His 'they' was a typical liberal 'they,' the others, everyone else but us—in this case the British. 'These people,' of course, were Africans. He might have said 'our,' or even 'my people,' but he was so dead white it was embarrassing.

Father Van Dam was probably right, but one couldn't help but feel that if a miracle happened—if 'they' did realize; if, for once, reactionary forces stopped battling progress and allowed themselves to be saved from their own folly, this good and charming man would be miserable.

When I left we passed through the plant, weaving through African printers slugging out paragraphs and locking in frames, who looked on us with the unsmiling superiority of all craft union men. As I got into my cab the Father said, a little

93

wistfully, "I don't suppose you could get me a good picture of the new Pope, could you? I have one but it isn't much. I mean, if you're going to Rome . . . Something for the front page."

Dinner was served at eight at the Kingdom-Hawkins' comfortable little modern house. We had a drink first and discussed cars, as he planned to retire in two years. They were torn between a DKW and an Opel Caravan. "We're not sure, yet," his wife said, "all we know is we don't want an *English* car." She was a small, pretty woman, very pale and usually quiet. She was Tabora's librarian. Letting one thing suggest another I commented on their hi-fi set and said that of course in New York or London it would be considered rather inadequate—with all the woofers and tweeters and what not they were putting on sets now.

"Yes," said Kingdom-Hawkins, "but you must remember that its hard to get things like that out here." The doors to the porch were open and I looked out into the black night at a huge pair of yellow eyes. Was one supposed to mention such things or ignore them? A moment later it proved to be the servant, carrying two lanterns across the yard towards the house. Casually I spoke of wild animals.

"Oh, there're plenty around," Kingdom-Hawkins said. "They stay away from Tabora because most of the natives have guns, but during the war when it was hard to get ammunition they started to move right in. There were elephants on the golf course . . . did quite a lot of damage. Then there were lion and leopard and other pests. We had a hyena out on the lawn just a little while ago." I glanced again towards the porch.

"But the driver ants are the most dangerous. They can come straight through a house—a swath about a foot wide. They eat anything that's flesh. If you leave a dog tied up in their path he's nothing but bones in a few hours—their jaws are so strong that sometimes they let them bite on a closed wound and use their heads as stitches. Some people we knew came home one night and found their baby's crib covered with them. They had to pick him up and toss him back and forth like a hot potato until they could get him under the shower. All bitten up even so. I can't think of anything worse than that unless it was that lion those nuns had in their privy."

At dinner I learned that lions are also especially prevalent in the neighbourhood of sisal plantations. The owners of the plantations encourage them because they have a tooth for bushpig which do thousands of dollars' worth of damage a year. Unfortunately, they also have a tooth for plantation worker, but this is the owner's calculated risk. The all-time favourite movie in Central Africa, I learned, is *Tarzan*.

Back at the hotel I had a final brandy before going to bed. There was an English party sitting at the back of the bar, having one of those conversations which so much puzzle people of other races.

". . . thought a great deal about this during the war and I don't think I could have stood torture."

"Well, I think if I could have gone through the first five minutes . . ." a woman said.

Someone broke in. ". . . the first minutes? I don't know—even at school—I mean bullying and all that sort of thing."

". . . I mean you get *angry*," the woman insisted.

"*Now*," said the wife of the man who had thought a good deal during the war, "why doesn't one play it very, very cleverly and say *every*thing and . . ."

"Look, darling, they've got a provision for that."

"They," in this case, was Anglo-Saxon for anyone else in the world who might be unfortunate enough to become involved in a war with England, provision or no provision.

The following morning I went for a walk, to pass the time

before Mr Maswanya was to call for me. At six-thirty the hotel garden was bathed in fresh light, as strong and clear as a northern noon. Oleanders and simple petunias nodded in the dawn breeze. Going down the road towards the market place (where I hoped to buy a pair of rubber bands because my nylon stockings weren't staying up) I noticed that some of the more prosperous young men flashed cowboy hats and leopard sneakers.

The women, as usual, wore shawls bright with flowers and loving-cups and footballs and spirited Swahili phrases. One young lady had a magnificent cloth with a picture of the Viceroy's palace, over which flew Indian and British flags; another had draped herself and her child in a bold sputnik print.

Before I had gone far, a taxi raced up behind me, with Mr Maswanya and a friend in it. They wanted to know if I would come along with them to see some TANU meetings. They spoke so casually and with such typical African understatement that one could have refused without realizing that they had gone to great pains to arrange these meetings.

The taxi driver, for instance, had volunteered his services for the entire morning and everywhere we went people were wearing their best clothes. They had also baked stony cookies, rehearsed songs and questions and gathered in multitudes to applaud and gape. Very soon I felt like an impostor, and before the morning was out Mr Maswanya seemed to have guessed that I was—at least as far as nationalist movements were concerned. But he took a certain mocking pleasure in the proceedings and we grew to be friends.

Our first stop was a small, mud-plastered hut, which contained two whitewashed rooms. These were lined with battered chairs and we filed in and took seats behind a table. The chairs were occupied by officers of the group. The leader was a

middle-aged, broad-minded, quick-tempered, lusty woman—
the sort who doesn't mind if her husband's friends get ashes on
the rug. We were in Tabora township still and all the people
in the room were clearly her friends and neighbours. Outside
there was a great crowd of people.

The Chairwoman wore one of her shawls over her head so
that a corner of it kept falling down over her eyes and she
habitually brushed it back as she spoke. Maswanya gave me a
running translation as she lit into the British. She stopped from
time to time to allow me to ask questions but I could think of
none. I was remembering something I had seen in the *Catholic
Times of Africa* in Archbishop Bronsvelt's office. Mrs Catherine
C. Byrne, the Lord Mayor of Dublin, had written:

In Ireland we have no colour bar and please God we never will.
One reason put forward for the exceptionally happy, united life led
by white and coloured in Dublin is that many of the immigrants
come from countries with much the same sort of history as Ireland,
evolving over the centuries to partial freedom or complete independence. The Irish, in consequence . . . go out of their way to
welcome the coloured.

At last the Chairwoman pointed with positively Celtic wrath
to the children buzzing around the doorway like flies. "Look at
them!" she said. "They need food and medicine and we can't
afford enough for them. Look at them—see how ragged they
are! That's why we want to run our own country."

I said, through Mr Maswanya, that it didn't seem to me that
self-government had much to do with what they could or
couldn't afford—not directly anyway. That is the sort of contradiction people don't generally like and, jammed in as I was,
it was hardly reassuring to remember that these people's
immediate ancestors had fought in Mirambo's army and had
treated Shiekh Khamis bin Abdullah very unpleasantly.

But as no one seemed to be angry yet I took heart and went

on to say that I had heard that the people of the Belgian Congo had even less self-government than those in Tanganyika and yet they were much richer. This freedom she spoke of might even work the other way around. Would she want it if it meant *less* to eat and *fewer* medicines for the children?

The Chairwoman gave her answer very quickly and as I had guessed what it was before Mr Maswanya told me, I smiled. The room burst into wild laughter and suddenly everyone began to sing and beat time. It sounded like a camp meeting. There was a familiar lilt to the music and I leaned over and asked Maswanya what the words were. He grinned and shouted back, "May the British go for ever, and *down* with the United Tanganyika Party!" It might have been *Onward Christian Soldiers* or *One More River to Cross*.

It was no good pointing out that it is very foolish to complain one moment that your children are starving and to say the next moment that you don't care if they are as long as you're the one who's responsible. Perhaps it isn't even safe. The object of revival meetings is to affirm a cause, not to reason about it. The room rang with joyous song and outside women gave ululating screams of triumph. Tea was served.

As we were about to leave, the Chairwoman asked Maswanya if I might be presented with an award. He said that I might, and gave me no chance to refuse. Standing before the taxi I was loudly serenaded while the Chairwoman came before me and put a red and blue Hawaiian lei around my deep red neck. There were more cheers and blood-chilling screams and I ducked into the car.

As soon as we were out of sight I took off the lei and put it behind the seat. Mr Maswanya smiled faintly and stared straight ahead at the hot, dusty road.

The second meeting-place was in a suburb of Tabora—a short, unpaved street with mud huts. Here the leader was a tall, grey-haired man. He and his fellow officers were wearing robes that were splendidly barbaric from a distance and close up were nothing but tacked-together bits of cheap cotton and leopard print, like stage costumes. But maybe that is all splendid barbarism has ever been.

We were crowded into a stifling room for more tea and cakes and songs while several hundred people pressed around the doorway. There were speeches and lively discussion. The chief complaint here was that the residents of the district had to walk a mile for their water. They said that they paid taxes and they wanted a pump. They had applied to the Government often but had heard nothing.

I whispered to Maswanya that *I* wasn't the Government and that I hoped he hadn't told anybody I was. Anyway, I said, a political boss worth his salt should be able to get a water pump out of the Government if he tried. Maswanya had only been in politics for two years and had been mostly concerned with the idealistic aspects of his work. But he was a sensible man and had lately begun to feel that principles alone were not enough. He was delighted by the practical possibilities of the pump and made a note to see Mr Dudbridge—not, I hoped, before I left town.

Riding out towards the bush for our next meeting I began to realize that the isolated native villages we passed, filled with yapping dogs and scurrying children, were just ordinary farm towns and that those women with bared breasts going to and fro with baskets on their heads were simply farmer's wives and daughters.

The farmers themselves, lean and nearly naked, are not different from men who cultivate the soil anywhere, though they may have a more difficult time here. They have the heavy, calloused hands of southern dirt farmers or Italian peasants and, when we stopped at one of the villages, I noticed that they had the same, stiff Sunday clothing—though more rudimentary. We were greeted by a chorus of the farmer's daughters wearing prim, identical frocks. They stayed just outside the meeting-house, while we took tea and cookies, and they burst frequently into song, like a flock of restless birds.

The Chairman, who was twenty-three years old, had gone to primary school and then had been apprenticed to a carpenter in Dar-es-Salaam, from which he had lately returned home.

Stanley would have remarked that this young man had very bad features, by which he would mean that he was as far as possible from the Hamitic or Semitic types one frequently sees in Africa—which are in turn closest to the Caucasian types of Europe. As most Europeans and Americans (including American Negroes) have adopted this standard of physical beauty it is very difficult to stand aside from it, even for a moment. He is ugly, I caught myself thinking, *but* very intelligent—just as Solomon thought that someone was black *but* comely.

Nevertheless he was very intelligent, and by far the most coherent of the TANU speakers I had met, including Maswanya. I asked if there was very much tribal feeling here. The boy smiled. "We don't think of tribes any more. We don't remember where we came from, just where we are going."

One of his officers was a young girl, with whom he seemed to be familiar, either as a sister or a wife. She, too, was very quick and spoke fluently of political events in North Africa and Europe about which I knew little.

Our final stop was a fair-sized village lying close to Tabora. It was half rural and half urban and I understood that there was considerable unemployment in the place. We sat out under a mango tree this time, and for a change drank Coca-Cola.

The whole population of the village gathered around us. The leader here was a rather sententious man of fifty or sixty. He made a long speech which Maswanya carefully translated—

all about unequal pay for equal work and other forms of discrimination. He was very angry with the British but, underneath, perhaps not as much as he pretended. A nationalist movement must have enemies as well as friends and sometimes in the beginning it is necessary to invent both. He said, at last, that he hoped Tanganyika would eventually join the Commonwealth.

There was no singing here and I noticed that many of the people were extremely poor. The shirt of one boy was little more than a white web hanging from a bony shoulder and his torn shorts were tied around his waist with a piece of twine.

I saw a young girl in tatters edging towards the table. She had large teeth, a lovely, full face strengthened by bold planes, and hair piled on top of her head in a black cloud. When the Chairman had finished she leaned forward and asked a question in a clear and unhesitant voice. I asked Maswanya what she had said.

His eyes sparkled. "She wants to know if the report of the United Nations Trusteeship Council has been published—and if it is true that Africans have as much trouble in Arkansas as they do in Tanganyika."

As I could not answer either of those questions we shook hands all round and left. At the hotel Maswanya reminded me, ironically, of my decoration. I fished it out from behind the seat and invited him for a beer. Before he left he gave me a letter to the District Chairman of TANU in Ujiji.

CHAPTER EIGHT

STANLEY only really got his column moving south on 27 September 1871, when he had rid himself of everyone he felt to be unfit for the journey. He was perfectly sure that he could reach Ujiji, but he had no idea if Doctor Livingstone was there or not.

By now he felt that his search was heaven-blessed, and when, on October 7 his men rebelled because they wished to stay longer in the rolling game country south of Tabora, Stanley put down the uprising with a remarkable show of courage. Standing with one armed man at his back and one at his front, in a circle of hostile soldiers and porters, he succeeded in disarming them both and then lecturing the entire party mercilessly until they were in agonies of remorse. They soon picked up their burdens and marched off 'with astonishing alacrity,' as Stanley said, unconscious of the wracking effect of his sermons.

Twice during October he had word from passing caravans that there was another European farther west, but only on the 27th was he sure it was Livingstone.

"A white man?" we asked.
"Yes, a white man," they replied.
"How is he dressed?"
"Like the master," they answered.
"Is he young or old?"
"He is old. He has white hair on his face and is sick."

But he still had a week of hard travel, made especially difficult because the petty chiefs in the neighbourhood demanded tribute at every stop. For the last few marches Stanley had to sneak through the country like a thief so as to save what was left of his supplies.

He was rather pleased to do this—though it was risky—because he was afraid that Livingstone would run away if he heard that he was coming. He was not only thinking of what Kirk had said—he had his own reasons . . . Of course the Doctor would be running from *him*. Months later, in a letter to a friend in London, Livingstone remarked with some surprise that when Stanley reached him at Ujiji he 'behaved as a son to a father.'

On the morning of November 3 (the official date is the tenth but that is an error), seven months and thirteen days after Stanley had left Bagamoyo, he put on a new flannel suit, freshly oiled boots, a chalked helmet with a new puggaree folded on it and set out on 'a happy, glorious morning' on his last march. Ujiji and Lake Tanganyika, now visible, lay just ahead.

Hurrah! The men responded to the exultant cry of the Anglo-Saxon with the lungs of Stentors, and the great forests and the hills seem to share in our triumph.

Stanley eagerly asked Bombay where Burton and Speke had stood when *they* first saw the lake. Bombay made the sensible reply that he hadn't the least idea but that he supposed it was around here somewhere.

Nothing could dampen Stanley's spirits. He was busy living the saga of Stanley finding Livingstone. He bore down on the good doctor so fast that the man would never have had a chance to escape if he had wanted to. It was really more of a capture—with the American flag flying over the striking force.

The presence of this flag rather puzzled Doctor Livingstone, as it has a good many Englishmen since. On the whole he was glad to see it. "I had thought you might be French," he said, later, "come to replace Lt Le Saint who died a few miles above

Gondokoro. But I was rather glad you were an American because I have no French and if he didn't know English we had been a pretty pair of white men in Ujiji!"

But this was on the following day when they had grown more accustomed to each other. On this first meeting Stanley approached the old man on the flank of a hill, overlooking the lake. It falls off rather steeply just beyond the point of their meeting, now marked by a dull monument, which takes what dignity it can from the description simple. After crossing a wilderness and displaying customary courage and fortitude, he was frightened to death.

Stanley was terrified of being snubbed, especially by an Englishman. This is even now a typical American reaction. The fact that he was born in the old country and ended his days with a knighthood only confirms the pattern. The most important thing in the world for him was to be well thought of, and a social affront at this moment would probably have reduced him to tears.

He said that he wanted to rush forward and throw his arms around the man but he had in mind the story of two Englishmen who passed each other with caravans in the middle of the Sinai desert and, having nothing to say, courteously doffed their hats and passed on, as though they had met in Bond Street. So Stanley, in this other wilderness, clutched at formality and became immortal.

He never ceased to regret his phrase that day, there in the shade of a mango tree, misunderstanding completely the springs of his own fame. It was merely the most correct introduction he could think of, and it hid a quaking depth of passion. He said later that if he had been rebuffed—had, as he fully expected, been asked for a letter of introduction—he would have turned on his heel and left.

No letter was required, but Livingstone perhaps outdid

Stanley's question by replying with the single word, "Yes."
Then he smiled and contact was made, though they didn't
unbend until the following day.

"Tell me the general news," Livingstone said when they
had retired to his house. "How is the world getting along?"
Then Stanley told him that the Suez Canal was no longer a
wild dream and that there was regular trade between Europe
and India. "That is grand news, what else?"

Well, the Pacific Railroad had been completed, a victorious
general had been elected President of the United States, the
Cretan rebellion had terminated, a revolution had divided
Spain, Prussia had humbled parts of Western Europe, and
France was in trouble again. *Plus c'est la même chose* sort of
news.

While these two were talking the Arabs of Ujiji sent around
hashed-meat cakes, curried chicken, stewed goat and rice.
Livingstone, whose digestion had been bad, ate vigorously.
"You have brought me new life," he said, "new life." Stanley
ordered the bottle of Sillery champagne to be served, and
handed the Doctor a silver goblet brimful of it.

"Doctor Livingstone, to your very good health, sir."

"And yours."

Then these implacable men sat through the evening, listening
to the thunder of the Tanganyika surf while insects, no doubt
deadly, sang. From time to time they spoke of their stomachs.
Their minds, Stanley assures us, were busy with the day's
remarkable events. At last, the Doctor said: "Good night, and
God bless you."

"Good night, my dear Doctor."

And they went stalwartly to bed, having found each other.

"Doctor," Stanley said before breakfast the next morning,
"you are probably wondering why I came here."

"It is true, I have been wondering. But I didn't like to ask you yesterday because it was none of my business."

Stanley laughed. "Don't be frightened when I tell you that I have come after YOU!"

Some months later, when Stanley had returned to the coast, Sir John Kirk said to Livingstone's real son, who had arrived at Zanzibar with another rescue expedition, "Stanley will make his fortune out of your father." Oswell Livingstone sent this comment on to the Doctor in a letter which he prudently gave to someone else to deliver at Ujiji—unfilial conduct which shocked Stanley.

Livingstone, who had remained in the interior to continue his explorations, reinforced by Stanley's supplies, wrote back: "He is heartily welcome, for it is a great deal more than I could ever make out of myself." There is no doubt that Stanley later considered his fame and solid if not absolutely leaden respectability to be a legacy from the old man to his heir apparent.

One of the best ways to insure that legacy, he saw immediately, was to get Livingstone to write a letter to the *New York Herald*, thanking the paper for his rescue. This would be the best way to handle the story and it would be irrefutable evidence that Stanley had gone where he said he had gone. Already, as his dispatches began to arrive from Africa, people were saying that he was writing the whole thing from a hotel room in New York. The *Herald* in its heyday was much less inhibited about such things than its successor. Even Livingstone had heard of it and thought it despicable. That made the thank-you note more difficult to get but, in his present weakened state, the Doctor—though imposing enough to cow any ordinary man—was no match for his young guest.

"Mr James Gorden Bennett, Jr . . . has commissioned me to find you—to get whatever news of your discoveries you like to give—and to assist you if I can, with means."

"Young Mr Bennett told you to . . . find me out, and help me! It is no wonder that you praised Mr Bennett so much last night."

"He is an ardent, generous, and true man."

"Well, indeed! I am very much obliged to him; and it makes me feel proud to think that you Americans think so much of me. You have just come in the proper time; for I was beginning to think that I should have to beg from the Arabs . . . I wish I could embody my thanks to Mr Bennett in suitable words . . ."

Stanley said that nothing would be easier and got him to agree to write a letter which would, of course, be published.

"And now, Doctor, having disposed of this little affair, Ferajji shall bring breakfast; if you have no objection."

"You have given me an appetite," Livingstone said, a bit dazed.

So began their first breakfast, the day after Stanley arrived in Ujiji. Livingstone said he had been having trouble with his teeth, which had been loosened by gnawing on green ears of corn. Consequently they had soft dampers, though Stanley would have preferred corn scones. This was a deeply serious matter for each of them. They were frequently so alike in their reactions that they would have been surprised to learn that any other sort of men existed.

It is extraordinary how many family traits these two did share. They were both authoritarian, teetotal, brave, stubborn, religious men. They had the same passion for the kitchen and for hot drinks and pompous conversation. They were intolerant of weakness, physical or moral, they shaved every day, both were inclined to be stout and energetic, each had a prodigious memory, and neither one could bear ridicule. Their only disagreement at this time was over Disraeli and Gladstone.

Livingstone put their likeness bluntly, if not accurately. "Americans and Englishmen are the same people. We speak the same language and have the same ideas."

A few days later Stanley wrote in his diary:

His manner suits my nature better than that of any man I can remember of late years. Perhaps I should best describe it as benevolently paternal. He . . . converses with me as if I were his own age or of equal experience. I get as proud as I can be, as though I had some great honour thrust on me.

As the days passed Livingstone began to confide in the young man. He had come to Ujiji from the Maniema country only a few weeks before, and he was full of plans to return to Nyangwé on the Lualaba River. He was morally certain that this river was the upper Nile; so much so, in fact, that he proposed to lead his critics in London astray by pretending to them that it was really the Congo.

As this was precisely what it was, it wouldn't have been a very effective trick, but Livingstone never lived to be disillusioned and Stanley—for all his outward similarity to Livingstone—did not have that sort of illusion.

The Doctor *wanted* it to be the Nile; he never wanted anything so badly—not only because it would confound his critics but because the Nile was a biblical river and the Congo was not. He persisted in error as strongly as he would have persisted in the right and it is perhaps a merciful thing that he died still dreaming of the lost cities of Zirah and Tirhaka— died two years later on his knees beside his bed in the middle of the African night, praying to his militant, abolitionist God.

"Have you seen the northern head of the Tanganyika, Doctor?" Stanley asked one day.

Livingstone replied that he had not—that the main line of

drainage in Central Africa was the Lualaba and he had considered that most important.

"Well, if I were you, Doctor, before leaving Ujiji, I should explore it, and resolve the doubts upon the subject; lest, after you leave here, you should not return by this way."

And so they decided to take a canoe and go off to determine if the Tanganyika had a northern outlet in the Rusizi River. They waited in Ujiji for a while, so that the older man could get his stomach in shape on Stanley's cooking (fresh-churned butter, eggs, roast mutton, eggplant, cucumber, white honey, beans and—at last—corn scones). For the Doctor, stomach trouble and nervousness was sure to end in diarrhœa, whereas with Stanley this produced excessive costiveness.

What with arrangements for a crew and a boat and earnest colonic conversations they did not get started for several weeks. The upper end of the lake is deep in what is now called Ruanda-Urundi, the Belgian trust territory, and the Rusizi River is not far from present-day Usumbura.

Both men enjoyed the pleasant days on the water, languidly watching the palm-fringed shore slip by, and occasionally trading in a fishing village. From time to time they would occupy themselves with soundings, but the water was so deep they lost much of their line.

They had no idea, of course, that this was the second deepest lake in the world and that thousands of feet down, where their line had parted, there is absolutely nothing alive —not a creature or a plant of any sort. Unlike the restless sea, fermenting with life, the water dies of its own stillness seven hundred feet down. And yet in the upper strata of the lake there are fish usually found only in the oceans, and no one can explain how they come to be here in the middle of the continent. In the forests, also, was a kind of prehistoric animal —an air-breathing fish-reptile that will even now attack a man, but which the surviving inhabitants of the region claim is delicious.

Very little of moment happened on this journey except that the two explorers grew to be firm friends. When Stanley had a bad attack of fever, his first since Tabora, Livingstone nursed him devotedly and the young man wrote that though the attack was especially severe he did not regret its occurrence, 'since I became the recipient of the very tender and fatherly kindness of the good man whose companion I now found myself.'

In fact, he had not spent such an idyllic time since his trip up the Mississippi with the Louisiana merchant who gave him his name. For Stanley, the experience was heavily emotional and was no doubt sufficient in itself. But he could not help being aware that when he returned to the world, this time, he would bring not only a name but a fortune.

Their only real trouble came from their employees. Released from daily lectures, now that these two tirelessly clean-living men had themselves to speak to, Bombay, and Susi, Livingstone's servant, sensing that they had a lot in common, got regularly drunk. One night, because of their inattention, or total stupor, some ammunition, a bag of flour and all of the Doctor's white sugar was stolen. At the end of another spree, Susi so far forgot himself as to crawl into the Doctor's bed. The old man made room for him, thinking it was Stanley and some really serious preaching went on the next morning.

The Rusizi River, which rose near a lake called Kivo—now called Kivu and full of Belgian resort hotels—was a disappointment. At this time of year it was little more than a few small streams sprawling over a delta. It was, as everyone seems to have known in the first place, an influent, not an effluent river and so could have nothing to do with the drainage system of any major river flowing north. This would hardly rock anyone at the Royal Geographical, but it was nevertheless Henry Stanley's first taste of pure exploration in the company of a master, and at this point the *New York Herald* and the world lost a magnificently incoherent newspaperman.

When he returned on his second expedition five years later Stanley was backed by his old paper and the London *Daily Telegraph*, but by then he considered himself primarily an explorer.

The adventurers did discover a small group of islands, which were locally called Kavunvweh. As this seemed too difficult, even for the islanders, they decided to re-christen them the *New York Herald* Islets, and after carefully noting that they were in lat. 3° 41′ S. they solemnly shook hands.

The rest of the twenty-eight days on the lake were fairly uneventful, though they did have several close scrapes with hostile natives. Stanley's account of this journey could have been written for *Boy's Life*, and contains a lot of good camplore. Both men, when not actually facing enormous obstacles, had the bracing emotional age of ninth-graders.

The Doctor had decided to go back with Stanley to Tabora, where he would collect the few supplies he had there. He would wait while Stanley went to the coast, outfitted another expedition and sent it back alone so that he could return to the interior.

Except for a five-hundred-pound draft from Livingstone, a great deal of this went on James Gordon Bennett's tab. Though the old man wrote a fervid note of thanks, and the *New York Herald* got what it paid for, Mr Bennett was understandably annoyed when he found that Stanley had been offered forty-five thousand dollars for a lecture tour in America—more than enough to cover the entire cost of the expedition.

It is doubtful that Stanley was ever aware of his displeasure. Both he and Livingstone moved majestically through the world of money, hardly noticing it except as a means to their ends, which were wildly expensive.

They reached Tabora after nearly two months' journey by the southern détour, and lived together for another month in Stanley's old *tembe* while Livingstone finished his journal which was to be brought back to civilization.

There the younger man suffered several severe attacks of fever, but the two found time to bury Shaw's body in a huge stone cairn, forgiving him the final weakness of dying.

On March 14 they rose at dawn for their last breakfast together, which neither could eat. Livingstone walked a way with Stanley (the latter implies in his book that this was a long stroll but it actually takes half a minute. For all their susceptibility to manly sentiment they were both eager to get about their work). They said good-bye under a great tree, since called the Tree of Parting, and Stanley, forcing back tears, turned and marched away. He had spent four months and four days with the Doctor, during which time, as he said in his diary, he was 'indescribably happy.' For the rest of his life March 14 was a solemn day.

A week later, on the trail, he received a note addressed to 'Henry M. Stanley, Esq., wherever he may be found.'

I wish I could give you a better word than the Scotch one to 'put a stout heart to a stey brae'—[a steep ascent]—for you will do that; and I am thankful that, before going away, the fever had changed into the intermittent, or safe form. I would not have let you go, but with great concern, had you still been troubled with the continued type. I feel comfortable in commending you to the guardianship of the good Lord and Father of all. I am gratefully yours, David Livingstone.

Stanley reached Bagamoyo in thirty-five days—three times as fast as he had come, and faster than any other European had travelled the distance. He had lost seventy-six pounds. He had also lost the obsession of his youth. His own hair was turning grey and he had found what he was looking for.

CHAPTER NINE

I ARRIVED at Lake Tanganyika on the morning of November 6 after sprawling all night in a coach with a Belgian cook who was going to work in one of the Kivu resorts. The railhead is five miles north of Ujiji and I took a taxi there through a forest glade. We sped around the boles of ancient trees, dodging naked children, bleating lambs and women pounding flour. Twice the axle nearly cracked.

At Ujiji, which is now merely a settlement—a few huts, some drab, half-dressed people and some scrubby animals— the TANU headquarters is in an old store, a few yards from the monument commemorating Stanley's meeting with Living- stone. I could see little but trees. A tall man stepped through the door of the TANU building and I approached him.

"Mr District Chairman?" I said, holding out my letter.

"No," he said, politely. "I am the Propagating Secretary." He led me into the building and into a dim room where a young man with gold-rimmed glasses was sitting at a desk.

"Mr District Chairman, I presume?"

"No, sir, I am afraid the District Chairman is not here at present. May I help you? I am the Recording Secretary."

I presented Maswanya's letter.

He read it and looked up. "Won't you have some tea?" he said. "I expect the Chairman will be back shortly."

I explained that my boat left soon for Usumbura and that I couldn't stay long.

"I am very sorry to hear that," the Propagating Secretary said.

The other pulled up a chair for me. "The District Chairman

will be *very* disappointed." He was wearing a clean white shirt, open at the neck.

We chatted a while about the work of their organization which had a very large membership here in the Western Province. I was going to ask them to accompany me to the monument, but I saw that this would be a mistake, like suggesting an ordinary Washington sight-seeing tour to an ADA group. Also, from the way they spoke of it when I asked the direction, I could see that the site had imperialist connotations for them. They saw me to the door, urging me to wait for their Chairman.

The memorial was set in a circle of pavement on a baked hillside. On its face a map of Africa was inscribed with a cross which stretched from Capetown to Tripoli and from Addis Ababa to Timbuctoo. Looking down the hill at the green tree-tops I could understand Stanley's elation at coming out on top of this leafy sea. A faint breeze from the lake stirred the branches and dry voices whispered:

"Doctor Livingstone, I presume?"

"Yes."

"I thank God, Doctor, I have been permitted to see you."

"I feel thankful that I am here to welcome you."

The cab-driver honked impatiently, as I was on a fixed fare, and we raced for the boat.

CHAPTER TEN

"**O**UI?"

The young man was dressed all in white and was obviously a member of that class of Congolese the Belgians once called *évolués*—though the word is now considered patronizing.

A wooden plaque on his desk identified him as a cashier. I put down my bag. The Belgian company which runs the Tanganyika boat service has an extra-territorial base at Kigoma, the British railhead. Stepping past the customs barrier is in some ways like stepping through the doorway of a middle-class Belgian home.

I told him in limp French what I wanted.

He blotted his ebony forehead with a folded handkerchief. "*Il faut voyager premier classe en ce bateau, m'sieu.*"

I tried to explain that I wanted to make the trip north to Usumbura and then across to Albertville as cheaply as possible, but he was unmoved and repeated that I had no choice but to ride first class.

I felt, for the first time, the stolid presence of this burgher government. There was no colour feeling involved here. Both racial discrimination and political awareness have been nearly rooted up in the Congo to encourage the growth of the profit motive, which may be predictably cultivated like a rubber plant.

I was invited to take a chair while he made out my ticket. He asked if I had francs.

I nodded sulkily. The trip on the lake was to last several days and the price was depressingly high, after Tanganyika.

I hadn't yet learned that one may avoid almost every inconvenience in this part of Africa but expense.

At last everything was arranged and I thanked the suave young man. *"Mais non, m'sieu!"* he said, leading me to the door. *"Ce n'est rien."*

The Africans under Belgian rule seemed to be a great deal better off than those under the British. They surely had more money and greater numbers had an elementary education. But I was to meet people—including some Belgians—who believed that this contributed to their unhappiness.

Of course the people just outside Ujiji, walking along the forest trails carrying bunches of fat bananas and baskets of cassava probably do not consider themselves particularly in tune with their sylvan surroundings. And if they could have heard the words of a priest in Stanleyville, speaking of the *évolués* in his parish ("You see, they are lost. They have nothing but the little money they make and they spend that all at the end of the month."), they would probably wish to God *they* could be so lost.

I had an African seminarist as a room-mate, but as the boat was not crowded he at last excused himself and asked for another cabin, saying that he had recently been ill and did not sleep well. He was learning English and carried a *Webster's Dictionary* instead of a devotional work. He couldn't have been more than twenty-two years old and had the languid, superficial beauty of a court favourite. His home was near Lake Kivu.

There was a fog on the lake and it was growing quite cool. We pulled slowly away from shore to the keening of railway whistles. My ex-room-mate asked me up to the forward deck to help him with his English, but I put him off.

Kigoma was disappearing in the fog and the captain wheeled about the bridge shouting *"salaud!"* and *"cochon!"* at any deck hand who dared to show his head. Behind me, in the tiny first-class mess, some Belgians were drinking beer and speaking a French that sounded as though it were being blown through mashed potatoes. It was difficult to leave Tanganyika. By any standards it was hardly perfect, but there was a curious sense of freedom in the air. The British, for all their insularity, accommodate exotic cultures just because they are so consistently themselves. They offer the prosaic protection that poetry needs to survive.

I remembered the café beside the pier in Kigoma. On the back wall was a giant official picture of Queen Elizabeth, standing in the midst of a tortured train of red velvet as though in a pool of blood. It was November 6, a few days before the British Legion's buddy-poppy day and the barmaid offered me a poppy with my beer. I handed her a bill.

"Sorry. Can't 'andle that. The missus's out and she always locks things up. You know how *they* are." I gathered that the proprietress was something foreign. "How's she expect me to make change, I wonder?"

I struggled through my khaki jacket. "Tell you what, dear," she went on, "you *could* try the bank across the street." She found this very funny and ran a damp hand through her platinum hair. "Well, I tried, didn't I? Can't say I didn't. Probably they'd say, hold on, what's 'ee doing 'ere. Git 'im out!" She patted her large chest cheerfully. "Still, you could try. Why not, luv? When you've 'ad yer glass. Hot, isn't it?"

I asked if she'd been long in Kigoma.

"No—we been up only a few months, from Rhodesia. 'Usband's got a contract 'ere. Getting north slow but sure. I could do with a nice bit of fog and snow. Too hot for me 'ere. But I suppose some day we'll wish we was back."

There was, of course, another class on the boat below first.

It was a sort of steerage, packed tight with noisy humanity—
all African. But there was never a question, as there might have
been in British Africa, that anyone with the price of a ticket
wouldn't be welcomed commercially to the top deck. Here was
a very real kind of tolerance, the logical by-product of the
traditional Belgian distaste for poverty. But it had its limitations.

I was introduced to these almost immediately, at lunch. I
asked the seminarist if he was coming in to eat and he said that
he was not allowed to. I assumed that this was because of his
colour, but he quickly reassured me. "I have not francs for
all the repasts," he explained. "And the captain will not permit
me to purchase one or two. *Vous comprenez? On doit manger
tout ou rien du tout.*"

I offered to lend him the money but he refused. As we
landed the following noon in Usumbura this prideful gesture
wouldn't really hurt him, especially if he had remembered to
bring a few bananas in his luggage—and I assumed that this
was why he had wanted a room to himself.

But at lunch I remembered that he had said that he was sick
and, as I was not particularly hungry, asked a waiter to take
several of my dishes to him in his room, in order not to em-
barrass him by calling him in.

No one seemed to want to do this, and at last I brought them
in myself, losing some temper. Later, I was charged for two
lunches and refused to pay. There was a scene and when you
are in such a situation there is always a moment when the tide
of public opinion turns for or against you. This time, in a room
full of silently chewing Belgians, it turned against. There
followed a sombre interview with the captain—a choleric
man with a face full of violence—and I was nearly deprived of
mess rights.

This was bad enough; but it was worse to be forgiven

because I was an American. Everyone knows how sentimental *we* are. I tried to point out to the captain that sentimentality had nothing to do with paying double for one's lunch but he dismissed this as a minor point. "Besides," he said, in English, "you cannot bring the plates to the cabins because they call the small beasts." I returned to my own, feeling like the American in Mr Greene's novel, a sower of social disorder.

During our discussion the captain had several times referred to the young priest, in the most condescending way, as a 'black fellow.' Obviously he believed he had no right to be on the upper deck and would have banished him to steerage if he hadn't already paid for his ticket. But the distinction was financial, not racial. The engineer of the boat, for instance, was partly African and he got on with his chief as an equal in all but rank.

The captain simply felt that the boy was rising above his station. He wouldn't have minded if he had been rich. This is perhaps not such a bad way of making distinctions if they must be made. It is at least a neutral one. But, as I learned later, it sometimes places those on the bottom under a double handicap. It is bad enough to be black in the Congo, but to be black *and* poor is misery compounded.

That night I awoke and began to climb out of bed for a glass of water, but changed my mind when the light was on. The captain was right about the small beasts. They were not even very small.

The northern end of the Tanganyika is surrounded by high hills; two large towns, Uvira and Usumbura, lie on either side of the Rusizi River mouth, which Stanley and Livingstone explored in 1871. Usumbura, to the east, is the administrative capital of Ruanda-Urundi, the Belgian Trust Territory.

This country, to the north of Lake Tanganyika and west of Lake Victoria, is another remnant of German Africa that changed hands after the First World War. In the beginning, the Belgians did little with it, but recently they have been pouring a great deal of money into the land, and no one, not even the Belgians themselves, can quite understand why, as they are merely administrators and are committed to leave.

The country is interesting because of its people. Three distinct races live in it, and originally they must have been a constant source of wonder to each other. They are the Tutsi, the Hutu and the Twa. The former are related to the gigantic Nile peoples, racially Hamitic. The Hutu are of normal Bantu stock and the Twa are pigmoid. Generally, the first are pastoral, the second agricultural and the last hunters of game. The Tutsi represent about fifteen per cent of the population and are the aristocrats; the Hutu make up the mass; the Twa, of whom there are less than fifty thousand in a population of five million, are frequently bound in service to the others.

For the rest, apart from customs peculiar to their modes of life (the Tutsi have a more precarious emotional balance than the others because they are generally brought up by nursemaids and lack the security of their mother's backs), they exist pretty much as other people, and have others' defects as well as virtues. Racial prejudice is a problem among them, as the Hutu believe they are superior to the Twa and the Tutsi know they are superior to everyone. But in spite of the shameful counsel of their elders the young people are tending to intermarry.

Their home life is also ordinary, and if a husband and wife wish for a divorce they must first try temporary separation because the interests of two patrilineal families have become involved. But most reasonable people would agree with them that valid grounds for a final break are habitual cruelty, refusal to cohabit, lack of support, non-performance of domestic duties and repeated adultery.

Many of them are very handsome and as a measure of prosperity has come to their land the men often deck themselves with double-pork-pie hats and black shoes with white piping. The women show their affluence by piling on gorgeous shawls. Some are very tall, and I saw one seven-foot lady with a huge and unconfinable bosom, strolling past crates of heavy machinery on the dock with the bemused and tolerant expression of the mother of the world.

In Usumbura I went to see M. Clement at the government information office. He was a brisk, likeable man and he kindly drove me around the town, speaking quickly, in excellent English, though with a difficult accent.

There was really an enormous amount of building going on, and in places the town looked like Scarsdale, twenty years younger. M. Clement said that when he first came here it was all very wild, and infested with carnivorous animals. They have since retired to the hills and elephants no longer come down to the lake. In 1930 the first road was built in Ruanda-Urundi and now there are over ten thousand kilometres of it.

In Usumbura, I learned, there were swimming-pools and tennis-courts for blacks and whites, several hospitals and sufficient inter-racial schools to give about ninety-eight per cent of the children some sort of education—a figure which is fairly consistent throughout the Congo, though it doesn't apply to higher schools.

The governor's mansion in Usumbura is surrounded by a low, decorative wall, but the one around the municipal playing-field is forbiddingly high and armed with shattered glass. Streets in the town have names like *rue d'Industrie* and *rue de Science*, and some of the best coffee in the world is processed here for the American market by making it soluble.

M. Clement was obviously proud of the work the Belgians had done and he had every right to be. Recently, the country has become a tourist centre and there are ten resort hotels at

Lake Kivu. Many people also come to see the Tutsi (Batutsi or, in Swahili, Watutsi) dancers, and a number of professional companies have sprung up to meet the need, though they will not wave a plume until the tourist puts down fifty dollars.

Back on the boat, headed for Albertville, I lolled on the deck through the afternoon, reading Colette's *La Vagabonde* and looking up from time to time at the hills, some of which lay out in the water like great, tired beasts. The land was dappled green and beige, and mango trees were stuck to it like children's cutouts. The lake was an impenetrable blue.

According to a legend, the Tanganyika was originally a small and bottomless well owned by a man and his wife. In its sweet water delicious fish sported. The couple had been warned, as such couples always are, that if they revealed the source of their good fortune disaster would follow. Unfortunately, the lady took a lover and, not content with simple infidelity, brought him some of the family fish. One inexcusable thing led to another and at last she revealed the well to him. The water flowed out, became a lake, and everyone drowned.

The following midnight we reached Albertville. The town lies across the lake, southwest of Ujiji, and is some miles below a forgotten village called Mtowa where Stanley landed at the beginning of September in 1876, headed for the great Lualaba River, which he intended to follow to the South Atlantic or to the Mediterranean, wherever the current and his own courage would take him.

CHAPTER ELEVEN

IN the five years that Stanley had spent away from Ujiji he had become one of the most talked-of men in the western world. On his return to Europe in 1872 he was given a triumphal welcome, temporarily marred by the refusal of the Royal Geographical Society to recognize his claims. In Paris the American colony gave him a banquet at the Hotel Chatham which appropriately featured *Poularde truffée à la Stanley*. In London, when the R.G.S. capitulated at last, the Queen gave him a jewelled snuff-box, the Turners' Company a gold medal, the eldest Miss Livingstone a silver locket, and the Duke of Sutherland a gold tie-pin embellished with a cairngorm in the shape of a heart, surmounted by a pearl coronet. America gave him money and wild acclaim.

Within weeks of his arrival in New York a play about him, called *King Carrot*, was produced; there were burlesque lectures on his trip at the Grand Opera House on 23rd Street; and a full-length saga, *Africa*, played at the Théâtre Comique on Broadway. It featured the comic team of Harrigan and Hart and a coconut shuffle by dancers reputed to have come from the Congo. Its backers took the entire front page of the *New York Herald* to advertise it.

But there was an undertone of laughter in the cheers, that spoiled the triumph for Stanley. In spite of Livingstone's own peaked consular cap, and in spite of his little black page, Kalulu, who had been presented to him by the Arabs of Tabora, and whom no one ever thought to call a slave, he felt people snickering. There was just something funny about him. People made up rhymes in Congress mocking his journey,

123

and undignified songs and sketches celebrated what was after all a great achievement. No one ever made jokes like that about Burton or Speke or Grant or Livingstone.

And, after eighty-nine years, the name Stanley still evokes a titter. This is not simply a response to his 'I presume' phrase, though that is funny enough when it is not touching. The reason is that this common little man was one of the first of our modern heroes, undeniably brave and strong and resolute, but at bottom a person no better than ourselves. He was popular democracy's wry answer to the princely adventurers of the past. As an explorer Stanley had already displayed greater will and endurance than most of those who had gone before him, but these very virtues were embarrassing in an *ordinary* man. He made people aware that ideals they had believed to be safely unattainable were, in fact, well within reach. Laughter is the only thing that can save such a man from being downright unpopular.

So the Royal Geographical Society was not entirely wrong in denying him admission to their roll of immortals. If Stanley was a great man no one was. Sir Henry Rawlinson, the president of the R.G.S., wrote to *The Times* and said that it was not true that Stanley had discovered Livingstone, but that Livingstone had discovered Stanley. And an eminent publication called for an examination of the American's stories by experts, and professed to find 'something inexplicable and mysterious' in the matter.

This wasn't merely British–American rivalry, as Stanley knew. They were attacking him, not his adopted country. Things were put right eventually; in the course of time the greying explorer was given the honour due a distinguished gentleman. But that took patience and three more expeditions and always, just beneath the surface, was a ripple of laughter.

After the first flurries of excitement he settled back to work as a reporter for the *Herald*, at no increase in salary. During the year and a half he had been in Africa, the German Empire had risen from the ashes of the Franco-Prussian war, Rome was taken by Garibaldi, a great fire raged through Chicago, and Dumas and Dickens had died.

Late in 1873 Stanley returned to Africa, this time on the west coast, to cover the Ashanti wars. On his way back to Europe he heard in April 1874 that Livingstone was dead and that his body was being taken to England to be buried in Westminster Abbey. He hurried to London and acted as one of the pall-bearers. Then, in three weeks, he turned out his usual turgid book on his most recent African experiences and set about planning another adventure.

It had occurred to him that if he were to return to Central Africa to finish Livingstone's work no one would dare laugh at him again. He wrote, peevishly,

What I have already endured in that accursed Africa amounts to nothing, in men's estimation. Surely if I can resolve any of the problems which such travellers as Dr Livingstone, Captains Burton, Speke, and Grant, and Sir Samuel Baker left unsettled, people must needs believe that I discovered Livingstone.

Thus he decided to return to Africa not to earn a name or money, which he had already, but to get people to take him seriously.

This time Stanley seemed to have guessed that James Gordon Bennett wouldn't foot the bill alone. He first got the approval of the *Daily Telegraph* in London and then wired New York. Bennett replied, 'Yes,' but it is probable that a letter followed limiting his liability. Henry Stanley's two-volume book describing this immense journey through the dark continent is dedicated to the proprietors of both papers and, in smaller type, to Mr Edwin Arnold, F.R.G.S., who had championed him in England. But this time he was going as an explorer and not as a reporter.

He proposed to do twice what anyone had done before. First, he was to follow the route of Speke and Grant to Lake Victoria, which he would circumnavigate. This was of lively interest to the geographical world; Burton and Speke had had a falling out over that lake and—while the latter lived—wouldn't speak to each other except in the columns of *The Times*.

After this, Stanley meant to come down to the Tanganyika, map its entire coast-line and look for a river draining it, and *then* he was to go across into the Maniema country and finish Livingstone's work. This involved proving whether the Lualaba River was a tributary of the Nile or the Congo.

Depending on which it was, Stanley could expect to emerge from Africa—if he survived—in widely different latitudes. There were about four thousand miles between the mouths of these two rivers. The man who successfully followed either one along its whole course could almost certainly count on being taken very seriously.

He set about collecting a staff. Convinced that Shaw and Farquhar had died because of drink and venery he got together three of the most innocent young Europeans Africa had ever seen. Two were brothers, 'young English boatmen of good character,' who had been recommended to him by his friend Edwin Arnold. Their names were Frank and Edward Pocock and they were the sons of an honest fisherman at Lower Upnor, Kent, who kept Arnold's yacht for him.

These lads were wild to go, and Stanley finally signed them on as assistants, after warning them of the dangers they would face. His third assistant was a clerk named Frederick Barker, whose entreaties were seconded by his mother until Stanley gave in. In addition, he brought along his page, Kalulu, who had spent the last few years in an English boy's school, and he recruited five dogs—two prize mastiffs, a retriever, a bulldog and a bull-terrier. On 15 August 1874, he again left England for Zanzibar.

Reaching the island in September he leisurely set about getting the expedition together. Stanley was determined to be properly prepared this time. He hired an African named Manwa Sera, who had been the chief of his second caravan in 1871, to command the native carriers and soldiers. He also took on Mabruki Speke, Chowpereh, Uledi and a few others from his previous expedition. The company had a boat called the *Lady Alice* which was so built that it could be broken into sections and transported overland.

The Pocock boys and young Barker were having the time of their lives and requested permission to fly the Union Jack over their tent. Stanley drew a deep breath and said to Frank Pocock, "My dear fellow, you surprise me by imagining for one moment that I could possibly refuse you. This is not an American Government or a British Government Expedition, and I have neither the power nor disposition to withhold my sanction to your request. If it will be any pleasure to you by all means . . ." Probably the boys' attention wavered before this speech came to an end a few minutes later, but soon they were observed patriotically snipping and sewing a little British flag, the size of a lady's handkerchief. In this they manifested much delight.

Before the expedition left Zanzibar, Manwa Sera and some of the other chiefs came to Stanley and asked to know precisely where they were going and when, if they were lucky, they might expect to return. On hearing what lands they were to visit they grew nervous, pointing out that the journey might take from six to ten years. Livingstone, they said, stretched a two-year trip to eight, and died on the shores of Lake Bang-weolo without *ever* getting back. Stanley replied that Living-stone was an old man, and that if he himself had made the round trip to Ujiji the first time in sixteen months he was not likely to be slower this time. "Was I not like a boy then, and am I not now a man?"

Thus reassured, they retired to enter into proper agree-ments before the consul. Stanley was right about the time. The journey didn't take anything like ten years. He was gone exactly nine hundred and ninety-nine days, about the time it took many of the Arabs to reach Ujiji. But when his band stumbled into the tiny settlement at Boma, on the other side of the continent in August 1877 more than half of the original expedition had died. Of these, smallpox, dysentery, battle and murder claimed eighty-one—while another thirty or so were carried off by crocodiles, insanity, starvation and the great Congo river itself. Those who survived this gruelling trip, Manwa Sera, Uledi, Mabruki Speke, Chowpereh and their wives, as well as Stanley himself, were those who had survived before.

On this journey Stanley lightened the customary loads of the porters, to gain speed. This later became a standard practice in the Congo and was one of the reasons the Europeans had greater mobility in their wars with the Arabs during the 'nineties. He had eight tons of material—two tons more than on his first expedition—and he had hired two hundred and seventy men to carry and guard it. His wage scale was lower this time, going from two to ten dollars a month and he had bargained more shrewdly for his supplies.

At the end of Ramadan, on 12 November 1874, the Expedition embarked from Zanzibar for the mainland. The 'charming, simple manners and manly bearing' of Stanley's young English assistants had won them a host of friends on the island. Many of these waved good-bye at the dock, confident that Stanley would bring the gallant boys through.

It was surely a sprucer company than that which had left three and a half years before to find Livingstone. But, apparently, stainless virtue offered no greater protection against the fevers of Africa than uncurbed vice. Two months later Edward Pocock died, beating even the dissolute Farquhar by a month or so. He was followed a short while after by Frederick Barker.

The first part of their journey shook down the crew. Of the Europeans, Frank Pocock and Stanley were the only survivors; among the Africans, desertions and death took their toll. Even the dogs dropped out, one by one. In the end everyone had to measure up to Stanley's 'respect for order and discipline, obedience and system (the true prophylactic against failure).' The order was *his* order and the obedience was to *him;* above all, it was his luck they were riding. Stanley was the leader and there was never any mistake about it.

This little band of people, who were shortly to open up the great heart of Africa to the slave-traders, caused still more havoc during their boat trip around Lake Victoria. Here they met Mtesa, Kabaka of the ancient kingdom of Uganda. His were very highly developed people by any standards on earth and Stanley sent off urgent letters to Europe for missionaries to turn them into Christians, much as Gordon did in the Sudan a few years later.

As a result, the Church Missionary Society and, on their heels, the White Fathers of the *Societé des missions africaines* descended on these feudal people and converted their leaders to Christianity.

When Frederick Lugard, one of the architects of British Imperialism and a friend of Stanley's, arrived in Uganda in 1890, he found a miniature Puritan War raging. Catholics and

Protestants were communicating only with battle-cries. The Kabaka of that time was an emotionally baroque young man, a venial member of the Catholic party, whose bias against the Protestants incited rebellion. But before a Cromwell could rise to complicate matters, Lugard stamped out the fighting by replacing men of God with nineteenth-century Englishmen.

From Lake Victoria the expedition headed south to Ujiji on Lake Tanganyika. Using this town as a base, Stanley explored the lake, and then, early in September 1876, two years after his arrival in Zanzibar, he crossed over to Mtowa and struck into the Maniema country.

Many of the tribes on this side of the lake were extremely poor, and so miserable they were hardly even hunted by the Arabs. In describing them Stanley rises to heights of hyperbolic condescension.

Though I knew quite well that some thousands of years ago the beginning of this wretched humanity and myself were one and the same, a sneaking disinclination to believe it possessed me strongly, and I would even now willingly subscribe some small amount of silver money for him who could but assist me to controvert the discreditable fact.

When they reached Uhombo, the frontier village of Maniema, they began to meet bolder and handsomer people. They were now on the edge of the Congo basin, a vast area which was once the floor of an inland sea. However, it maintains an altitude of a thousand to fifteen hundred feet, and though it lies entirely within the tropics it is not all steaming jungle, nor is it always hot.

The people of the Maniema country were warlike, and were armed with a light, balanced spear which Stanley says was the most beautiful weapon in the world next to the spear of Uganda. Their villages consisted of one or more broad streets, a hundred to a hundred and fifty feet wide, flanked by low, square huts. At one end of these streets were the council- or gossip-houses. Here, also, the women pounded their grain. Besides corn, they lived mostly on bananas and plantains and cassava. The Guinea palm supplied them with oil and wine.

Within the first month Stanley was asked three times by Maniema chiefs to help them in local wars. He had had enough of that back at Tabora, fighting Mirambo, and refused. He learned that this was a custom among the Maniema. They would frequently invite the Arabs to fight for them, offering the women and children and ivory of the enemy as an induce- ment.

This was very short-sighted. Frequently their own women and children and ivory were taken as well. In turn, large numbers of people were displaced and joined the Arabs as mercenaries rather than starve to death. It was with these troops that Tippu Tib and his companions fought their last bitter battles with the European invader in 1892.

In October the Expedition arrived at the confluence of the Luama River with the great Lualaba. The latter was about fourteen hundred yards wide. It was a pale grey colour, and Stanley likened it to the Mississippi before the Missouri poured its rusty brown water into it.

Somewhat farther on, in fact, the Congo becomes dark red. Stanley was rapturous.

The great mystery that for all these centuries Nature had kept hidden away from the world of science was waiting to be solved . . . now before me lay the superb river! My task was to follow it to the Ocean.

It was a task a good deal more difficult than he expected and he nearly died completing it.

CHAPTER TWELVE

ALBERTVILLE on a Sunday morning has the sickly calm of almost any European or American city over the weekend. On the wharf a small party of middle-aged Belgian men wearing pith helmets and carrying brightly coloured plastic pails and collapsible fishing-rods were climbing into a motor-launch. The harbour smelled of sewage, and I hurried towards town.

The people seemed prosperous. A number of Africans were driving great, hell-bent American cars and the streets were a peril of bicycles and motor-cycles. The men were frequently dressed in Western clothes, but none of the women wore anything but shawls, some of which were printed with bright yellow lions crouched above the words *Bonne Année*.

These women generally carried at least two babies, one on the back in a tight little hammock, and one in the womb, and for both purposes their shawls were perfectly adapted. The infants are constantly being swung as the mother walks, and crying is practically unknown. The older children are extremely well-behaved and when with their mothers are usually occupied in carrying things.

Watching them, it is clear why cloth was money in nineteenth-century Africa, as it was in Europe during the Middle Ages. It has a great many more uses than most of us remember. Besides clothing, it serves as rope, as a container, webbing for other bundles, a shock-absorber for carrying objects on the head, and shade.

African women, therefore, surround themselves with as much material as possible. It forms a part of their riches and, worn loosely, may shelter them from the heat. A few wear simple dresses, of course, as Epis did, but that was because she was ashamed of the old ways, just as she was embarrassed by the tattooing on her forehead.

Albertville is built along the lake and consists chiefly of one main street near the water, lined with hotels and shops and bars. From one of these bars, called *Cabaret Albert*, I heard crashing music and went in. It was simply a large room with many tables. People sat here listening to a record-player turned on full volume, bathing their spirits in beer and throbbing music.

It was the first of many such places I was to see. About all that varied in them were the labels on the beer-bottles. Here people drank Simba. Further north it was Stanor and Primus (Queen of Beers). The music, generally Latin–American, is enjoyed gluttonously and the louder it is the better. African talent for music extends to listening to it, as well as playing it. And if the visitor allows himself to get caught up in the spirit he discovers that a single, banal record, played over and over, acquires a complex tonality and rhythm that certainly was never put there by the composer. For this reason it seems to make very little difference what is playing as long as something is, and the night-clubs of Stanleyville boom just as enthusiastically with recorded as with live music.

I sat down and ordered a Simba, attracting some attention because I was the only non-African there. One of the few pleasures to be salvaged from the separation of races is that a person from the opposite side is always *noticed*. It is a great luxury to have waiters, ticket-sellers, postmen, cab-drivers and political leaders pay attention for once—always provided they don't do so in order to discriminate against you.

Over samba music I carried on a shouted conversation in high-school French with a young man who worked as a cashier in a bank. I asked if he could direct me to the White Fathers' mission in Albertville. He replied that he could but as it was Sunday it would be best to go in the afternoon. The train didn't leave until evening and I promised to meet him here again at five o'clock. Apparently he intended to stay in the cabaret all day.

In wandering around the town I ran across an Italian who invited me to a friend's house for a Sunday afternoon *polenta* dinner. We rode out into the country in an old G.M. truck and stopped at a place that seemed to be a combination farm and machine shop, very badly run down. I was welcomed by the other Italian and after several toasts in vermouth we went to the table. A bottle of chianti was passed around as a sentimental reminder of the old country, but the *polenta*, as well as their Italian, had acquired a Belgian accent. Neither had been home for over thirty years.

They said, apparently without spite, that Africans were untrustworthy, that they had no sense of time, were carefree, warm and vain, and that they could never work on their own initiative; everything, in short, that North Europeans and Americans usually say about Italians when they are trying to congratulate themselves on having survived the Industrial Revolution.

But like those patronizing tourists who flock every summer to the most backward parts of Italy, they could not hide a deep nostalgia for the old, simple ways. African women, they said contentedly, were a good deal finer and more sincere than European ones. This fortunate state of affairs had been troubled recently because the ladies were no longer content with small presents. My two companions darkly hinted that this was the fault of the Americans.

I asked *how* African women were finer. After long thought the older one said that it was because they were more conservative than European women. By this he explained that he meant old-fashioned, not modest. They were at once more female and less bold. They would not be likely to swear in public, for instance, and when they made love they practised few erotic refinements but were on the whole more passionate. They also talked a good deal less than European women and were not so nervous. In his youth in Turin, he said, there were still a few like that, but they were becoming very rare.

At this point the younger man began to get drunk and I persuaded him to drive me back to town before he passed out. We were almost there before he confided to me that he had no brakes.

At the White Fathers' mission I spoke to a priest from the Veneto who said that here in the Congo, as in Tanganyika, his society tried to stay on the side of genuine nationalist movements. He added that in ten years fifty per cent of the population would be literate and in another ten everyone could expect the same education they might receive in Europe or America. Therefore, he said, enormous changes are inevitable no matter what the policy of the government might be. The society also published a number of papers here, the most extreme of which was *Temps Nouveaux*, though it had a small circulation.

That night, on the train bound for Kindu, on the Lualaba, I shared a compartment with an elderly Indian who had retired from active business in the Congo to play the stock market. He made, he estimated, about four or five thousand pounds a year on widely spread investments. In India he got six or seven per cent and the Government paid his income tax on all profits. He valued his wife, to whom he had been happily married for forty years, now chiefly as a tax deduction on other speculations. At bed-time he stripped off his pure white outer suit and revealed an identical one beneath, which he slept in. Before we dozed off he calculated that travel in Tanganyika cost a shilling a mile while in the Congo it cost two shillings. Unfortunately he had to travel a lot because he had interests in Bombay. These were . . . It was like being read to sleep with *The Times* business section.

In the morning we woke stranded in the midst of a vast forest. Something had gone wrong with the train and, at a quarter to seven, the dining-car sat primly in the jungle smelling of fresh toast. Brilliant birds shrieked outside, and I thought I heard a heavy body crashing through the underbrush. The wife of the Belgian man in charge of the dining-car was English and she made me a nice cup of tea as the sun rose in a savage vermilion sky.

We started again after breakfast and reached a town called Kabalo. In the station, as usual, the efficiency and grace of the women was most striking. One, a very tall person with a slim neck adorned by a delicate, small face, carried a metal suitcase on her head, another in her hand, a number of bundles and a pineapple. She had to get this luggage and three children packed into a third-class carriage and she did it smoothly, with perfect confidence, and with never a sign of distress.

We travelled north all day through a thicket-forest. The occasional clearings were full of young, sweet, yellow-green grass. There were many glades which would have been ideal for picnics if one had been armed. Here and there ant hills grew from the ground, like tumours, and dead, white wood gleamed through the green shadows. It began to rain but the light remained and coated the jungle with an eerie fluorescence, as in a supermarket.

Occasionally we passed a village and in some of them one could see that the only touch the inhabitants had with the outside world was this train that whistled by twice a week. Great, strapping men and women would stand by the tracks, hands to their cheeks, naked and quivering with excitement. The children, believing the railroad to be something military, stood at rigid attention.

The next morning we arrived in Kindu, which lies near the third parallel south of the Equator. Down on the Lualaba a small stern-wheeler was building up steam for the journey north. I hurried over with my bag and got a cabin in what turned out to be a floating Belgian boarding-house.

Most of the passengers in the upper section of the boat had the relentless respectability of the continental middle class. They were good-humoured people, the sort who do not stand on ceremony and who look forward to dinner as the most significant event of the day.

The English woman from the train dining-car came on board to chat with the captain's wife. She introduced me to a Yorkshireman who had taken a Belgian wife and now travelled up and down the Lualaba repairing office machines. "*Vous avez la mauvais compagnie!*" she said, forgetting for a moment that I spoke English. "*Est terrible, ce type-la.* Really, I mean it, he's *terri*ble."

The captain's wife, a fat, energetic woman of about thirty-five broke into screaming laughter as the Yorkshireman tried to hug her while she loaded the ice-box with butter. He was a great favourite on board, especially with the ladies, not because of his scandalous behaviour, but because he was a little boy at heart. On his arm a dagger was tattooed and across it ran the words, 'True Love—Mother.' He had a quick smile and crimped, sandy hair resembling wool. He told me that there was always a good bunch riding up to Ponthierville.

He was surely right about that, though some people take to ladies in print dresses and domesticated men addicted to horse-play more easily than others. One of our passengers, for instance,

137

was an Arab in a long, blue kanzu carrying a mysterious brass-bound chest and some tusks of ivory wrapped in dirty canvas. He may not have understood all those screams of laughter.

Below was the steerage, though not many were travelling there. It was a small boat and much of the space was devoted to cargo and to the logs which were used as fuel for the boilers. A steel lighter was lashed to our port side with still more wood. This was the old method of travelling on the Congo, as wood could be cut at any point of the journey. Now most of the vessels are diesel-powered.

The Africans who lived around here travelled on the river in pirogues, long narrow craft hollowed out of logs. They are very superior boats, can attain a great speed and will take almost any kind of abuse. Later, on a more prosperous stretch of the river, I saw some fitted with Evinrude motors that could outrace anything on the water.

Looking out towards shore as we beat downstream I was reminded that these people had been cannibals a short time ago. Many of them denied this, even in Stanley's time, but when people race out at you in pirogues, as they did at him, and shout, "Meat, meat!" it is hard not to draw uncharitable conclusions. It therefore made me uneasy to see that many of the villages along the river had large, black pots boiling merrily in their squares; these were actually oil-drums and undoubtedly had some philanthropic function. Behind the villages giant, red flowers nestled among the tree-tops and black fishing birds floated above.

At lunch we had Brussels sprouts, and the captain's wife directed the conversation. She seemed afraid of not having an opinion about everything; small opinions, for the most part: what was the best cut of veal, how to get children to go to sleep, where to buy sheets. But sometimes her judgments extended to other people's morals and she was particularly set against unauthorized sexual activity. Her husband, a man with little to say, looked like an ex-football hero run to fat. She herself was not attractive; such women often marry childishly handsome men and spend the rest of their lives in terror of losing them.

She was in the midst of telling a story of a family who went thoughtlessly off to the movies and left their daughter and her fiancé at home alone together, when the Yorkshireman, who had mischievously devoured all the bread and butter and all the dessert, pushed back his plate and said, "*Je n'ai pas faim,*" with a small boy's pout, so that no one but the Arab could keep from laughing.

The captain's wife wasn't to be cheated of her indignation. "*Tous les jours la même chose. Il est arrivé chez soi-même et il a trouvé* deux *hommes avec la fille! Hein? Tous les jours— aurrhhh! C'est incroyable!*" Her voice had grown very high.

There was an embarrassed silence and an old lady sitting next to me said, "*Ah, non!*" That was all she ever said, except once, that evening, when someone told her that she looked as though she were dressed for a ball. She blushed prettily and replied that she hadn't been to a ball for twenty years, casually lopping off fifteen.

The captain's wife frequently dieted. For lunch she would limit herself to one piece of toast spread with about a sixth of a pound of butter, a boiled egg, and a bunch of bananas. As her weight soared, she grew even more disapproving of unofficial love-making. She was only really at ease when talking about small children who had not left the age of innocence.

Towards evening we passed a very large native town, stretched out along the river for nearly a mile. At its beginning, two young boys swam out and expertly caught on to the props of the paddle-wheel as the boat passed. They hitched a ride to the far end of the town where they dropped off and raced each other back to shore. Stanley was perfectly right in comparing this river to the Mississippi, and somewhere along it, perhaps here, reincarnations of Tom Sawyer and Huckleberry Finn must now be living.

The air was fragrant with rain. A wind had put a scruff on the water and clouds gathered on the horizon. From time to time they were cut by lightning, and a sweet, smoky, mouldering odour rose from the expectant land. It was raining towards the west and the sunset was blurred; though a storm was clearly on the way, it was moving slowly.

As dusk deepened, sparks flew from our chimney like fireflies, and the sounds of the wind and our crashing stern-wheel blended together. Still there was no rain and even the crimson river seemed parched for it. Sparks were whipped across the deck and, with them, the sharp taste of burning wood. Several of the crew began unloading the lighter to keep the fuel dry.

A few big drops fell like coins and the air suddenly grew gentle. Behind us, there was a pink band of unclouded sky, some forty miles away. Then, with no more warning, the wind slapped the little boat over at an angle and water fell so thickly that the river's waves were beaten flat. It came warm at first, as from a hose left in the sun, then colder and scented with flowers and the freshly broken stems of leaves. Palms on the shore waved their plumes in it and dead trees held up their bony arms, while the corners of the forest grew silver with fog. Clouds of rain raced across the river and sheet-lightning threw a tungsten glare on the heaving forest as the sky went from grey to black, the rain stopped, and the passionate wind departed.

The following morning we passed a really elegant village with a large council hut which would have served very well as a movie house and perhaps was. These people had a *blue* pot boiling in their square, and seemed in every way superior. They greeted us with drums but took no other notice.

We were due in Ponthierville that night, from which a train was scheduled to take us to Stanleyville. I sipped coffee and watched banks of fern, and trees festooned with creepers drifting by. The engine of the boat was revved down and its noise was like muffled sobbing in an adjacent room. That fitted the mood of the river very well for the moment. The water was red-brown and the forest a sullen green.

We arrived in Lowa an hour later and docked before the A. Houdmont & W. Thuysbaert Company, whose great, whitened concrete buildings bulked back into the forest. A number of porters streamed on to the boat with bunches of bananas and sugar cane, a mimeograph machine and a cash-register. When they had delivered these they retired to the shore with a bucket of banana beer, which they drank from the rim.

The cash-register was for the Yorkshireman who immediately began to strip it down. "This is one of yurrrs," he said to me, indicating the American brand-name. He told me that he had spent some time in Toledo, at the scale company there. He had liked the United States but preferred Belgium. He couldn't stand England. He gave a number of reasons for this, but the real one was that he hated the British class system, or hated being at the bottom of the British class system.

When I met him in Stanleyville a few days later and had a glass of beer with him, I asked what were his relations with the Africans. "Oh," he said, airily, "I don't notice 'em. I just look right through 'em. You do, after a while." He wasn't blinded only by their race. Different classes tend to see no one but their own members. It is almost a matter of vision; they will accurately describe what people in their own group are wearing and hardly see others walking around naked. This applies to higher classes as well as lower, though men strain to look upward more than down. The Yorkshireman had been looking up for a long time and it was naturally hard for him to glance in other directions, even for a moment.

Ponthierville is a rail terminus of the line which runs up to Stanleyville and by-passes the seven cataracts, which took such a terrible toll of Stanley's expedition. The chief attractions of the town itself are a bowling alley and a scrubby hotel which has a bar and a game room with expiring philodendrons in green-and-gold ceramic wall-vases. I waited for train-time in a wicker chair staring at a false Egyptian tapestry on a baby-blue stucco wall, listening to a malaguena being played on a little lame phonograph.

The train rattled on all that night, across the Equator, towards Stanleyville. Everyone has a place in the world he believes to be his home, not necessarily one he admires or even wishes to remain in. After nearly forty years I was ready to see my own.

CHAPTER THIRTEEN

HAMED BIN MOHAMED BIN JUNA was called Tippu Tib, men said, because the name imitated the sound of spraying bullets; but it also means 'gatherer of wealth,' and they were simply confusing his means with his end. At the time Stanley arrived on the Lualaba River in 1876 this remarkable man had been established at Nyangwé for two years. That town was to become the focus of Arab power in Central Africa, after Tabora fell to the Germans. It is some miles up-stream from present-day Kindu where the steamer leaves for Ponthierville.

Tippu Tib descended on his father's side from a line of rich and influential merchants at Zanzibar. At an early age he went into Africa to make his own fortune. Many other young Arabs did the same, but few had his detached view of their work.

Slaving, he saw, is a difficult profession because people have a congenital love of liberty. Therefore a good deal of killing is necessary. But taking a man's life is one of the ultimate demands one may make on him and nothing short of overwhelmingly superior force can guarantee success. Such force, Tippu Tib knew, could be supplied by modern weapons. He armed a hundred fighting men with the best rifles he could find and plunged into Africa for slaves and ivory.

He turned his profits into more arms and with these he took more lives, more ivory and slaves. He began to penetrate isolated regions where people were unsophisticated about the uses of ivory. Some villages were partly constructed of it— pillars, fencing, etc. Others had heaps of tusks which had been rotting for generations. A little guile, here, wouldn't have exceeded the trade practices of most people, but Tippu was also after slaves and more soldiers. Destruction ideally served his purposes and he pillaged with murderous efficiency.

Yet he was not a bestial man, merely a logical one with no pity. Stanley describes him as tall and black-bearded, with a black skin and fine, intelligent features.

He was . . . straight, and quick in his movements, a picture of energy and strength . . . neat in his person, his clothes were of a spotless white, his fez-cap brand-new, his waist was encircled by a rich dowlé, his dagger was splendid with silver filigree, and his *tout ensemble* was that of an Arab gentleman in very comfortable circumstances.

He was one of those men, made for certain kinds of greatness, whom Stanley admired because he saw himself in their eyes.

To achieve these comfortable circumstances Tippu Tib did not always bludgeon helpless people himself. There were other ways of encouraging disorder and misery. One of his favourite tactics was to stir up local wars so as to come in on the winning side and claim the spoils, including the persons of the vanquished and even of the victors, if they had been enough weakened.

Though he didn't like to take chances he was a courageous man, and once, when his ammunition was low, he walked into a strongly fortified town and declared that he was the king's nephew, who had been taken in a slave raid some years before, possibly one of his own. He then persuaded the ageing king to abdicate in his favour.

Finding himself the acknowledged sovereign of thirty or forty thousand souls he declared war on contiguous kingdoms and soon was absolute master of the whole district. Opposing chiefs sometimes tried to bribe him to treat them leniently but he considered everything they owned to be his anyway, including their flesh.

At the height of his power in 1891 he controlled an area the size of France and Germany combined, though it was sadly depopulated. He achieved all of this through unashamed greed and his rapaciousness was probably matched by only one other man then living, Leopold II, King of the Belgians.

Tippu Tib was naturally a very popular man as well as a rich one. He was surrounded by attendants and troops whose fierce loyalty he could count on because they were afraid to think of him as an enemy. He was eventually to meet men who were not afraid, and his forces were finally routed—though his own person was never touched. The European army's victory was gained by superior weapons, used in accordance with his own principles, and he was probably not at all surprised at his defeat.

But if he had known in 1876 that Stanley was destined to bring the Congo Free State into being, the rivalry which would culminate in the Arab-European wars sixteen years later might have begun with something more spirited than a foot-race. In that race Tippu Tib beat Frank Pocock by fifteen yards to win a silver goblet and a cup, which hardly consoled him in his old age for the loss of an empire. Henry Stanley should have run this race, not young Pocock. Tippu was ten years older than Stanley and the match would have been far more sporting. But the leader was so muffled in a cloak of paternal dignity that it would have been unthinkable for him to play such games, though he considered them fine lessons in manliness for the young. Both camps would have been surprised to learn that he was only thirty-five years old. After spending the first years of his life as a fatherless child he was spending the last as a childless father.

The two men met near Kasongo, some miles up-stream from Nyangwé. Tippu Tib had been out in the Maniema country avenging the murder of one of his men by hostile natives. In view of his own propensities this was more of a routine police action than a show of indignation.

Stanley was anxious to know what obstacles there were to a journey down-stream. He suspected that the greatest of these was Tippu Tib himself. Though the Arabs had not yet penetrated the Congo they considered it their zone of influence and did not like Europeans encroaching. Livingstone and, two years before Stanley, a man named Cameron, had been held up at Nyangwé and never got any farther down the Lualaba. Why?

He learned that 'Daoud Liviston' had been refused boats by the Arabs who said that the trip was so dangerous they didn't want to be held responsible for his death by the British Consul at Zanzibar. Also, the Doctor's own men balked, probably incited by the Arabs, but all the more ready to do so when they heard that the natives along the river were addicted to human flesh. This had been enough to discourage Cameron and, with Tippu Tib's paid help, he turned south-west and went across the continent to Portuguese Angola.

"I suppose, Tippu Tib," Stanley said, "having offered the other white man your assistance, you would have no objections to offer it to me for the same sum?"

Tippu hedged, and pleaded that he lacked men. Besides, he said, he didn't see *why* Stanley wanted to go down the river. "If you white men are desirous of throwing away your lives," he said, "it is no reason we Arabs should. We travel little by little to get ivory and slaves, and are years about it—it is now nine years since I left Zanzibar—but you white men only look for rivers and lakes and mountains, and you spend your lives for no reason, and to no purpose."

Knowing his own motives so well, Tippu Tib simply couldn't believe that the Europeans didn't have a more practical reason for making these trips. He was perfectly right, and if he had followed his instinct to hold Stanley up, the centre of Africa today might be occupied like the Sudan by a huge Arab nation. But he also had an instinct for making money, and when this rash young man offered him five thousand dollars to take him sixty marches, in any direction Stanley chose, he accepted. He foolishly agreed to forfeit his five thousand if he gave up before he had made the full sixty marches through a country said to be infested with boa-constrictors and leopards and a kind of gorilla that would seize your hand and bite off the fingers, one by one.

Stanley had entered into these negotiations without consulting his own people. But the night before the contract was signed he called Frank Pocock into his hut for pipes and coffee. Stanley had become very fond of the boy and confided in him in the manner of a scoutmaster with his favourite eagle-scout. "Now, Frank, my son," said this hoary thirty-five-year-old, "sit down. I am about to have a long and serious chat with you. Life and death—yours as well as mine, and those of all the Expedition—hang on the decision I make tonight."

Their chat *was* serious and certainly it was long. Stanley pointed out that both Livingstone and Cameron had been well equipped to attempt the river—the first by experience and the second because he was very well armed. But they had both been forced to turn back. There was no doubt that the trip would be extremely dangerous. An alternative to making it therefore, Stanley said, would be to head south to the Katanga; another would be to go north-east and cut across Uganda.

To all of these suggestions Frank, whose vocabulary was severely limited by the blameless, athletic life he had led, replied, "That would be a fine job, sir!" or one-syllable words to that effect.

Yet the river was tempting. Should they dare the Lualaba, Stanley continued, and gain glory? The young man struggled

147

with an idea. "I say, sir," he burst out at last, "let us toss up! Best two out of three."

They took a rupee. "Heads for the north and the Lualaba; tails for the south and Katanga," Stanley said. Frank beamed and threw.

"What is it?"

"Tails, sir!" Frank said, disappointed with fate for trying to save his life.

"Toss again."

They tossed six times and tails always came up. Then they drew straws, short ones for the south, long ones for the river, and poor lucky Frank got a run of short ones.

At last Stanley threw away all the short straws and, with them, Frank Pocock's last hope of getting home to Lower Upnor.

"It is of no use, Frank. We'll face our destiny, despite the rupee and straws. With your help, my dear fellow, I will follow the river."

"Mr Stanley, have no fear of me. I shall stand by you. The last words of my dear old father were, 'Stick by your master.' "

Reassured by this canine display of loyalty, Stanley signed the contract with Tippu Tib the next day.

On October 24 they left for Nyangwé, which they reached in three days. The Expedition was in remarkably good condition considering that they had made the journey from Lake Tanganyika in forty-three days. The Arabs generally took three or four months to do it. Only Kalulu, the little page Stanley brought from England, was ill. He had an accidental gunshot wound and his master nursed him tenderly, in spite of the fact that he had tried to run away some weeks before.

On November 5 they left Nyangwé behind, heading north overland to by-pass the three falls that blocked them from the lower reaches of the river. Tippu Tib accompanied them with four hundred men, about half of whom Stanley was pledged to support on the journey. The slaver had also brought along the twenty women of his harem and about fifty boys between the ages of ten and eighteen whom he was training to act as servants, scouts, carpenters, blacksmiths and leaders of raiding parties. One of these was Gongo Lutete who, at the time of the Arab-European wars, became Tippu's chief lieutenant in the Maniema, and whose defection to the European side marked the end of Arab dominance in Central Africa.

They plunged into thick forest which was sometimes so dark Stanley couldn't see to write his notes. Within ten days the porters were complaining loudly and even Tippu began to grumble at the unexpected resistance of the land. When they occasionally came out on a hill they could see nothing but forest around them. They were also being harassed by pythons, green vipers, puff-adders and large, howling baboons.

On the 16th Tippu Tib said he was quitting. "Look at it how you may," he argued, "those sixty camps will occupy us at the rate we are travelling over a year, and it will take as much time to return. I never was in this forest before, and I had no idea there was such a place in the world. The air is killing my people, it is insufferable. This country was not made for travel; it was made for vile pagans, monkeys, and wild beasts. I cannot go further."

Stanley talked him into coming twenty marches further, for two thousand six hundred dollars, paying all expenses himself. He did this not so much because he needed Tippu Tib's help here in the jungle but because he wanted to get far enough away from Nyangwé to be sure that his own men wouldn't desert.

In the native villages they occasionally passed they saw a great many skulls and other bones lying around cooking sites, looking uncomfortably human. The residents swore that these

149

were the bones of delicious chimpanzees, but Stanley brought two skulls back to England and Professor Huxley told him they were of a higher order. These same people, when not eating, made a kind of primitive furniture which would now be in great demand by decorators.

Fourteen days out of Nyangwé they swung west and reached the Lualaba again. Stanley decided to rechristen it the Livingstone. Here they camped on the right bank. The leader had his tent put up by the river, a mat spread on the ground before it, and the tall reeds cut near the water's edge to give him a better view.

He began to meditate, always a ponderous process with Stanley. What of the future? What of the River?

Downward it flows to the unknown! to night-black clouds of mystery and fable, mayhap past the lands of the anthropoids, the pigmies, and the blanket-eared men . . . I seek a road. Why, here lies a broad water avenue cleaving the Unknown to some sea, like a path of light! Here are woods all around, sufficient for a thousand fleets of canoes. Why not build them?

He sprang up, told the drummer to call to muster, and delivered one of his more tiresome speeches to people who were already exhausted from a long march. The burden of it was that the Voice of Fate had decreed that they should go down this river.

"You who have followed me through Turu, and sailed around the great lakes with me; you, who have followed me, like children following their father, through Unyoro, and down to Ujiji, and as far as this wild, wild land, will you leave me here? Shall I and my white brother go alone?"

That was precisely what about three-quarters of his children were thinking. They were frightened and they had good reason to be. Of his one hundred and thirty-three men, ninety-five made not a move when he called for volunteers. Stanley was a bit shaken by this and said that there was no hurry about deciding. Perhaps they would change their minds. Tippu Tib's contract wasn't up yet and he hoped to be far along before it was.

They launched the *Lady Alice* and, after a quarrel with a local tribe, shifted the entire company to the west side of the Lualaba. The bulk of the people proceeded northward along the river by land, while about thirty travelled in the boat. The inhabitants of the district were extremely hostile and frequently attacked both the land and river parties. The men were sickened by dysentery and smallpox, and thorns tore at their legs, causing dreadful ulcers. Stanley found six leaky canoes that he said had been abandoned. He lashed these together and made a floating hospital.

Just below the site of present-day Kindu they came to the first of the river's many unnavigable stretches. The great disadvantage to travelling by boat was that its occupants had to carry it almost as often as it carried them. Tippu Tib was ready to quit again at the sight of the rapids but Stanley dissuaded him and manœuvred the boats through the rough water.

On December 4 they came upon a huge canoe, very much in need of repair. The men set to work on it day and night, as it was needed to carry the increasing number of invalids. Smallpox, dysentery, ulcers and pleurisy raged, and there were some cases of typhoid. Every day several bodies were thrown into the river. Seventy-two of their number had to be carried in the boats.

Attacks from the natives were growing each day more determined. When they reached Vinya-Njara, about two hundred miles above Nyangwé, they had to hole-up in an abandoned village and fight for their lives. One reason for the persistent enmity of the inhabitants of this region was that they thought the expedition was a party of Arab slavers. They knew enough about these *Wasambye*, or uncircumcised, as they called them, to hate them without being too afraid to fight.

In the midst of the battle Stanley organized a night raid, cut loose most of the enemy's pirogues, and at last persuaded them to discuss a truce. This was facilitated by a crude form of miscegenation, frequently practised in primitive Africa, called 'blood brotherhood.' The chiefs of the opposite parties cut their arms and allowed their blood to mingle.

Tippu Tib's patience was exhausted. He was still eight marches from fulfilling his revised contract but he told Stanley very firmly that he was leaving. He demanded his full pay and Stanley couldn't refuse because he knew that Tippu would take more than half of the Expedition with him if he didn't get it. So he agreed to give the Arab a draft for two thousand six hundred dollars, a riding-ass, a trunk, a gold chain, a great deal of cloth and beads and one thousand six hundred cowries, plus two hundred rounds of ammunition and fifty pounds of brass wire if he would undertake to keep the men of the Expedition from deserting.

That ended their association. Stanley's goal was entirely too impractical to interest this pragmatic man. On the day after Christmas 1876 Tippu Tib gave the Expedition a banquet of rice, roasted sheep and palm wine. Then Stanley took his men, augmented to one hundred and forty-nine by last-minute recruiting, to a tiny island and built a separate camp.

He was elated; already he smelled the salt sea. But about ninety of his men felt condemned, and the others couldn't have failed to notice that their camp was very like a prison. Even Frank Pocock was as downcast as his plucky nature would permit, maybe because of the blanket-eared men.

He became relatively talkative. "Before we finally depart, sir," he said, "do you really believe, in your inmost soul, that

152

we shall succeed? I ask this because there are such odds against us—not that I for a moment think it would be best to return, having proceeded so far."

Stanley replied at great length, resorting to that heavy-handed optimism with which Victorian men and women so frequently entered darkly pessimistic situations. "There is an enormous risk," he conceded, "but you know the adage, 'Nothing risked, nothing won.' " He was now fairly sure that they were on the Congo and he promised that they would be in the Atlantic Ocean by April 1877. He was only four months out, but those four months were fatal to Frank. Just before they went to bed Stanley cheered the boy up by saying, "Good night! and may happy dreams of the sea, and ships, and pleasure, and comfort, and success attend you in your sleep! To-morrow, my lad, is the day we shall cry—Victory or death!"

Tippu Tib was sure that death would come to Stanley very much sooner than victory and so left him with an untroubled heart. But he had sown the seeds of a war that would destroy his power sixteen years later.

CHAPTER FOURTEEN

STANLEY'S trip down the Lualaba, from Vinya-Njara past the seven cataracts of Stanley Falls, was an unrelieved horror. On the day they started out, 28 December 1876, Stanley gave all hands one of his pep-talks, to which, he says with rare perception, they responded wanly. "Lift up your heads and be men. What is there to fear? All the world is smiling with joy. Here we are all together like one family, with hearts united, all strong with the purpose to reach our homes. See this river; it is the road to Zanzibar!"

The very next day some people farther along the road to Zanzibar tried to eat them, shouting Bo-bo-bo-o-o and reciting their favourite recipes as they circled the Expedition in their canoes. Stanley, now travelling by water with all his men, withheld fire for a while—thinking that it was ridiculous to be angry at people who regarded them simply as capons—but was at last forced to clear the river. The party picked up a number of floating shields, which they fastened to their boats as bulwarks.

On the 30th they camped in a drenching rain at the present site of the A. Houdmont & W. Thuysbaert Company, taking no more comfort from that than the Dutchman who bought Manhattan Island would have taken from sleeping on the site of the Stock Exchange. Proceeding down the river, they were attacked again on New Year's Day and four more times on January 2.

One battle in the morning lasted for three hours; though no one was killed and spears were no match for guns, the prospect of going through this for many months to come was terribly depressing. They were growing tired of being considered some-one else's meat and being told in detail how they were to be cooked.

Some of the tribes along the shore were more peaceful, or at least not so uncompromisingly carnivorous. They traded palm-wine, bananas, potatoes, cassava and an occasional dis-gruntled chicken to the voyagers for beads and cowries. If everyone along the route had been like this they might have made the whole voyage to the Atlantic, counting portage at the rapids, in a few months.

But some miles below these pleasant people another group of culinary-minded natives came into view, painted half-red and half-white, navigating monstrous pirogues. One of these, which Stanley and his men captured, was eighty-five feet long, They christened it the *Great Eastern*. The Expedition had twenty-three other boats, most of them named after British Cruisers familiar to the African East Coast. There were also the *Telegraph* and the *Herald*, the *London Town* and the *America*. On the 5th, just above the first cataract of Stanley Falls, two men were killed. They were now at the site of present-day Ponthierville.

From here they had to haul their canoes two miles overland, on a path fifteen feet wide which they cut through the bush and forest. By January 8 they were in calm water again, only to reach the second cataract by evening and to run into more hostile natives.

From this point Stanley began to display that amazing stub-bornness and deep faith in himself that raises him far above the ridiculous figure he so often cuts. Like many modern men, he was unable to cross from absurdity to greatness except by a leap. When things were absolutely hopeless he could reach nobility, but only then. During the next four days he repelled a great force of warlike natives, drove them from their villages, then turned and cut a three-mile path through dense forest round the cataract.

To do this he established six camps on the proposed route, one at each half-mile. Then he formed pioneer battalions to work day and night and applied cane, smeared with gum frankincense, to the trees as torches to work by. They rushed from camp to camp as the road was built, dragging their canoes, while the rear-guard fought off the hordes of cannibals. These marches were made with women, and even some children who had been born on the trip. In the Africa of those days women were not considered dispensable, even for short periods.

When enemy attacks threatened to halt road-building altogether, Stanley turned and chased them deep into the jungle. The battalions again took up their axes and, after seventy-eight hours of almost constant work and fighting during which Frank Pocock put every subsequent eagle-scout on earth to shame, they were back in the water.

At the foot of these falls they were 1,630 feet above sea-level, a figure Stanley arrived at by measuring boiling-points. The Expedition was just 270 geographical miles south of a spot where the Nile was known to have an altitude of 1,525 feet. A decline of 105 feet within that distance was easily possible and Stanley wondered if they weren't on the Nile after all, especially as they were still going North.

Between the fifth and sixth cataracts, where there is a considerable stretch of clear water, they camped one night on the right bank and woke in the morning to find that a net had been placed over them by enterprising natives. The paths around them were planted with splinters which pierced to the bone. These people were simply after meat and when Stanley's party captured some, after breaking out of the net, they confessed that they lived, whenever possible, on old people and strangers.

The Expedition cut its way around the sixth cataract on

January 20, unaware that there was only one more ahead. They were now exactly four miles north of the Equator. On the 24th they heard the booming of another stretch of rapids and the whole company was in despair. This neighbourhood was also populous and they could expect to fight every inch of the way. The party's guns could usually cut the enemy to pieces, but the natives' very ignorance of the effect of gunfire made the situation more dangerous, not less.

The final falls in this series do not merely drop, they are *pushed* downward by the force of the water. Stanley, at this point, again took the altitude and found that they were 1,511 feet above sea-level, so that there now could be little doubt that they were on the Congo. This was dispiriting. If it had been the Nile they could have expected some sort of aid within a few weeks. Now they knew they had months more of travel and perhaps hundreds of rapids to shoot.

But Stanley maintained his optimism. He took soundings of the river and made sketches of the fish in its waters, in order to enrich the world's knowledge of these parts. He also compiled a tiny lexicon of the local language, heavily loaded with words like, 'foot,' 'arrow,' 'knife,' 'fire,' 'food,' 'run,' 'canoe,' 'dead,' and 'darkness.'

Once he heard Frank singing, dolefully,

"The home land, the bright land,
My eyes are filled with tears,
Remembering all the happy band,
Passed from my sight for years."

Stanley reprimanded him and ordered him to sing something more hopeful. With determined cheer and shining countenance the boy sang,

"Brightly gleams our banner,
Pointing to the sky,

Waving wanderers onward
To their home on high."

Stanley explained that this smacked of another sort of defeatism, however pious. "Sing, my dear Frank, your *best* song." Young Pocock rose to the occasion and made the forest ring with,

"Onward, Christian soldiers,
Marching as to war,
With the cross of Jesus
Going on before!"

At the end of the seventh falls they found many tall poles placed in the river's channel, supporting woven baskets to catch fish. Even now this structure is seen at the south-east end of Stanleyville. On January 28 they cleared the last obstacle in the river, while constantly attacked by savages. The Expedition emerged exhausted into clear water, at the juncture of the Tshopo River with the Congo. This is the present site of the throbbing, vulgar, touching, frontier town that very properly bears Henry Stanley's name.

CHAPTER FIFTEEN

W<small>E</small> arrived in Stanleyville at dawn. It was raining heavily and the railroad yard was grey and lonely. I stepped from the train to a gleaming cinderbed and hurried across a sheaf of tracks. The main part of town, I had heard, was over the river and I would have to get a ferry. The fog was low here and it was hard to tell which direction was north, but somehow, as Melville said, one always knows where the water is.

The rain fell harder and there were comforting port smells in the air—creosote and honourably rusting metal—which make one long for a cup of coffee in a pallid all-night café. Then the great, brown river showed itself. From here on, the maps call it the Congo, but it had earned that muscular name long before. It was very like the Mississippi, inexorable and majestic, as no river in Europe knows how to be.

Coming closer to it, picking my way between abandoned freight cars, I looked down and saw steel cranes standing on the piers like praying mantises. Except for a person in the distance, riding a bicycle down a glossy cement walk, the entire yard was deserted. The fog was lifting, though it still rained, and faint outlines of buildings were visible across the river.

Black hand-cars on the sidings were filling with water and looked like drinking-pans for forest monsters. Rain dripped from the sides of a flat-car and blue-purple oil film swam on the tracks. The spoor which industry leaves in the jungle blends into it far more easily than do the smallest traces of our domestic lives; so that a coal barge on this side of the Congo lay patiently in the driving equatorial rain, practically indistinguishable from its surroundings, but the little carts of the

Boulangerie l'Avenir peddling liverwurst sandwiches on the other side offended the wilderness by their very existence.

In any case it always leaves one a little sad to see Nature so manhandled, whether by warehouses and slag-heaps or by chunky modern buildings with air-conditioned doctors' offices. It might have been better to leave it all as it was. Except that this kind of nostalgia applies to any city, and a person who says that Paris and London should have remained meadows with rivers maundering through them may be right without being particularly helpful. Besides, there is a perverse beauty in the artificial landscapes men create that God, in His classical severity, can never quite bring off.

The one thing that doesn't change in Stanleyville is the river. In this it is like all the other great rivers of the world. They are indifferent to St Louis, or Aswan, or Omaha; they would just as soon reek of naphtha and sewage as of mud and rotting trees. Sooner or later they will carry all the forests and cities on their banks off to the sea.

The person on the bicycle turned out to be the ferry pilot. He directed me down a wooden ramp to a small motor-launch, where I ducked into the empty cabin, wet to the skin. He followed slowly, ignoring the weather, and busied himself checking gauges. I noticed that this young man was wearing transparent plastic beach-sandals. These are ideal for Congo weather and, I believe, are also considered smart. Many Africans of the *évolue* class wear them, and are especially proud when the plastic turns a bilious yellow—much as we like hats to be a little stained. At six-thirty, sharp, he glanced casually around the rail-yard and we roared away from the wharf.

The boat headed diagonally upstream to compensate for the current. Above and below us other boats skated across, packed with people on their way to work. In three thousand miles the river has no bridges and is so broad in most places that it would be a massive engineering feat to build one. It stopped raining and a few minutes later a powerful sun drew up the last of the fog. Then it grew hot. Walking up from the opposite embankment into town I nearly stepped on a beetle, about the size of a dessert plate, which seemed to have been drowned in the gutter.

I got breakfast in the *Chutes Hotel*, where I had been advised to stay. It was a comfortable place, though a bit expensive, and was a splendid example of the success the Belgians are having in their vast scheme for banalizing the Congo, though this is as yet confined to the European quarters of their cities. Here Belgian culture spreads like a benevolent sore, as supermarkets and florist shops spring up filled with canned fruit and sickly north-European flowers. With any luck this land will become a huge, comfortable, electrified suburb in fifty years. In this the Belgians are much superior to the British who have never quite managed to turn East Africa into a tea-garden, maybe because their standards were impossibly high.

In order to encourage Africans in the Belgian way of life, the authorities have established what are called *centres extra-coutumiers*. These are groups of detribalized persons which have formed around European settlements. Such people are not *évolués* in the strict sense of the word, though many among them are. They simply have no common origin and would be a disorganized mass without this recognition. The Belgians have encouraged these centres, and the effect has been to create a large population (more than three million now) who can step into modern life without any of the handicaps a person long nurtured within a tribe would suffer—and, naturally, with none of his safeguards.

In Stanleyville there are four *centres extra-coutumiers*, *cités Belges 1* and *2*, *Bruxelles*, and *Mangobo*. In these, especially in the *cités Belges* and *Mangobo*, there is a good deal of public housing: long rows of concrete huts, tin-roofed, each about twelve feet wide and ten feet deep, having two rooms, public water, and a lavatory for every two families. At least this was the kind I became acquainted with. They offered a minimum of comfort and cleanliness and were rented very cheaply. The people who lived in them were pleased to be there and would surely have said, if anyone had asked, that banality was a very small price to pay for their homes.

I had stopped for a bottle of beer that morning in an African bar near the market. Here a young man had promised to take me to see one of the leading figures in *cité Bruxelles*, a certain Chief Sidanou. I returned that afternoon to the *Café des Sports* on the *rue du Marche*, but could not find him. The place wasn't crowded at this hour and to pass the time I ordered another beer at the bar and watched a man getting drunk at a near-by table on a grim mixture of stout and Coca-Cola.

The girl behind the bar reversed a stack of records on the café's poor, overworked machine and in this rare interval of silence I asked her if anyone had left a message for me. The music began again and she came down to my end.

"*Avez-vous un message pour moi?*" I repeated, nearly shouting. "*J'avais . . .*"

The girl stopped me with a raised hand and spoke to the stout-and-Coca-Cola man in Swahili, interlacing a few words of French. She evidently found it difficult to understand me and was asking for help. When she turned back I heard her say, "I don't know. That's the truth."

"Why didn't you tell me you spoke English?" I said, a bit ruffled.

She shrugged and turned to arrange a box of bazooka bubble-gum and a glass of dusty paper poppies before the bar mirror. Without being at all taciturn, it was Epis's custom never to speak if her meaning was already clear. I hadn't *asked* if she spoke English.

"Will you have another Stanor?" she said, taking my empty bottle.

I nodded and asked if she would have one with me.

She looked at the clock and shrugged again. "Yes, now I take a Stanor, thank you. I don't take Primus, it makes me drunken." As she went to get another glass I noticed that she was very tall, nearly six feet in her flat slippers. Unlike most of the other African women in Stanleyville she never wore shawls, except in the house. She was dressed now in a cheap red-on-white cotton print, held in at the waist with a red leatherette belt. She was very slim, built on the lines of an antelope, and had a calm, immobile face with a good strong chin, which some anthropologist would be sure to call prognathous.

She came back with two bottles of beer, both Stanor. I asked if this was her regular work, as she seemed unlike the other women one saw in these bars—more withdrawn and independent. The room rang with electric guitars playing a cha-cha-cha.

She shook her head. "No—I got to work at the tables. My friend has this work and she is sick. But I can do it very well. I tell you. No one can fool me."

I asked her name. She picked up a rag and wiped a ring off the bar. "Epis," she said, looking towards the door. Whenever she spoke she seemed on the point of leaving.

"Epis what?"

She looked around, apparently surprised to find me still there. "What?"

I asked what her last name was.

She hesitated, then looked over my shoulder. "Noel," she said. "Epis Noel."

Another customer came in and she went to him. She seemed to have forgotten that I was there, except that her glass stood beside mine, barely touched. At last I saw the young man who was going to take me to Chief Sidanou in the *cité Bruxelles*. He seemed unsure of himself now, and denied that he knew the man. As I had come here on purpose to get the introduction I was disappointed and a little angry. Then I saw that he was drunk and went back to the bar.

Suddenly Epis was at my side. She picked up her glass and sipped her beer. "I tell you something. These people around here. You watch out. They just think you will buy them a Stanor. That's true. I tell you, sir. And the girls. Some are not clean."

The cha-cha-cha came on again. This particular record was the rage of Stanleyville that week and before I left I heard it many hundreds of times. I explained to Epis that I had been trying to see a man in *Bruxelles*.

She turned half away and sipped her beer, saying nothing. "Instead of telling me whom I should look out for," I said, "you could show me around yourself. Where do people go at night? Is there any place for dancing and music?"

She looked at me and shook her head. "I cannot. I must go home."

I tried to explain that I wanted her as a guide, mostly because of her English, and that if she had anyone who would object she could assure him . . .

"No, that's not it. I have no man who lives with me. You mean to say that, don't you? I can do what I want. I tell you. But I have my daughter." She glanced to a row of chairs along one wall and I saw a fat little girl with a head of honey-blonde curls sleeping blissfully through the clanging steel guitars.

Epis had gone again, but as her glass was still by mine, I waited. It took a while to learn her rules of conduct. They were, I discovered later, a bit like the rules of dancing—intricate steps and elaborate rhythms performed almost without movement. The best dancers would hold themselves within a circle no more than two feet in diameter.

She came back again. The bar was now growing crowded. "Her name is Ann," she said, proudly. "Her father was an Italian man." She pronounced both 'Ann' and 'man' with a long 'A.' [1]

I asked if there was anyone at home to leave the child with, promising to pay her for her time if she would come with me as a guide. "Yes—I have my sister, if she will be there. But . . ." Suddenly her eyes caught mine, then she looked away quickly.

"What?" I said.

She turned and arranged some cartons of Viceroy and Belga cigarettes before the bar mirror. "That's all right. I go with you. I know a nice place. Very nice music."

Then she turned and drank her beer indifferently. "I must lock up at nine o'clock," she said, "you come then." With this she picked up our glasses and took them to be washed.

When I came back for Epis she was carefully balancing out her cash. There was no one there and she let me in at a side door. The owners of the café lived next door. They were Belgian. When she had counted her cash in a cigar-box and snapped a rubber band round some papers, she left her daughter in my care and went to deliver them.

[1] I haven't tried to reproduce Epis's pronunciation because it is too much like the burlesque speech ascribed to American Negroes. She very clearly said 'dat' for 'that' and 'das' for 'that's,' for instance. She also used 'de' for 'the' and possibly 'hab' for 'have,' though it sounded more like 'haaav.' This would be offensive to many Americans and probably to many citizens of the British Commonwealth, though dialect English hasn't yet been made a crime, and what is good enough for Ronald Firbank—as far as the English language is concerned—should be good enough for anyone. But many people are sensitive on that point and should not be forced to enrich our tongue against their will.

The child and I stood beneath an arc light in the deserted street. We were not far from the centre of the European town, but the rudimentary buildings were scattered among vacant, weed-strewn lots and there was a feeling of despair about the neighbourhood one finds at the outskirts of all cities that have grown too fast. When Epis came back she perched the child, who was about four years old and heavy as a dumpling, on her hip and we walked away. She said she had a friend with a taxi and asked me if I could afford a trip to *Mangobo*, where she lived.

The taxi had gone a number of miles into the country when Epis told me that we would first stop at the home of another friend of hers. This turned out to be a young woman with a light complexion and large, vague eyes. As Epis said later, "She is my *best* friend. You will dance with her, mmm? I will thank you very much if you do. She is not very intelligent but she is very good. Very nice. That's right."

The young woman lived in a small, concrete hut, in *Mangobo* also, such as I have described. She was apparently supported by an *évolué* who was a government clerk. He lived here most of the time, he said. The inside of the house was dimly lit with kerosene lamps and contained a battered couch, a table and several chairs. The walls were bare and the floor was cold cement. A curtained doorway to the right led to a tiny bedroom. There were now about six of us inside, including the cab-driver.

People came and went, evidently with some purpose, though I couldn't fathom it unless it was to see me. In the meantime we sat about the table consuming Primus beer (though Epis wouldn't touch any), looking like conspirators in the long-shadowed light. Then we left together to go to a cabaret up the road. Little Ann was temporarily put to bed in the other room, in charge of a couple who were staying behind, though they could probably be counted on for nothing but their presence.

The lives of these young people had a certain aimlessness that made one uneasy. Epis felt it also, and normally sat a little apart from the others. But, as she told me later, they were her only friends and she couldn't spend all of her time alone. None of them, it seemed to me, had very serious interests, or even very frivolous ones. The conversation of the men—when they would speak French—was spiritless and humdrum. They seemed to want to do nothing but drink beer and, from time to time, to make love.

Most of the women were wholly or partly kept, but this had no especial significance. Only when everyone was dancing or when music was playing did they seem to come together. Otherwise the society was formless, a community of strangers held together by money. It might have been one of the towns in our own West just after the Civil War.

In fact, there is something *extra-coutumier* about many Americans. Having left our tribes on other continents we are more adaptable to change and social disorder. We are also most at home in a world of plastic and flashing glass, though hardly responsible for the fact that others imitate it. But there is a danger. Unstable mixtures are explosive. The Belgians may be making a mistake in deliberately fostering these settlements of the dispossessed. The few riots which have erupted in the Congo so far (especially in Leopoldville, where the *extra-coutumier* settlements are oldest) seem to be parochial, without national organization. But the pile is being set up and a reaction will surely take place, whether or not it is controlled.

The cabaret was nothing but a large, floodlit cement floor with tables set around and a record player booming the cha-cha-cha. From time to time people got up to dance, not necessarily in couples. The best and most serious dancing was done alone, and sometimes the entire floor was filled with people who were not touching or even looking at each other. It then approached folk-dancing, and the performers moved with great precision, staring down at their feet as though they were playing difficult passages on the piano.

At such moments I always sat down. Our table was littered with bottles of Primus, though Epis had a Stanor to herself. It was important for her not to be drunken. As always, she sat apart. She was pleased to answer any questions I asked or pass them on to others. She was never sullen or even ungracious, but she remained detached from all that was going on.

Epis danced very little and when she did she barely moved on the floor—though she moved perfectly—holding her long body in rigid control. Even in this she managed to seem withdrawn and danced by herself, for herself. I admired her, perhaps especially because she often attained a motionless, obsidian beauty that made one catch one's breath; but I was beginning to think I had made a mistake in hiring her to guide me. I had wanted someone *typical* of this place, and she seemed more of a stranger to Stanleyville—and even to Africa—than I.

Once, when a waltz came, I tried my luck with a large, voluminously shawled lady who was brimful of beer but whose balance was far better than mine. We hadn't made more than four turns when she stopped and mutely drew my attention to her bare feet.

Some time after midnight Epis and I walked back to her friend's house, just ahead of the others. The road was lit by nothing but moonlight and the night echoed a fading samba. "Your taxi is gone," she said, at last.

"Oh? Can I get another?"

I could see her shake her head in the faint moonlight. She

168

walked very straight and, though I am tall, her eyes were always opposite mine. "I think they make a joke at me."

"Why?"

"Well, they think . . . It's because I don't see these boys much, you see. They leave you alone with me because I say they *must* take you back to Stan."

"But I can get another car. There was one back there at the cabaret." It wasn't pleasant to be left alone here in the Congo night, four or five miles from town.

"No, they are going the other way. I ask them."

"Then . . . ?"

"You could stay with me—but I don't want to be in the bed with you. Do you see that?"

I said that I did, easily. I didn't particularly want to spend the night in one of those huts. They were all very fine, viewed as housing for others, but not as places one stayed oneself.

Epis was silent for a while. From time to time the moon passed under a cloud and then only the white of her dress would be visible. "Yes, you would like it. I know, most men do. And I don't mind. Sometimes. That's the truth. But I will tell you something, sir. I am twenty years old. That is not old, I tell you."

Behind us the voices of the others rose in laughter. They were a bit drunk. It was chilly.

"In the last five years I have birthed four children. You believe that? Since I was fifteen. Now I have my daughter and I got to work. I don't mind that, if I am free. It's not bad to work. But when you birth children it make you tired. That's right. So that is why—not now, maybe next year all right but not now. You see, there is just one way not to have children." The moon came out and I saw that she was staring levelly at me. "Stay away from the men," she said, and glanced

169

back at the others who were coming up to us. "Even the boys."

We picked up her child at her friend's house and walked about a mile down a dirt road until we came to some more files of concrete huts. In almost total darkness she singled out one from the others and we went in. I seemed to have caught cold from my wetting that morning and was not very cheerful about this adventure. Epis's sister was sitting with her friend at a table, in a circle of kerosene light. A bottle of beer stood before them and they were talking in low voices. He was a large, serious, dull young man who worked in a hospital. He wore an open white shirt and plastic beach shoes. A few minutes later he rode off on a bicycle, guiding himself by a flashlight. I gathered that he stayed here some nights, but not always.

The other room, I found, was divided in half by a curtain. In each section was a pallet. Epis put me on her own, and she, her daughter and her sister slept together on the other. I was nearest to the tiny sitting-room. The house was so small that we could hear each other breathe in any part of it. But on the whole I was comfortable, though the blanket smelled bitter and the pillow was lumpy (the only other pillow was given to the daughter, who had a cough). I fell asleep almost immediately.

During the night I woke with a fit of coughing. Then, as I lay in the cold darkness, I heard a voice directly above me. "Will you like some water now?" Epis said. "My daughter want some too." I felt a glass placed in my hand and I took a sip. "You are not afraid?" she said.

"No," I said. "Thank you—thank you very much," but Epis took the glass and left without speaking. In Swahili the word for thank you is seldom used, as people are taught to be generous enough not to need it.

When she pulled the curtain back a shaft of moonlight came

into my side of the room and I saw that she was naked, though simple nudity had less significance for her than it had for me. But I noticed that she *did* look like an antelope.

Just before I went to sleep again I heard some cats bounding across the roof, as they frequently do during the night, but it seemed to me that they had very large paws.

The next morning, as I was thrusting into my trousers, balanced on one leg, Epis's sister walked briskly through the curtain and said, *"Bonjour, M'sieu!"* I fell back on the pallet but she hurried through, and soon I heard her breaking wood to build a fire. When I came into the other room I found that Epis was up also and had been giving her child a wash behind the house.

I mean *houses*, for no one's demesne could be defined. Long, unbroken lines of identical structures sat on naked fields of red earth, which still bore the scars of bull-dozing. Two files of houses were separated by a dirt road, then came an interval of forty or fifty yards and two more files. Some families in Epis's row had tried to plant kitchen gardens, and across the way a few had marked out front yards with tired bushes and flowers, though these seemed intimidated by the trackless Congo forests surrounding them.

Epis had been up before dawn, but everyone in the community began to stir when the first light came at five-thirty. Here, near the Equator, the times of dawn and dusk don't vary appreciably, and one can count on thirteen hours of light every single day, all year long.

Epis came into the house, cleaning her teeth with the end of a stick. We shook hands. "How do you do, sir. I think you are not well all night, no?" She turned suddenly to her child who was down on the floor following some kind of insect. *"Nunú Hapana-pana."* The girl looked up and smiled with the automatic sweetness which is children's weapon against their parents. Her blonde ringlets were damp. Both she and Epis were wearing clean wash-dresses, and Ann had little red shoes.

A woman passed the doorway and peered in. She was pregnant, and her brazen belly rode comfortably outside her shawls. A small, naked boy followed her. Suddenly, across the road, another woman began to scream. "That is nothing," Epis said, seeing me start. "That man there he always beat his wife, every morning. That's just like that. Every day. Most men they take their wives in the bed or they go for a walk but not him! Don't worry, she like that, maybe. Don't listen."

In trying not to listen I glanced at a calendar on the wall, advertising beer with the smiling countenance of a fat, African friar. Beneath each of the red figures on the face of the calendar someone had written, 'happy days.' On a table near by were a strapless Tissot lady's watch, a Swahili bible and some loose cigarettes.

Epis's sister wandered into the room, hitching up her shawls and combing her hair with a thick wooden comb shaped like a fork. She sat on the stoop working pomade into her scalp and humming South American songs. I wished I could have got *her* to show me around. She seemed perfectly typical. Her finger-nails and toe-nails were dyed flaming red and she was afflicted with giggles. By contrast Epis was severe and regal. She wore her hair in a neat cap on her head, about as deep as the joint of a finger, and no ornament of any sort.

I had thought the sticks were being broken to make a fire for breakfast, but when I wandered into the cubicle that served as a kitchen, with a flue for an open fire, I noticed a pot of greens just coming to a boil. There was a can of Danish crab bisque on a shelf, and I was told that this was to be the sister's friend's dinner. When the pot boiled the manioc leaves were taken out and pounded together with hot peppers and leeks in

172

a mortar made from an up-ended log, with a pestle about the size of an oar. These ingredients were again cooked slightly and mixed with palm oil. There was nothing else to eat in the kitchen, not even fruit, and I was glad when Epis said she was ready to go.

We walked slowly up the road, and I noticed that my colour was attracting very much attention. This became more pronounced when I offered to carry Epis's daughter (homesick for my own), and the child, after riding on my hip and staring at me deeply with her grey-green eyes, suddenly began to cry, "Papá! Papá!" using the Italian inflexion. I asked Epis if it did her reputation any good to be seen with me here, at this suspicious hour of the morning.

She took her child back. "I don't care what they say. I am free, that's all. I have to work and I got my daughter. So if we have a place to stay that's all I care. I tell you, that's like that."

"Is that all you want? What about the child's father? Won't you see him again?" We were coming into a main road now and several hundred people were going in our direction, on their way to work.

Epis looked straight ahead, expressionless. "No, I would not go with him now. He is nothing to me. Not if he gave me two thousand francs. Fuuiii!"

Two thousand francs were just forty dollars, and I wondered why she was so specific about the amount.

"That's all right," she continued, relenting. "He wasn't a bad man. He send money sometimes. Then he forget. I don't care, just so I am free."

We were coming towards the highway, where there was a bus-stop. There were now over a thousand people before and behind us. Many of these were women, carrying bundles on their heads for the market.

I asked about her other children. "Two are dead," she said

unemotionally. "*He's* got one. The boy. He will put him in the school, I think now in Ruanda. I take the girl. We have what we need. Only, I just want . . ."

She turned suddenly to me. "There is that boy who run away last night. If you like to go in the taxi back to the hotel you just call him. Maybe you don't like us with you. That's all right, I tell you," she said, not too sincerely, looking longingly at the taxi. We hailed it and got in.

As she and her daughter were going to the market to buy some fruit before she went to work (she had no regular schedules for meals; her day was like a clock without a face) I said that I would drop them off. Epis spent some time lecturing the unrepentant taxi-driver, and finally sat back in the seat with a sigh as we sped into town.

"What was it you said you wanted, back there on the road? You said you had all you needed, only . . ."

She nodded. "That's just that," she said, looking boldly out at the poor people who could not afford the bus to work, let alone a taxi. "We got to get up very early. And then at night, lots of times we walk home. One hour—two hours, sometimes, when I carry Ann. *Nunú! Hapana-pana.*" Ann was sweetly pulling the stuffing out of the back seat.

"Yes?"

"I saved something, just in four months. Maybe later, next year we will have one. You can pay a little, and then some every month. I have to work, so that's all right, I tell you. We have the house, a hundred and fifty francs a month and I forget how much the water. That's right, then we will be free all the time. I tell you. *Nunú! Hapana-pana.*" Ann was wetly kissing my cheek.

We were in town now and coming around by the far side of the market. "But *what* do you want?" I said, impatiently.

Epis picked up the handkerchief tied at four ends which she

174

used as a purse and prepared to get out of the car. She dragged her amorous daughter out of my lap. "A bicycle," she said, quickly. "*Nunú!*"

I went, that afternoon, to *cité Belge* to visit Father Rommens, a parish priest. I heard that he had been stationed here and in other parts of the Congo for a long time, and a trip to his parish offered a pleasant walk to the Tshopo Falls. On the way out I passed several neighbourhoods that looked like cribs, in the old Southern sense, except that the women lived in thatched mud huts. I believe there wasn't anything official or even semi-official about the district. It was a natural outgrowth of what the Father spoke of several moments later, when I arrived at his parish house.

"You see, there *is* a kind of slavery left here," he said, puffing on a curved Flemish pipe. "It's not all stamped out yet. The women are slaves—that's about all it is, slavery. Especially the women of the *évolués*, or whatever you want to call them." Father Rommens paused and offered me a cold drink. He was a good-looking grey-haired man, just on the far side of middle-age, but lean and active.

"It works like this. A man goes out in the bush or the forest —to a tribe, perhaps his own. There he arranges to purchase a wife. He pays very little—just a trifle to her family. Then she comes with him, say here to Stanleyville. Well, your *évolué* makes a great deal of money by her standards. (And starting next year they will have equal pay with Belgian workers.) But he doesn't tell her what he makes. He gives her just enough money to buy food for herself and her children, when she has them.

"For fifteen or twenty years she works for him, for nothing . . . she and any number of others, whatever he can afford. Sometimes she can save enough out of the house money to go

175

back to her parents. That's what she dreams of. But she must leave her children behind. They are his property."

Father Rommens stood up and went to the window, where he knocked his pipe out on the sill. His parish house was built right on the Tshopo River, and was mostly surrounded by high cane and grass. There was a small lawn to the front.

"That doesn't make the women very moral, you know," he said, sadly, but with no particular rancour. "Money to them means freedom, that's all. They are right, there. Marriages like that are just slavery, you see. And, most of the time, the only reason the men get legally married at all is to get the *allocation familiale*. That means about seventy-five francs a month to them—sometimes more." He sighed and came back to his seat. "*L'homme est toujours libre*, I'm afraid. But what is bad is that the women are slaves."

He pointed out that he was speaking generally. There were many exceptions. I asked if he found the members of his parish to be individually different from the members of a European parish. He shook his head, again sadly. "I wish they were. There are just about as many Christians here as in Europe, if that's what you mean. They are better than some of the people in *bad* European countries and worse, maybe, than some of the people in *good* European countries." He seemed pleased to have avoided a ten-letter word beginning with 'P.' "Some are very good and some, I'm afraid, are not." Father Rommens heaved a great sigh and quickly refilled his pipe.

"Sometimes it's not even the *Christians* who are fine. But we try. We have only had trouble with two of the Commandments," he said, with fixed optimism. "The first and the sixth. The first is not so badly broken, now. I really think we've got graven images under control. But.. .." He frowned and blew out a great cloud of smoke. ". . . the sixth. Sometimes I think

176

it's hopeless." Then he brightened somewhat. "Even the Protestants can't handle that one."

When I returned to the hotel I began thinking of Epis. I had promised to drop by the *Café des Sports* to pay her the money I owed her, as I hadn't had change this morning. She made no nonsense about not accepting the fee—she was very glad to do so. I was going to add something more for her hospitality and leave it at that. I would find someone else to show me around. She was just too serious and self-centred for me to handle, if I was going to handle anything else.

The trouble was that I already *knew* Epis. I had recognized her as soon as she began to speak. She was my grandmother. Possibly she was yours, too. She had just the proud, awkward, noble bearing of an ancestor, brought to indignant life from the bottom of a chest in the attic. In their photographs such women wear high-necked, ruffled dresses and they have a cool, indomitable beauty.

"You wouldn't believe it to look at her," the descendant says, turning the pages of the album, "but by the time she was twenty-five she was supporting seven children with her pastry-cooking while she put herself through college. She was really a remarkable woman." It comes as no great surprise, then, to learn that at the age of sixteen, when she and her husband went to the Yukon, she killed a savage Kodiak bear with a kitchen knife. One also expects to hear that she was dead-set against profanity and alcohol, and that people complimented her right up to the day she died on her tiny feet.

Though these women often attain awesome respectability they do not hesitate to defy convention. They may brave the jeers of the crowd in picket lines or uphold the right to free love, if not the practice. Their chief qualities are strength and courage, and what they want most in the world—what they will have if it kills them—is freedom. They want to be emancipated, with honour, and a country that has a few millions of them, as the United States had at the close of the last century, is headed for revolution. I went to the hotel desk and checked out, leaving my bag behind. If only Epis hadn't mentioned that bicycle . . .

On the *Avenue du Marche* the cha-cha-cha was going full blast. Epis noticed me the moment I entered the café, but I had to go through the elaborate ritual of greeting. I sat at the end of the bar and looked around, keeping her always in the corner of my eye. She seemed to ignore me completely, even when her work brought her to within a few feet of me. Then, just as I was getting impatient and was about to call her, she appeared beside me holding out her hand. I shook it.

"Are you well, sir? I think you probably don't come. My daughter ask and I say he probably stay away. Will you like a Stanor?"

I nodded and she left again. Ann was wandering around the room, looking for something to eat, to take apart or to be fond of. She came to me and put her arm around my leg. "Papá," she said, contentedly.

When Epis returned, I explained my plan, quite certain that she would agree. I hadn't much money left, but if she could put me up, charging what the hotel charged, and worked for me from time to time as a guide and translator, she would have earned enough in the few days before my boat left to buy a bicycle.

"What does one cost, by the way?"

"Two thousand francs," she said quickly, wheels gleaming in her eyes.

I told her that I had seen a very high English lady's bicycle for considerably less than that, though it was a bit old-fashioned.

178

"That isn't a good kind," she said, wiping the bar nervously.

Two thousand francs was about what she would have, but it did seem silly for her not to keep something aside, if she could, and I advised her to get the English one. Also, I thought she would look splendidly Edwardian on one, but Epis understood such antiquarian sentimentality no more than my grandmother would have.

She was desperate. She stared past me towards the vacant lot across the street. When you long for something—really yearn for it—it is better not to have it at all than to have an inferior substitute. She shook her head, stubbornly. "I cannot do that, sir. The Belgian bicycle is what I must have." She paused and added, ". . . because if it is broken I always have the pieces to put into it. But not if it is English, sir. Then I have no pieces. That is the truth, I tell you." There was silence, while she searched for a better argument. At last she nodded quickly and said, "I tell you, every one in Stan got the Belgian bicycle. So if I sold it, it would have to be Belgian or no one would buy. You see that? It's like money in the bank!"

This clinched it for both of us. It is better to have good reasons for doing what you intend to do anyway. She told me to come back at closing time and returned to her work, maintaining, probably with difficulty, an air of total indifference.

That night we went to another cabaret, after leaving Ann with Epis's sister. This time we were alone. The place was like an old-time frontier dance-hall. We might have been in Cheyenne or Albuquerque in the 70's, if one can imagine those places made still more raucous by electric guitars. Here there was a live orchestra which sometimes played along with the records, sometimes against them and sometimes alone. Among the instruments was an old piano, its wires prepared with bits of string, pencil and tape. There were also some horns, and some drums tuned like a harpsichord.

Frequently the music was as good as anything you may find in the States. Once or twice it was much better. But I heard another band like this some time later in Leopoldville and the music in each case was generally not up to good American jazz, simply because it lacked coherence. The individual performances were expert and sometimes amazing, but after a few minutes the group would coast on its own momentum. What they wanted was a conscious tradition, and in this they were like all the other *extra-coutumier* people I had seen. They seemed to lack any organization or purpose.

The dance floor—it was *all* dance floor and people even danced outside—was packed so tight you could hardly move. Thousands of bottles of Stanor and Primus were being shoved across the bar at the rear, and here I saw a pair of demure mulatto whores seated at a tiny table fanning themselves with snakeskin purses. They were dressed in identical skirts and boleros cut from a material of stars and sickle moons and other appropriately celestial motives, and they were exquisitely bored. Standing at the bar was a young woman who would have answered to the name of Lil in any dance-hall on earth. She was jet black, dressed entirely in white organdie, and wore a giant rhinestone butterfly clipped into her hair at the back of the head.

Seeing her, I must have made some move to rise because Epis put a hand on my arm and said, "No. I don't do that, I think. You would not be wise. I tell you, that's like that. She is a friend of a very *big* man." It wasn't clear whether she meant big physically or big with influence, but there was a note of urgency in her voice and I sat down.

Epis herself wore her usual wash-dress, but this gave her a certain distinction. Any person out for the evening who can look poised and splendid in a threadbare rag, with no cosmetic or ornament, may safely go anywhere in the world smart people gather to intimidate each other. She could have managed as well on Manhattan's East Side or in Mayfair. Epis had a number of friends of both sexes milling around the cabaret, but she seemed not particularly close to any of them. When they broke into laughter she would look away and wait for them to stop.

We danced once or twice, but I decided, at last, to give up this form of entertainment, being too far outclassed. The people here took to dancing with a seriousness and a devotion which few other races of the world can know anything about. It was not wild, ever, and even the most uninhabited drunks applied themselves to the intricate movements with miraculous severity and control. Everyone *worked* at it. Dancing was less a thing to enjoy than to live, and when a squad of soldiers came in they barely paused to order a few bottles of Primus before they got up to dance, each alone, staring down at clumsy boots as they caught on to the music and grew light as the ringing air.

At last Epis leaned over to me and said, "You like to go, I think." That was exactly what I had been thinking, and I was surprised that she was so observant of me. She rose quietly and walked towards the door, holding her fine head a good six feet high.

We stumbled home down a rutted road, occasionally lit by a clouded moon. I asked Epis if she intended, ever, to get married and saw her nod quickly. She had evidently thought about this before.

"Oh yes, I think I will. That's right. Only, I tell you something, I got to *see* him first." She turned to me and I could just make out her face as she put one finger to her eye. "You believe me. I tell you, I got to see him. I got to know what he like. That's all. I got to see him very, very good before I marry him, I tell you. That's just like that. I don't stay in the house when he goes out, no sir, I don't do that. I don't got to be grateful if he give me a bite to eat, you see.

"I don't mind to work. Only it is hard to have children, that's all, when you got to work. Then you want a husband." She guided me past a ditch. "There are good ones and bad ones, I tell you. I don't want the one who think he own me just because we married. I got to *see* him first, before I marry him. That's all."

Just before we reached home she reminded me again, in case my new status had caused me to forget, that she did not expect to occupy the pallet with me. I protested my innocence, but she seemed not to notice it (chiefly, as I saw with some shock, because it had ceased to exist). She fell into a long silence and then, just before her door she turned and said, "I will have it on the back, I think."

"What on the back?"

"The chair for my daughter, sir. I can have it on the front or the back, but the back is best."

"Are you speaking of your bicycle?" I said, a bit dryly.

"Yes, sir. On the back is best." We went in.

That night the heavy cats ran up and down the roof and I didn't sleep at all well.

The next day Epis had a half happy-day, so that we were able to avoid the great crowds going to work in the early morning. After that first rush *Mangobo* remained fairly quiet. Even the wife-beater had apparently gone for a walk. As Epis and Ann and I walked towards the bus she told me how she had come down from Uganda with her sister. This was a bit confusing because apparently the word 'sister' meant to her any female relative of approximately her age. It was not the sister *I* knew but another she had come with. Also, her family had not looked on European borders with the proper gravity, and often did not know whether they had been living in British or Belgian territory. However, Epis had gone six years to a British Protestant school and had come out neither very British nor very much of a Christian, though in every other way excellent.

She had been here in Stanleyville a little more than a year, she said, and had been ill for a while. This was after the birth and death of her last child. She had come into the Congo with her daughter because she had relatives here and because she had heard that one could earn a living. In the beginning she had been afraid, especially during one terrible period when she had been left alone and had been continually sick.

"Not to work I wasn't afraid," she said, "only to be sick. That is very bad. I tell you."

While checking my bag at the hotel I had taken with me Colette's *La Vagabonde*. I took it from my pocket now and read,

Vivre seule, on s'en tire, on s'y fait; mais languir seule et fiévreuse, tousser dans la nuit interminable, atteindre, sur des jarrets défaillants, la fenêtre aux vitres battues de pluie, puis revenir à une couche froissée et molle,—seule, seule, seule! . . .

Epis's French was better than mine, but Colette isn't always easy and she took the book from my hands and had me point out the passage to her. Ann had wandered into a ditch and a great red sun was beating down on the scraped earth of *Mangobo*.

At last she looked up. "How he know that?"

I explained that Colette was a woman.

"How he *know* that," Epis went on, paying no attention. "That's the truth, I tell you. Just like that. When you sick then you just can't be alone. I tell you, sir. That's just the truth!"

It is a consistent fault of young people to believe that no one in the world has ever learned anything but themselves. The circumstances of Epis's upbringing and education made her even more provincial in this respect. I read her other parts of the book, there in the merciless sun, not to further her knowledge, merely indignant that she should think she was the only person in the world who had ever felt different from her fellows.

But then I began to realize that in this story of a woman freeing herself from domestic slavery fifty years ago in France, Epis saw herself quite clearly; and that it was probably written more for her than for me. She especially liked the description of marriage as, 'noue-moi ma cravate, prépare-moi un lavement, veille à ma cotelette, subis ma mauvaise humeur et mes trahisons.' She borrowed the book and stuffed it in her handkerchief before she went to pull Ann out of a puddle of mud.

Late that morning we went down to the last of the Stanley Falls, just to the east of town. Here the Wagenia fisheries stand below the rapids as Stanley first saw them, after his harrowing ride from Vinya-Njara. We had bought some fruit in the market and, in a picnic mood, had hired a dugout canoe to take us across to an island in the boiling river. Epis sat in front, very straight and tall, looking particularly ancestral. I, too, felt the generations drop away. She should have been wearing a large hat and a veil and I badly wanted muttonchop whiskers. Our boatman, however, an emphatically *coutumier* member of the Wagenia Tribe, was a few hundred years behind us and grimaced fearfully through filed teeth because Epis had knocked down his fare by half.

Later we returned to town, as she had to go to work at noon. To pass a half-hour we went down to the river again and sat on the wall before the Belgian Congo Bank. We stayed about three or four feet apart as she didn't like us to be seen too much together in white neighbourhoods. There was, of course, no law against this, but it was a question of class to some extent as well as colour. These things are so difficult to explain just because they make so little sense. I believe Epis also did not want the owner of her café to get word of our friendship.

That about describes the feeling we had for each other. We had become rather close but not exactly as a man and a woman —in spite of my near-lapse the previous evening. That was hardly to be wondered at. It is really quite difficult to sustain libidinous feelings for one's grandmother, even when she is young enough to be one's daughter. But we *were* close. We had learned the habit of each other's thoughts and our conversation had become a series of silences punctuated by remarks which would make less than complete sense to others.

The river was a tawny red, and at this point about a mile wide. It had the uncanny *flatness* of fresh water and today insistently reminded me of American rivers. I remarked how beautiful it was. Epis nodded absent-mindedly and I could tell that she was thinking about herself. A few delicate fishing birds floated in a porphyry sky. Ann was eating a liverwurst sandwich.

"You know the ocean?" Epis said, at last.

"Yes, pretty well. But I know more about rivers like this." Two little wren-like birds with scarlet heads hopped on the wall beside us.

"Where you live, people wear little tight dresses to bathe themselves in the water, don't they?"

I said that they did.

Epis nodded. "Where you live does the ocean come into the town?" She looked down at Ann. "*Nunú! Usiwe mbaya.*"

"No—but it's near by."

"How would I be if I went to your ocean in a little tight dress? What do everybody think?"

"You would probably cause a riot," I said, sincerely, looking at two faint, tattooed lines on her forehead.

"Ah, I know. You have big fights with African people, don't you?"

I stared out at the flat, sombre river. "That wasn't exactly the kind of riot I meant."

She looked at me curiously for a moment and then slid down from the wall, adjusting her dress around her long legs. She took up her handkerchief-purse and called her child. If Epis didn't immediately understand what one was saying she didn't bother to pry. It was one of her most restful characteristics. "I got to go now. You will pass me tonight? Ann! *Njoo!*"

That afternoon I bought a Congo colonist's magazine called *Pourquoi Pas?* and settled at a table outside the *Chutes Hotel* to read an article called *M. Rosebud Découvre Le Congo*. It was about an American who had risen above the handicap of his name to become one of our nation's crack political reporters, chiefly by making a good thing out of anti-colonialism. He rode to fame on the backs of the poor colonists of Indonesia and Indo-China and cynically took the part of the indigenes. Now he was turning on the Congo.

Rosebud arrives with a bandolier of cameras slung across his sports shirt, and his third wife, who clutches a box holding all the jewels she hasn't been able to pile on her person. He is irritated not to find an army of photographers but (*Hélas!*) he has forgotten to inform them of his arrival. At a dinner that night Mme Rosebud is in very bad humour because she has been served in a perfume store near their hotel (*ô horreur!*) *after* a Negress. Rosebud makes a particularly fuzzy-headed and tasteless speech and asks questions about the Congolese parliament. This is awkward because he apparently is not aware that there isn't any. He also asks what names the Republican and Democratic parties have in the Congo and what is the native's favourite comic strip.

186

Rosebud (his pink complexion comes either from drinking whisky before his meals or milk during them) buys a copy of Gunther's *Inside Africa* and goes off to see the country. He is particularly worried about the strides Communism is making in this land because he sees an ice cream called Sputnik and an omelette mysteriously called Siberian. Flying home, Rosebud notices that his wife is depressed.

"What are you thinking about, dear?"

"About that Negress who was served before I was."

"Bah! Don't give it another thought. We'll take two weeks' vacation at your sister's in Arkansas. You can be sure that nothing like that will happen there!"

No doubt this is a wildly accurate description of some Washington reporter-columnist—except for the part about his wife not getting on all her jewels. But the interest of the piece lies in the anger of the author, so out of proportion to the provocation. Or it would be out of proportion, if the character of Rosebud were not supposed to represent the United States. We are, for the moment, so enveloping that Belgians, as well as many other Europeans, must have the feeling that we are about to colonize *them* (*Hélas!*). Then they, in turn, would become indigenes and would be forced to accept Mr Rosebud's bumptious support.

I had been hoping to meet the owner of the *Café des Sports*, and that evening the opportunity came. I arrived at about closing time to pick up Epis and found all the lights still on and a Belgian policeman speaking to several of the patrons. There was abnormal tension in the room—the atmosphere of a command post before zero hour—which became incomprehensible when I was told the reason for it. A number of boys had been throwing stones at the windows. This, of course, is serious for the one who has to pay for the windows. But in this case nothing had actually been broken and the situation hardly seemed to warrant the grim deportment of the Belgian officer, or even, so trivial was the offence, his presence.

Epis kept as far away from these inquiries as possible and went about her accounts as though no one were there. She spoke only a word or two to me.

The owner of the café then appeared, a fat, infantine man of about thirty-five. His face was charged with the helpless rage of those whose natures are both limited and violent. One could see that, for him, it was intolerable that the boys had *not* succeeded in breaking anything. Now he was left with his anger and no place to spend it; he was suffering the pangs of frustrated hatred, which are worse than those of frustrated love.

At this moment, from the dark street, two African policemen appeared, escorting three handcuffed boys. I had expected that they would be teen-agers, but their combined ages didn't reach that of any adult in the room. The youngest was eight, maybe seven, the oldest no more than twelve. One frequently says that boys of that age should be locked up—and only half in joke—but it is at first ludicrous and then enraging to see it actually done. Handcuffs pushed all the way up to the last notch on unformed wrists are a great deal more degrading to the policeman than the criminal.

The owner of the café stepped forward and hit one of the boys so hard on the side of the head that he would have been knocked down if he hadn't been chained to the others. The child did not cry, and there was nothing frustrated about the hatred in *his* eyes. The assailant's large and well-upholstered mother had come out in the meantime and was looking on with the brutal righteousness of those who normally feel themselves to be inferior—perhaps with reason. The scene was a little too much, and I entered into an argument with the café owner and was soon being closely questioned by the Belgian policeman.

This was a dry and schoolmasterish man, in no way cruel or even unkind. Such people are especially useful in giving maniacal situations the stamp of humdrum sanity. Looking at the world through dun-coloured glasses they cannot tell blood from dish-water. This otherwise normal man was going to put three small children in jail all night, presumably without informing their parents, because they had been accused, without proof, of trying to do something—not, in any case, very serious—that they hadn't succeeded in doing.

In fact he told me, with no sense of mental unbalance, that the children would be perfectly safe in jail and that they would be well-treated. There was a certain North-European hyper-legality about this that was chilling. It seemed to occur to no one that the boys should be soundly whipped and sent to bed.

In the midst of this disturbance, however, I began to be aware that Epis wished desperately that I would shut my mouth and leave. As there was nothing else to do anyway, without landing in jail myself, I stepped away as the boys were triumphantly led off and the café-owner and his mother went back into their house.

Epis delivered the accounts to them, and a few moments later we were walking down the dark street. I asked if she hadn't been angered by what had happened, but she shrugged and said it was none of her business. She was exclusively concerned with her own affairs, and the one time I asked about her political opinions she didn't even bother to answer.

The following days fell into a pattern. I would see Epis to work in the morning and call for her at night. We knew each other quite well, and knew that we might know each other better, but did not make the effort. Again, this was more or less the feeling of people who are compatibly related. Nothing more.

Once, however, when Epis came to meet me in the European

quarter of town I saw her from a distance walking down the street holding her daughter's hand, stopping to stare in windows and moving aimlessly through busy crowds. It was dusk and the two of them seemed especially forlorn and somehow symbolic, like a shot from an old Charlie Chaplin film. But making symbols of people is one way of withholding friendship, no matter how much honour it does them. Epis would surely not have appreciated it. She was too frail for such a burden, though a great many mothers and their children have been even more so. It is no comfort to remember that the strongest people in the world—those who undertake to represent human solidarity to us—are not always the most robust.

Before I left, I saw Chief Sidanou. He was an old magistrate in the *cité Bruxelles*, and was considered the leading political figure of the *centres extra-coutumiers* of Stanleyville, perhaps because he was about the only one. Belgian control of *extra-coutumier* political life was nearly complete. There were chiefs and native Consultative Councils, but these were hand-picked. The Belgians argue that complete democracy would not only be silly but disastrous and that is probably true. But there are many degrees short of complete, and when they accuse the Africans of being impatient they are, as the White Father's paper *Temps Nouveaux* puts it, trying to break down an open door.

Chief Sidanou was personally as well as politically toothless and his breath stank. He seemed a garrulous and mendacious old man, but there were sparks of life in him. When I mentioned the three boys who had been arrested his eyes twinkled, and he told me not to worry unduly about such things. I protested until I saw that he had not meant to be callous. He meant that the administration's legal decisions were strongly tempered in practice. I gathered that the boys had been sent home the night they were arrested, to parental discipline a good deal more severe and less eerie than anything they had expected.

As my boat was to leave on a Wednesday morning and I had many last-minute things to do, I arranged to stay with Epis only through Monday night. We spent that evening with her sister and the burly young hospital-attendant until I grew bored and suggested to Epis that we go for a walk. She seemed disturbed and said, as soon as we were outside:

"I think you will cry when you leave, is that true?"

"You mean will I be sorry to go?"

"Yes."

"I may be sorry but I won't cry. It has been very pleasant, here."

"All right. I will tell you something, Thomas. I like to talk to you, that is true. But I don't mind that you go. If I have to work and can be with my daughter I don't care. If I have the bicycle I can sleep at morning and that is very good for me. But . . ."

"Yes?" The moon had been shrinking the last few days and I could not see her at all, walking beside me.

"It will rain tomorrow," she remarked.

"You were saying?" I stumbled in a rut.

Her voice came from just ahead of me. "When you go down to Leo you will send me a telegram, I ask you that. From down there. Just before you go away you send a telegram to me. When I have it I won't think of you again. You see that? Just a telegram when you go from Leo. That means you are gone. I like to know."

It was the closest thing to sentiment I had ever heard from her and I asked why.

"That's just like that. I don't mind. I just like to know when you leave Leo. Then I don't think of you again, Thomas. You see that?"

"Yes, I see," I said to the black night. "That is very kind."

She didn't answer, and I might have been absolutely alone

until I returned to the house, except that from time to time she guided me. We found the sister's friend preparing to leave, and as the kerosene in the lamp was drying out there was nothing else for us all to do but go to bed.

One undertakes, writing of oneself, to hold to matters which are likely to interest other people. If I therefore say that I awoke that night to find Epis on my pallet, sobbing, it is my duty to point out that she was not doing so because I was leaving—however flattering that would be to me—but because she was being left. It is bad enough to lose a friend, but generally one can bear it. Loneliness is quite another thing, and she might have said with the grief of Colette's René Néré, "*Tout le monde me laisse! . . . Je suis toute seule! . . .*" For all I know, that's what she was saying, in a language I didn't understand. In any case, at such moments one becomes strangely impersonal and does whatever one can to help.

I drew her close, and when my hands touched two lines of erotic tattooing on her back she recoiled as though I were rubbing in an irritant, as her mother had done, a few years ago, to bring the marks out.

"You will like a cup of tea?" she said the next morning. I awoke and saw her standing over me, holding a steaming cup. No breakfast was ever made here and I accepted this as a special going-away present—though Epis acted as distant and as unconcerned as usual.

Though it was raining hard we made a final visit to a bicycle-store. In the last few days we had gone to a number of these but the machine she wanted had to be ordered. It had not yet come and I gave her the money for it now, which she put at the bottom of her handkerchief. Later that day, however, finding that I hadn't enough for my ticket down-river and being too late for the bank, I went to the *Café des Sports* and took most of the money back again. Epis lent it with grace and with only a momentary tremor of doubt.

That night we went to another cabaret, having nothing else to do, and not wishing to be alone. She was looking even more like grandmother Stanley than usual. She seemed to be craning her neck for a posed photograph, glancing out of the corner of her eye at the man with the black cloth over his head. She sat with her long, fine-boned hands folded in her lap, listening calmly to the wild music. I had always wondered what had been going on in my grandmother's mind as she sat there in her stiff chair so many years ago, waiting for the shutter to click. I looked again at Epis. She was thinking of her bicycle.

I saw her home in her friend's taxi and said good-bye at the door, where she shook my hand. "Good night, Thomas. I see you tomorrow, before you go." She turned and went into the house.

I came to the *Café des Sports* the next morning, as soon as I had been to the bank. It was about nine o'clock and my boat left in an hour. Ann greeted me with a moist kiss, and Epis nodded to me curtly, though there was no one else in the café. She asked if I wanted anything to drink and I ordered a stout.

"So you leave me, eh?" she said, without a trace of coquetry. We all deplore sentimentality in our friends, but are disconcerted when they don't show it.

"Yes, I'm afraid so," I said, handing her the money I owed.

"Why you afraid?" She went to the record player and put on a whitened stack of sambas and mambos and cha-cha-chas. Looking up, I saw a little sign over the bar which read, '*Demain on boit pour rien,*' evidently a reply to those who asked for credit. We spoke casually for a while and at last I got up and started to say good-bye.

Epis anticipated me and came around the bar. She held out her hand. "Good-bye, Thomas. I know I must say thank you very much. I like you to remember me. Please, you will tele-gram me from Leo that you go. Good-bye, Thomas." She shook my hand as though I were a delegate to an insurance convention and turned back to her work. I had now learned enough to do the same, but it was difficult. I walked out of the café and went up the street, looking back only once.

CHAPTER SIXTEEN

STANLEY didn't stop at the site of his city on his first trip down. It became a terminal later, when steamers began to ply the Congo. From the foot of Stanley Falls all the way to Stanley Pool, where Leopoldville is now situated, there is an unobstructed stretch of river nearly a thousand miles long. The present trip takes only five days in a steamer, but even the very first stern-wheelers could make it in a little over a week. It took Stanley's party almost a month and a half to travel this route, though they were obstructed only by the men who lived along it.

In this consistent, armed opposition the savages were being merely prescient. If someone had succeeded in picking Stanley off, literally millions of people would have been given an indefinite reprieve from the most appalling deaths imaginable during the next thirty years. Furthermore, if the struggle for power in the Congo had come a few years later, England, France, Germany and Egypt would probably have divided it between themselves. Then the King of the Belgians would never have acquired this vast land as a private park and, for a great many, the reprieve would have become a pardon. Speaking actuarially, therefore, it's a pity someone didn't get Stanley.

He was saved by his luck as well as by his courage and skill. From Nyangwé to the bottom of Stanley Falls he had fought twenty-one times with hostile tribes along the river. From the present site of Stanleyville to the mouth of the Aruwimi River, a distance of about a hundred miles, they endured eight more battles, and once Frank Pocock, game as ever, was almost skewered on a spear-blade.

The party had only forty-three guns left, pitifully inadequate to repel thousands of warriors attacking in mass. They were probably saved as much by the noise of their gunfire as by its effect. They had also collected sixty-five great shields which the women, children and non-combatants held up as bulwarks along their canoes.

But their secret weapon was Stanley himself. He held them firmly together and sometimes would turn his guns on his own men and threaten to fire when they were ready to scatter. He also knew, more than any of them, the logic of despair. When there was nothing else to do but fight he fought with all his heart; it was useless to retreat. Probably none of the others, European or African, had begun life in the black mental misery he had known, unlightened by hope or even fantasy. Over and over again in his later life Henry Stanley collected indemnities on the lacerated spirit of young John Rowland.

The constant fighting wearied and embittered Stanley's men. They often had no more than three hours of peace a day. What was also maddening, the river offered clear sailing and they should have been able, riding with the current, to make hundreds of miles a week. On 1 February 1877, at the confluence of the Aruwimi, they were attacked once more by a great fleet of war-canoes. There were fifty-four of these monstrous boats and each one carried eighty oarsmen and had a bow-platform crowded with warriors.

Stanley managed to drive them off, mostly because of superior discipline. Then he turned around and attacked their village which contained a temple made of ivory and an idol painted with bright vermilion camwood. They sacked the town, taking away wedges for splitting logs, war-horns, pestles for pounding food, armlets, and mallets to beat fig-bark into cloth, all fashioned of ivory.

Stanley returned to this district ten years later, in 1887, on his way to rescue Emin Pasha. He went up the Aruwimi and established a base camp about sixty miles north of what was already known as Stanley Falls Station, and would one day be Stanleyville. On *this* expedition he forswore both debauched seamen and clean-living youngsters and took along a group of army officers and gentlemen. He went from his base camp, up the Aruwimi and across to Lake Albert on the border of present-day Uganda, leaving behind half his force to follow at a slower pace. This rear column was placed under the command of Major Edmund Musgrave Barttelot, of the Seventh Fusiliers. As assistants, the major had William Bonny, an army surgeon, and Mr James S. Jameson, who had travelled in Mashonaland and Matabeleland studying birds.

Tippu Tib had promised them extra porters for their vast supplies, though Stanley was sceptical and advised Barttelot to come ahead in relays if the porters didn't show up in a reasonable time. This, of course, required further palavers down at the Falls with the old slave trader, whom Stanley had made governor of the district before he left.

The Arabs were well established on this part of the river now and had brought along, as usual, all the amenities of home. The trouble was that some of these amenities were exceedingly rare in the major's home; the traditional role of the English-woman being less temptress than goad. Barttelot felt duty-bound, therefore, to make every effort to get the porters Tippu Tib had promised, even though it meant months of delay and a great many trips to the Falls Station.

The months stretched to a year and the conscientious major never did get started. He was shot, at last, by a native, for no very good reason, though the argument appeared to have something to do with the native's wife. No doubt Tippu Tib was actively responsible for this delay, both by withholding porters and putting the venereal facilities of his Station at Barttelot's disposal. He was flatly opposed to any further European penetration of his district.

Of course the major was an old campaigner and he shouldn't have been held up for a *year*, so it is likely that his dalliance merely contributed to a fatal relaxation of discipline—as any Englishwoman could have told him. In a year the base camp lost about three-quarters of its supplies and half its men, without ever moving from the spot. It was probably here, or somewhere near Stanley Falls, that Kurtz, in Conrad's *Heart of Darkness*, lived. He enjoyed the pleasures of being a God, not a rake, but the end was so similar for both men they might have been trying for the same prize.

Tippu Tib had probably tried this ruse on Stanley, with disappointing results. The Arabs at Tabora had done the job better with food. How was Tippu to know, after all, that the only woman in Stanley's life was to be a respectable English girl named Dorothy? With her he would spend his declining years at Furze Hill, his estate at Pirbright, thirty miles from London. There he would pretend that his fields, a wood, a quiet lake fed by a little stream, were places he knew in Africa. He called the lake Stanley Pool and the wood the Aruwimi Forest; the stream, of course, was the Congo. No African Arab, however wily, would offer, or would ever think to offer, this.

As a result of Barttelot's splendidly military defeat, Stanley had to come all the way back from Lake Albert through hundreds of miles of dense jungle where food was almost impossible to find, to rescue what was left of his own rear column. It took him three months to reach his base camp, after meeting, and then leaving, Emin Pasha. He found the camp in the charge of William Bonny, who seemed less fond than the others of soldierly excursions to the Falls. Jameson, the bird-watcher, was there at the moment.

In this final expedition Stanley was once again searching for *someone*, and as he describes that search some of the old excitement of the Livingstone expedition comes back to him. To celebrate his success with the Pasha he carried five bottles of champagne wrapped in old stockings.

In spite of his Arabian Nights name Emin Pasha was a handsome, studious German Jew from Silesia born Eduard Schnitzer. On graduating from medical school at the age of twenty-four, he went to Albania and had a love-affair with the Turkish Governor's wife. This, for some reason, endeared him to the Governor who gave him a series of important posts in the Near East. Following these, he was stationed in Trieste, then Cairo and Khartoum. He wandered about Africa for a number of years, becoming a legendary figure, elegantly bearded, wearing a fez and the gold-rimmed lozenge-glasses of a scholar. He was at last appointed Governor of Equatoria in the Sudan by General Charles Gordon.

When Gordon was killed in Khartoum by the Mahdi's dervishes in 1885, Equatoria was cut off from the civilized world, and a cry went up, especially in Britain, to save the solitary and mysterious man who controlled the last vestiges of European power in the Sudan. Stanley was chosen as his deliverer and once again set out to rescue a man who didn't really want to be rescued.

At the end, after going back across the Aruwimi Forest in the winter of 1888 with the remnants of his rear-column, Stanley dragged Emin Pasha and six hundred of his followers to safety practically at gun-point. The two men were not each other's cups of tea or even champagne.

To placate the Pasha on the overland trip south, past Lake Victoria, into Tanganyika and so to Zanzibar, Stanley appointed him naturalist and meteorologist of the Expedition. This was an astute move. Emin was passionately scientific and set about stuffing birds and collecting insects, preferring their company to Stanley's. The latter had outgrown his father-finding proclivities and simply loathed his guest.

He delivered Emin and his little half-Abyssinian daughter Ferida to the German authorities at Bagamoyo, opposite Zanzibar, and then looked on in disgust as a banquet was organized, champagne toasts were drunk, the Pasha got blind and fell off a roof, and the object of three years' backbreaking work and physical horrors nearly died of a fractured skull.

These events were all seminal, as was practically every incident involving Europeans in Africa during the last quarter of the nineteenth century. Emin Pasha's dislike of Stanley caused him to go to work for the Germans instead of the British in the scramble for East Africa. Two years later, when Lord Lugard was trying to sign a treaty with the Kabaka of Uganda, he found himself hard-pressed by Emin and other representatives of the expanding German Empire—as well as by the French.

It is a testament to the superb eccentricity of a good English education [1] that Lugard was unwilling to open one of the Pasha's private letters which may have had a crucial bearing on his work, but he did not hesitate to open fire on the French Catholic party of Uganda when they opposed his assumption of power. Of course, they were about to fire on him, and the Wa-Ingleza and the Wa-Fransa, as they were called by the

[1] At this very moment, Sir Alfred Moloney, Governor of Lagos on the Guinea coast—called the white man's grave—was demonstrating his own regard for the important things of life by publishing an article entitled 'Butterflies and Moths of Yoruba.'

natives of that country, had been doing this sort of thing regularly since the battle of Hastings.

The affair caused a fuss in France, though, because Lugard's decisive weapon was a Maxim automatic and it seemed to the logical French mind too much of a coincidence that it should just *be* there without the connivance of the British Government. Nor did they care for the explanation that Stanley had dragged this gun into the centre of the continent on his way to rescue Emin Pasha. Clearly Anglo-Saxon hypocrisy was involved, even if Stanley *was* an American, which no one believed for a minute.

But these events came at the end of Stanley's career in Africa. In 1877, when he was going down the Congo for the first time, he was thirty-six years old and at the height of his powers. This was fortunate for him; probably no one else in the world, and not even he a few years later, could have managed it.

Aside from the physical hardship involved, his position itself was enormously dispiriting. He was nearly certain, for instance, that he was on the Congo. This meant that he could calculate with fair accuracy the minimum distance he would have to travel to that river's known mouth. On February 3 their latitude north of the Equator was 1° 29' and their longitude was about 23° east, so that even if the river went straight southwest towards its mouth they could not have less than a thousand miles to go. But they were headed *north*west.

Also, they were approximately one thousand five hundred feet above sea level; that meant one thousand five hundred feet of falls, somewhere. He could only hope that these would come all at once, so that he could get them over with. It was like being given a choice between fifteen or twenty ordinary accidents and one big-smash up. He had little hope of coming out alive in any case.

In the meantime, they were harried by warlike, hungry savages. He wrote:

Livingstone called floating down the Lualaba a foolhardy feat. So it has proved, indeed, and I pen these lines with half a feeling that they will never be read by any man; still, as we persist in floating down according to our destiny, I persist in writing, leaving events to an all-gracious Providence. Day and night we are stunned with the dreadful drumming which announces our arrival and presence on their waters. Either bank is equally powerful. To go from the right bank to the left bank is like jumping from the frying-pan into the fire. As we row down amongst these islands, between the savage countries on either side of us, it may well be said that we are 'running the gauntlet.'

At last, on 8 February 1877, Stanley's party was driven by want of food to force their friendship on one of the tribes, at the risk of becoming a source of food themselves. They offered so many shiny gifts and conducted themselves so peacefully that they were allowed to contract blood-brotherhood with the chief, who then sold them supplies. They asked the name of the river. "*Ikutu ya Kongo!*" the chief said. Stanley now knew past all doubt where he was going—if he could make it.

At this place, also, the party discovered that there were four ancient Portuguese muskets. For hundreds of years these guns had been coming up-river by means of trade and war. The men were delighted to see them because it proved that the river led to civilization. They forgot that this was a mixed blessing; from here on more and more of the natives were armed, obeying the rule that says that men become deadlier as they grow less savage. As yet, none of their enemy had got past the fifteenth century and their weapons discharged slugs of metal which would not penetrate their shield-bulwarks except at close range.

On February 18 they were on the Equator again, just below the present city of Coquilhatville. They were headed due southwest at last, having travelled in a great loop through eight degrees of equatorial longitude and six of latitude, or roughly the distance from Budapest to London via Copenhagen. They hadn't eaten since the 10th and were starving. Just below the Equator, at the confluence of the Ubangi River, they bought food from two drunken chiefs. From here they drifted down in comparative peace. The Expedition stopped nine days in a friendly village to recuperate, then continued, arriving at a great lake in the river on March 12, which Frank dutifully suggested be named Stanley Pool.

In these days motor-ferries scoot across this plain of water from Leopoldville to Brazzaville and back, joining Belgian and French Africa. It is a natural site for cities, lying at the lower end of the long, clear stretch of the river, above two hundred miles of intermittent rapids between it and the sea. Both ends of the navigable Congo, therefore, celebrate Stanley. Nearly three months later and only one hundred miles farther down-river, Frank Pocock was to have a pool of his own, and a suitable woodcut in Stanley's book reading,

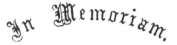

In Memoriam.

CHAPTER SEVENTEEN

A<small>T</small> the Stanleyville dock there were many African women waving good-bye to their friends with festive handkerchiefs. I stood at the rail of the boat for a while and then went to my cabin, very much resenting the knowledge that I would not see Epis again.

Towards evening familiar night odours began to rise off the river, and the green forests on the shore filled with shadow. We were now travelling almost due west and the sun went down in the water, leaving a bright orange stain which faded off near the boat in metallic blues. There were twists of silver clouds in the sky, like the tortured paths of worms in old wood, and violet banks of rain piled up on the horizon. Then there seemed to be a radio chattering deep in the jungle and some boys called to each other across the water.

At this point the language of the Congo changes from Swahili to Lingala, roughly dividing the eastern half of Central Africa from the west. Both are Bantu, but the former is strongly modified by Arabic and its name is derived from a word meaning coasts, as it originated near Zanzibar and Mombasa on the east coast. It has now spread over a great part of Central Africa and is one of the twelve major languages of the world.

Lately Swahili has shown signs of disintegration because it is so badly spoken by Europeans; their numbers are insignificant but they are economically powerful enough, still, to enforce their own standards, good and bad. The same thing would probably happen to modern English or French if the situation were reversed.

This five-day journey down the Congo was a measure of

the enormous changes which have taken place here since Stanley's time. It was as monotonous as an ocean voyage and produced a lethargy which passed for rest. The interminable forest slipped by, trees occasionally marked with river-traffic signals. Safe channels in the river were indicated by buoys, and now and then we passed an industrial town where self-confident young *évolués* in beach shoes shifted our cargo with the aid of giant cranes called *les Titans Anversois*. Sometimes the smaller boats were lifted wholly out of the water by these cranes so as to move their goods faster. Little tugs, operated by rakishly nautical crews of Africans, roared back and forth across the river. Here, also, one began to see dug-outs powered by outboard motors.

In the small towns along the river there seemed to be less racial tension than in the cities, maybe because of the many Portuguese living in them. These people are more at home in Africa than any other Europeans. They are industrious, prosperous traders and they carry racial tolerance to its logical conclusion which is, as racists never tire repeating as though it were an argument against it, miscegenation.

In Bumba, for instance, a couple of hundred miles down from Stanleyville, one may see white women with coloured children; this is not unheard-of elsewhere, but the surprising thing about it here is that the women are so conventional— the sort who go to bed in cotton nightgowns and consider talk about sex and psychiatry to be in bad taste. I saw one woman, who looked as though she made wonderful pies, dividing chocolate between her two sons. The boys had evidently had different fathers, one white and one black, but they displayed no more than the usual amount of sibling rivalry.

Often the river broadened into a lake, patched with islands, black as rubbed ebony, reflecting trees. And when the sun set, the forest seemed curtained with green velvet, like a

205

tremendous theatre. There were occasional, lonely villages on the island shores with fishing pirogues drawn up, and women lounging in doorways. It was like Louisiana bayou country, heavy with vegetation and silent with life.

Though the forest was usually a solid mass near the water's edge, there were clearings behind, in which one could occasionally see patches of orange flowers. The sky, except at sunrise and sunset, was pearl grey and looked like the underside of a huge bird's wing. Our boat pushed stolidly through the water, hour after hour, and the river gathered in wrinkles behind us like the skin of hot milk.

From time to time, towards evening, we were besieged by butterflies, especially where the river was very broad and unobstructed by islands. They were trapped by the night winds and blown too far out over the water to make land. For some of them the boat was a haven and they would drop exhausted to the deck, flexing their tattered beige-and-black wings. But for every one that found temporary safety, hundreds more fell into the water. This was particularly agonizing when they flew to us with all their strength and fell short, a few inches from the deck's edge. They dropped behind, struggling to rise, as the engine pounded on to the rhythm of a cha-cha-cha.

I remembered one day in Stanleyville, waiting for Epis before a hotel. It was very hot and as she wasn't due to come for another ten or fifteen minutes I ducked inside. The place had a cabaret for Europeans, and as it was then about 11 a.m. the bar was deserted and the little stage looked like an unmade bed.

To the rear a man was playing Mozart on a grand piano, and just before the open door of the veranda another man rehearsed passages on a guitar. They were Europeans and had the unmistakable air of professional entertainers. A well-built woman in black slacks, plump with approaching middle-age, finished a tomato-juice cocktail at the bar and strolled over to them, if one can be said to stroll in bedroom slippers. Clearly she was used to high, silver heels.

The three of them gathered round the piano and discussed an arrangement. They had the child-like sweetness of people who stay up all night and sleep all morning. They also looked a little strained, probably from too much dieting, not all of it voluntary.

There are hundreds of these people, perhaps thousands, in Southern Asia, the Middle East and in Africa. They have no particular nationality and no hope for one. They are dancers, musicians, acrobats, clowns and torch-singers. They worry about their costumes, their weight, their bookings and notices, and—above all—their health. They hold hands at motion pictures in the early afternoons and give each other surprises of fruit and sometimes candy. They seldom drink or even smoke and they live together, two, three, and four in a hotel room, often sleeping in the same bed to save money and lying with arms curled round each other, chaste as babies. They are very like butterflies and most of them fall into the water.

Our boat was called the *Baron Liebrechts*, a name which seemed familiar. Unlike the middle-class boarding-house that churned down the Lualaba, this diesel monster recalled a second-rate hotel. Not third, second. It was thoroughly Belgian and operated with great efficiency. It had only first-class cabins and *luxe* first-class cabins, which meant that the first was really second. It also had a great barge lashed to its flat bow which contained other, lower classes, for Africans. This was owned by an African concessionaire who paid the shipping company a fee for the privilege of tying on.

That didn't mean that Africans were barred from the

Baron Liebrechts. A Portuguese man with two extremely dark children was travelling *luxe.* The classic Anglo-Saxon approach to the matter, which we define as separate-but-equal, is replaced in other parts of Europe by a simpler philosophy of economic-togetherness. It is as brutally superior to our method as their metric system to foot-yard measurement, replacing illogical with logical discrimination.

However, most of the passengers were Belgian. Many of these, especially the younger ones, resembled Americans and wore brush-cut blonde hair and tropical shirts. I think the similarity was mostly external; older men tended to be more formal and to look as though they were working in banks or shipping offices, even when they were eating. The women were softer and more permissive than Americans, and dressed in quiet bad taste. This made some of them attractive, but others merely looked as though they had been drinking *béchamel.*

At table people followed the north European practice of buttering a whole slice of bread and cutting it in half to make a little sandwich. These were always micrometrically neat, and were consumed in great quantities. Two priests opposite me went through ten slices of bread in a few seconds, using them as soppers. They were both good men and looked like old Flemish portraits, but one felt that the most difficult thing about joining their order would not be taking a vow of celibacy but enduring three times a day the official licentiousness of the refectory.

One of these men had a great, broad face, a cast in one eye and a white goatee. He was going home to Holland after twenty-six years in the Congo because his spine had begun to decalcify. He said that when he reached the coast he would take a very slow boat back. He felt that he was going to his death. But it was not only at table he was valiant. He smoked smelly cigars, gleefully read an obscene book, and went every morning—before breakfast—to the African barge to hold mass.

His companion was an older man, not, I believe, a simple priest, and was travelling *luxe*. The Dutchman teased him about this and promised to stop only if the other bought him a bottle of wine. He hadn't any right to do this, as the old fellow was the head of a group of schools with a total registration of over fourteen thousand and his position and years of service gave him the right to such a simple luxury. He was much disturbed, however, and spent several sleepless nights on his extra-comfortable bed before he paid up.

On board I got to know a Belgian psychiatrist and his wife. Dr Vyncke was on his way to a psychiatric congress in Brazzaville. He was a fat man, getting fatter, and wore an uneven, tooth-brush moustache that begged to be straightened, like a picture on a wall. He had charge of a mental hospital, or department of a hospital, in Usumbura. The doctor was thoroughly devoted to his work and consequently neglected his wife. She was inclined to be a nervous woman, anyway, and was easily driven to drink.

All of us, except for the very good and very evil, seem ridiculous when viewed dispassionately, so I must add that Dr and Mme Vyncke are my firm friends. If he neglects her she isn't unable to see the reason for it or above reminding him of it sharply from time to time. She sometimes suffers, but a great many tortured men and women benefit from that; and if enough people in the world are well-shod it is often worth being a shoemaker's child—or even his wife.

Mme Vyncke sometimes sat with me while the doctor pored over his *Psychoses et névroses en Afrique centrale*, which he was going to present to the congress. She herself came from South Africa and spoke English, though after many years here some of it was beginning to go. As she explained, it had been tinged with French from the beginning, as that was her mother's nationality.

"I met my husband in a psychiatric hospital," she said one afternoon, running her finger round the rim of her glass. "That's where I worked too, during the war. Now we are here ever since, in the Congo. He likes work very much here. Can you see? I mean he studies, studies, studies and I never get to see him any more, and now in a few years even my children will grow up. Then they will go away." Mme Vyncke took up a fresh cigarette with slightly trembling fingers and glanced across the bar, near which her husband was sitting silently, at a table full of papers. He looked wonderfully like a psychiatrist.

"I sent them . . . my children . . . to the inter-racial school at Usumbura, but I had to take them out. You see, when they have a vacation time, the black children go to very poor homes where they all sleep in one room and there they learn too much about some things. Then they come back and tell *my* children and there are just some things I don't want them to know yet." She sighed and called for another jigger-bottle of Johnnie Walker.

"And now I'll tell you. I was ashamed to keep them in that school because, you see, they were always behind. Oh, they are not stupid boys, believe me, but those black ones are *picked*." Mme Vyncke glanced at me with watery defiance. "I mean, only the smartest ones go there—out of maybe five million. What chance have my boys got? They were always last. The others said they held everyone back. Maybe they *could* have studied harder, maybe it was good for them—that's what my husband says—but I took them out anyway."

She leaned towards me and lowered her voice. "Once my child said to his friend, '*J'ai soif*,' you know, 'I'm thirsty,' and the other boy said, 'Why don't you go home and suck your mother's . . .' You see what I mean? God knows what else he's told him. Not that my boy didn't know *that*, but you just don't talk that way, do you?" She sat back and emptied her glass. "The trouble with that school is that you learn *too* much. Have you finished your beer? Have another one with me, and then I can have some more. God, it's hard to be a good mother in Africa."

A few rounds later Dr Vyncke packed up his papers and joined us. He had the disconcerting frankness of a man who has spent too many hours in the consulting-room ever to treat personal matters personally again. "She has been telling you her troubles?" he said, settling into a chair. "She says I work too much and neglect her, I know. I tell her I can't help doing my work the best way I know how. There's just too much of it. She ought to have something to do, I say, but she can't be a nurse any more because of the children. She tried painting once and gave that up and she won't do social work for some reason."

"No I won't," Mme Vyncke said, stubbornly, twisting her glass on the table.

The doctor sent her down to their state-room to get some books. He wasn't being peremptory, merely kind. She really liked to do things and was feeling lost, away from her home. "She says she wants to go back to South Africa but I don't think she'd be able to get along there any more. Things have changed. Will you have another bottle of beer?"

I had been keeping up with Mme Vyncke and had to refuse. "You must not misunderstand," he said, signalling to the waiter. "It isn't always as bad down there as people say it is. I am Flemish but I'm not talking like an Afrikaaner now, believe me. After all, Africans *still* slip into that country clandestinely, for the higher wages. No place is ever all good or all bad."

The doctor gave his order. "You should see this from the African point of view as well as the European. Do you think that they notice as much difference between South Africa and —the Congo, for instance, as *we* do? Some of them, of course. The *évolués* are more or less accepted here, though perhaps they pay for that in other ways—mental stability, for one thing. You see, when it comes to racial discrimination there is only one European country in Africa that doesn't practise it. That is Portugal. *All* the rest of us do, even when we say we don't, and all of us are heading for trouble."

His beer came and he drank off half his glass at once, after which he wiped his forehead with a handkerchief. "Speaking as a doctor, I can tell you there is only *one* solution to this problem—miscegenation. It's the simplest, safest, most reliable way to reconcile men to each other that was ever invented— it was the first and it will be the last. When people of different races intermarry they do away with mass neuroses and settle down to individual ones." He smiled triumphantly, his spectacles gleaming purple in the late afternoon light.

"And I can tell you that the individual psychoses here are just exactly what you will find in Europe—and in America, of course," he added hastily, as though afraid of offending me. "So that husbands and wives in mixed marriages will have exactly the same battles they have everywhere else."

Dr Vyncke beamed, managing to look like a mad scientist crossed with Oliver Hardy. He finished off his beer. "I must lend you my book. I'm going to present it to the congress. It may cause quite a flurry. People used to say that Africans didn't ever have true schizophrenia. Imagine! I've got some really *classic* cases. And manic depressives too, of course," he added, proudly.

Mme Vyncke came back and sat quietly at the other side of the table. The doctor glanced at her professionally, then

212

ordered a drink for everyone. He began to speak of a trip he and his wife had taken to the United States, for another congress. Several times he referred to coloured Americans as 'natives.' When I corrected him he explained that he hadn't wanted to use the word 'Negro,' because, in Africa, it is not considered polite. Both he and Mme Vyncke appeared to have been terrified by America and still half-believed it to be a savage country. Many times, while they were there, they had longed for the safety and civilization of Usumbura.

To begin with, they had had a cold reception in New York when they arrived with a Belgian professor friend at the St Regis Hotel wearing rucksacks. Fortunately they had reservations and got safely to their rooms. Then they put on street clothes and went to what had been described to them as a real French restaurant in the west Fifties. Having completed that ordeal they came out into the street and the men of the party were accosted by a lady of the evening. Dr Vyncke's objection here was that they were approached in mixed company. He had been in Africa since the early 30's and was used to more conservative behaviour.

In New York, also, which they had really expected to be quite civilized, they saw a man being choked in the street— a native, as it happened. " 'I'm getting cold, I'm getting cold,' the man said. At least I *think* he said that," the doctor added. "I wanted to help but the friend we were with—an American— told us to come away. I didn't know. I thought perhaps that happened all the time and we were in danger, you see. Otherwise . . ."

The Vynckes then went out in the bush, to Detroit. There two men asked the doctor for a hand-out and when he didn't give it to them they threatened to beat him up. "I ran. Just ran up the street, you know. It wasn't really very dignified. I saw a policeman and went to him, but he did nothing." He paused.

213

"The men just walked away. I expect they were desperate for money," he added, charitably.

But the couple's nerve was beginning to give, and in a middle-western state they had been told was dry (after learning with wonder that there were states that were wet) they went into a café and found the patrons blind-drunk, half of them lying on the floor in their own filth. That did it, and as soon as the congress was over they ran back to the Congo. Speaking of the drunks in the dry café, Dr Vyncke said, trying to draw a medical moral, "Probably they were people without social roots, like our *évolués*. They seemed to lack emotional stability."

That evening I took a copy of *Psychoses et névroses en Afrique centrale* to bed with me. Most psychiatric case-histories have a family likeness. Obs. No. 43-B Bernadette—age thirty years, might just as well have been made in Poland or France as in Ruanda-Urundi. Bernadette had been abandoned by her husband at the time of a new infant's death, leaving her destitute with five other children. Her mother and father had also died, some time before. "All of them killed by God," the girl said, lapsing into prayer. "God pardon me, what have I done? Now God is silent—he is going to judge me. God took my child and he had committed no sin. When I am dead I can rest a little. He will take my heart and close my nostrils." No doubt that is a case of melancholia, but it is anybody's.

The more serious histories, the schizophrenic and paranoic psychoses, are so often beyond our ken that they at first seem less touching than odd. A boy named Dahana killed his mother because she reproached him for being lazy. When he was arrested the authorities asked:

"Have you any brothers?"

"I had, but they all disappeared when they were young.

214

We slept together, and the next morning I found the bed empty."

"What was that tree you were speaking about?"

"That was my mother, my real mother, who begot me with my father and he is my size and my age."

"Who brought you before the judge?"

"Those who want to eat. But I no longer know any of them."

" 'Those who want to eat.' What does that mean?"

"Evidently the husband of the woman who is my father."

It is probable that he is deadly serious and that the world he lives in has even more agonies than ours.

But the most interesting cases are just a *little* sick, like the rest of us. They are sometimes so familiar that we would swear they weren't sick at all. For instance, a man of forty-five named Biti said, "I never throw off my clothes and I never insult anyone, my intelligence is normal. My neighbours treat me as though I'm mad but the doctor will show them it is not so. The only sickness, which I have during the month of Ramadan, is that I sometimes see my mother's ghost, who wishes to kill me . . ." (at the sight of her he would run through the forest shouting senseless words) ". . . but now I am completely normal."

There was also a poor man who was treated for a minor ailment by his native doctor. Shortly after, he began to feel intense pains in his back and chest and at last jumped out of his bed and, for three days without stopping, ran screaming through the forest. Then he returned home and went to bed but couldn't sleep. So he called for medical help again and the doctor prepared the same medicine he'd given him the last time. The sick man had a sudden stroke of common-sense and jumped out of bed, and tried to kill the healer. Then he went back to sleep and woke up feeling fine.

215

These men stood well within the border of sanity, as did the man whose second wife said she would put something in his food to make him impotent—and did. (Cure: narco-suggestion —You are *not* impotent.) Also uninhibitedly sane was the woman who ran a cabaret in a *centre extra-coutumier*. She had cashed a counterfeit thousand-franc note for a customer and when he was finally arrested her right hand, with which she had counted out the change, began to dance for joy. (Diagnosis: conversion-hysteria.)

And one final case, perhaps more typically African than the others, is really only an example of robust refusal to adjust to dementia. A mentally ill man committed a crime and was put in jail. He escaped, was captured again, and escaped again. In a short while he had broken out of every major prison in the Congo, in spite of handcuffs and strait-jackets and solitary cells. He was at last shipped to Dr Vyncke's clinic as hopeless. There he was given an unlocked room and stayed docilely until he could be cured.

Europeans and inhabitants of the *centres extra-coutumiers* appear to be most frequently afflicted by mental diseases, and both for the same reason—because they have been uprooted. Dr Vyncke is severely impartial in his clinic and keeps black, white, cases of worms and malaria, cases of anxiety-reaction and depression, all together in the main waiting-room. Looking around, you never know if your neighbour has liver trouble or if he is just crazy.

At Coquilhatville I got off to mail a letter. It is a large town, though smaller than Stanleyville. It used to be called Equator Station and, as the name suggests, is terribly hot. I wandered around for a while, liking the place very much for a certain dreary, incomplete urbanity—a quality it shares with Stanleyville. Unable to find the post office, and seeing no European, I

216

walked up to a wonderfully barbaric man with bright orange polish on his toenails and the lithe stance of a warrior or a basketball player and said, "*Où est la poste, s'il vous plaît?*"

He smiled. "*Je ne sais pas, m'sieu. Je suis étranger ici.*"

He suggested that it might be down a certain road which seemed to be the main one, and there I found it. When I came back to the boat I found the Dutch priest on deck speaking to the psychiatrist in Flemish.

Vyncke turned to me at last. "We were talking about the old days. I was telling him that I once had the complete records of a station here on the Congo, before 1909, you know. But there were orders from the government to burn them, so I did. I'm sorry now; I suppose they would be very valuable."

The doctor didn't mean that he could get money for them, though perhaps he could. He meant simply that there are few sources of information covering the period of the Congo Free State any more. Their scarcity is deliberate, though some reports have slipped through the net.

I turned and looked at the bridge of our boat as the warning whistle blew, remembering, at last, who Baron Liebrechts was. As we edged out into the current the water churned up behind us, red as crude-oil. A man on the wharf was selling spearheads stamped directly out of sheet-steel in curious flat, baroque designs. The baron was one of the King of Belgium's three principal Congo secretaries at the turn of the century. The name Liebrechts, therefore, is ignominiously tied to that of one of the greatest monsters to have lived.

CHAPTER EIGHTEEN

ELDERLY people in Europe still remember the days when Leopold II was called the King of Maxim's, and when the Mediterranean coast of France, particularly at Cap Ferrat, was largely supported by his munificence. Most of us now do not like to think too ill of such a person, as many didn't in those days. He was an old reprobate—a skirt-chaser; a clever financier; a cynical, sophisticated, handsome, vigorous man with a great, big, beautiful beard and a healthy, sensual appetite. We live too greyly these days to do without at least the memory of such a frank hedonist.

Also, we are tempted to feel that a man who has so many obvious vices is fundamentally at peace with the world and therefore needs to be no worse than he seems. He liked women and he was tremendously rich; it seems to us grandly nineteenth-century that he should combine the one with the other. So his memory is protected, along with the era in which he lived, in a swathing of sentiment born of our small frustrations. That's as it should be, surely, if that were all. But on the day people begin to refer to Hermann Goering as an incorrigible old rascal, someone—in the name of all the decent scoundrels and reprobates in the world—should bring up the facts.

In September 1876, three and a half months before Stanley and Tippu Tib parted on the Lualaba, Leopold II called together representatives of various nations for a conference on Africa deceptively named *Conférence Géographique de Bruxelles*. From this was created the 'African International Association' which was vaguely committed to establish bases in that continent to help explorers on their lonely way, and to fight slavery.

At this distance Leopold II looks extremely embarrassed as an abolitionist. In his lifetime he induced—by the most brutal methods imaginable—about twenty million people to work for him almost without wages, and when he died in 1909, from five to eight millions of them had preceded him unnaturally.

In comparison, it is refreshing to hear a man like Lord Lugard say in 1895—and this is from the lion's mouth—"It is essential to bear in mind that this annexation of Africa by the white races was no outcome of missionary or philanthropic zeal. It was the natural outflow of the nations of Europe into the waste places of the earth, following the law which has guided and, indeed, formed the history of the earth . . . Settlers driven to seek their fortunes in new Colonies . . . do not embark for Africa with the primary object of benefiting the natives, but of benefiting themselves . . ."

If the air at the Brussels Conference had been cleared by a statement like that no doubt a great many lives would have been saved. As it was, Leopold was able to control the Association by playing off the rivalries of each participating nation, while hiding his own ambitions under the guise of sweet philanthropy.

When Stanley returned, triumphant, in January 1878 he was met at Marseilles by a representative of the Belgian king, and in June of that year he agreed to return to the Congo as agent for the *Comité d'Etudes du Haut-Congo*, another euphemistic organization, designed to attract venture capital for Leopold's schemes. Stanley headed an expedition from the west coast of Africa this time. He established Leopoldville at Stanley Pool and made treaties with all the natives he could find farther up the river.

The *Comité d'Etudes du Haut-Congo* dissolved in turn and

became the 'Congo International Association.' This was getting closer. All Leopold had to do now was to persuade people to drop the words 'International' and 'Association.' He could not, of course, have aspired to anything like that if the great powers around him hadn't agreed that he should.

They did so precisely because he was politically weak and could be expected to hold the territory neutral while they fought it out among themselves. At a conference in Berlin in 1885 the International Association was confirmed sovereign of the Congo basin and Leopold, who owned the Association, was made King of the Congo Free State—a name which had not yet acquired a grisly irony. He was the first ruler of that land since the seventeenth century, when the four-hundred-year-old Bakongo Empire dissolved. The delegates to the Conference were near tears as they contemplated the 'humane and civilizing work of His Majesty the King of the Belgians.' One by one they delivered panegyrics and encomiums on this awful sovereign.

Leopold had control of the Congo at last but he couldn't begin to consolidate his realm until it was cleared of Arabs. He was very much beholden to the European powers in the beginning and needed their approval. Therefore he took up the cause of anti-slavery, an acceptable tactic, even a laudable one —if one discounts the Arab point of view, and a rudimentary respect for honesty. On the strength of his crusade, and of his promise to will them the Congo after his death, the Belgian Government gave him a twenty-five million franc, interest-free loan; it was followed by another six and a quarter million francs a few years later.

The anti-slavery societies of Britain and France (the latter guided by Cardinal Lavigerie, founder of the White Fathers) had become the spearheads of Colonialism in their two countries, for the most part unintentionally. The governments simply found them convenient for whipping up sentiment, and Leopold's use of them was similar, but with a new twist. If the anti-slavery, anti-alcohol groups could be enlisted on his side he knew they would fight off their *own* governments for him and confirm him in a position which was still very shaky.

He was successful at this. But he was one man, not a nation and could not practise the saving deceit that comes naturally to large political bodies. In Britain and France foreign policy might make use of anti-slavery sentiment, but this sentiment remained as a constant check to any individual's ambition. As Leopold's critics later pointed out, when responsible public opinion can be marshalled for or against a policy, that policy has to be temperate. The king was his own law.

In 1886 the Stanley Falls Station, now Stanleyville, on the upper Congo was attacked by Tippu Tib's men. His power had increased enormously in recent years and he was acknowledged as chief of all the Arabs and their forces in Africa. *He* saw the purpose of all these conferences and committees and associations, if no one in Europe did, and this attack was his answer.

But things had not yet come to open warfare, and when Stanley returned to the Congo once again in 1887 to rescue Emin Pasha, and incidentally to strengthen the claims of the Free State to land in the northeast, he was forced to make Tippu Tib governor of Stanley Falls, under the King of Belgium. This was a dangerously strategic position and Tippu was subsequently replaced by a Belgian officer and a small armed force, but by that time he had built up a great deal of support in the district and continued to do so until the war.

In 1890 and 1891 the lines of battle were drawn. European steamers could now go up the Congo from Leopoldville in the southwest, to Stanleyville in the northeast. They could also go southward down the River Kwa. Therefore the fighting would surely take place in the Maniema country. The Arabs' objectives were first to destroy the State forces and then the Stanley Falls Station. From there they could come down the river to wipe out the European garrison at Leopoldville and take over the State themselves.

One speaks of Europeans and Arabs in this war, but both sides fought almost exclusively with African auxiliaries. As most of these were at least part-time cannibals a great many battles were literally fought for food. The slain would be dragged off and eaten. It was even worse to be captured. The men of the Bangala tribe, for instance, had a tradition that game was tenderer if it was allowed to suffer. This applied to all fauna, including men. Three days before a war-prisoner or a slave was to be eaten, his arms and legs were broken and he was placed in a stream chin-deep, with his head tied to a stick to prevent him from committing suicide or simply drowning.

The Europeans tried to control this in their camps, as probably the Arabs did also. But they couldn't stop their troops from eating those slain in battle, and often they didn't want to. There was not much else to eat, and this kind of scavenging prevented epidemics.

The reason cannibalism was so widespread in the Congo was hunger. Except in its symbolic, religious aspects it was simply another one of the masks of poverty, as was savagery itself. Such poverty may be borne by men in fairly well-organized societies, where the rich are always ready to help them bear it, but when people live in an untamed land, battered by wars, weather and disease, and when they are further demoralized by the institution of slavery, then slavery itself becomes an enormous temptation for them to turn on their own natures, and to destroy their sense of identity with fellow-beings. This is a sense man shares with most lower animals and it is truly a frightful aberration when he loses it, as Europeans have seen in the most recent war.

There were degrees of this. Eating a man who has died a violent death in battle, even if that violence was your own, is perhaps not as dreadful as it is unappetizing. But killing a slave to cook (human flesh was never eaten raw) *is* dreadful, almost as much for the eater as for the eaten. The next logical step would be to roast your own hand.

There were children in the Congo who ate their aged parents, and no doubt parents who ate their children. A great many people, especially during wartime, thought of everyone they saw as a possible dinner. On one occasion two members of a squad of soldiers who were down with fever were cut up and smoked by their companions, as provisions for a march. And there were villages where everyone was young and vigorous and able to defend himself. The old, the cripples and the timid had been devoured, and it is terrible to think how lonely, as well as frightened, the survivors must have been.

This complete and conscious cannibalism, as distinguished from battle-scavenging, occurred more frequently among peoples with a high social development. Most Europeans acquainted with the subject, including that wonderfully garrulous old man, Trader Horn, agreed that cannibal villages were cleaner, more orderly and a good deal pleasanter than non-cannibal villages.

Captain Hinde, who was with the Belgian expedition of Baron Dhanis during the Arab Wars, mentions that the Maniema people seemed to be superior in everything but their avowed cannibalism. They even had recipes for cooking human flesh—a heart chopped up with goat meat, or a hash prepared with bananas. This meat had the advantage, they said, of being a bit salty, so that no other condiment was needed, and some grew so addicted to it that they would eat nothing else. During the war Hinde found a volunteer drummer-boy in a hut, with the half-consumed body of an enemy at his side, dead from over-eating.

The war actually began when Gongo Lutete, one of the Arabs' most important African allies and a former protégé of Tippu Tib, lost an engagement with Baron Dhanis and decided to change sides. The Arabs were enraged. They retaliated by murdering several Europeans in the Maniema at the time, one of whom was Emin Pasha, the man Stanley had gone to such pains to rescue.

The Arabs then organized a large army, numbering about ten thousand, armed with guns and swords, marched westward from the Lualaba River to attack Baron Dhanis and a few hundred troops. They were led by Tippu Tib's son, Sefu, and they demanded, literally, Gongo Lutete's head. The Baron brought along all of Gongo instead, with his men. Just before a skirmish on the Lomani River, it rained, and the caps of the Arab's guns were wet. Nearly helpless against the Europeans and Lutete's people, they panicked and about three thousand of them were killed. What was more important, the victors gained many new allies.

Successive victories gave them still more strength, and at last Commandant Dhanis felt able to attack Nyangwé, which he took in March 1893. Here the Arabs practised a sort of germ warfare by sending people with smallpox into their midst. A short while later Dhanis marched against Tippu Tib's son at Kasongo, up-river from Nyangwé, and captured the city immediately. The Arabs had withdrawn all of their goods to this town and the State troops slept on silk and satin mattresses and rejoiced in shower baths and other luxuries they had nearly forgotten.

In another battle, some months later, Sefu was killed and a strong Arab force from Ujiji was routed. Tippu Tib himself was apparently on his way back to Zanzibar at this time.

The war was now almost over and the Europeans, with their usual thoroughness, executed their faithful ally, Gongo Lutete, for suspected disloyalty. This had repercussions among his own people, who were without protection and therefore eligible for anybody's pot. Probably the allies of the defeated Arabs were in the same fix.

Surely, no Africans won that war. The two barely human creatures who had started it were destined to live out their nearly identical lifespans in egregious peace and luxury, one in Zanzibar and one in Brussels. For all the difference it made in their personal lives few could have noticed that Leopold II had gained an empire and Tippu Tib had lost one.

Leopold probably meant *his* rule of the Congo to be more enlightened, though he clearly never intended putting it on the rarefied moral plane his missionary supporters expected. Very likely he said to himself that if the pious frauds in the world were going around talking about the white man's burden he could do the same and do it better. Why should they grab all the choice plots with their hypocrisies?

For sixteen years, until his death in 1909, Leopold was as piously fraudulent as any man has succeeded in being before or since. He tirelessly rode the hobby of philanthropy, and when accused of personal ambitions he was a model of wounded dignity, and quickly got his side of the story to his supporters. He was probably the first man to set up an information bureau, on modern lines, to distribute misinformation.

His real trouble was money. Though the king was a rich man, and had made a fortune in Suez Canal shares, he wasn't rich enough for such an enormous undertaking. The Congo could be expected to pay for itself in time, and possibly a good deal extra. But, as France and England and Germany were discovering, a large initial investment had to be made and had

225

to be supplemented for many years before a colony became even self-supporting. These countries had the money to put up, when pressed; Leopold hadn't. Therefore, when normal methods of exploitation were insufficient the king resorted to abnormal ones.

Reports of atrocities had begun to reach Europe from the period directly following the Arab Wars, and as early as 1897 a recommendation was made in Britain's parliament for an International Conference to discuss the administration of the Congo. This was not necessarily presumptuous of the British, as they were one of the fourteen signatory powers of the Berlin Conference giving Leopold control of this territory, and a review of his administration should have been automatic.

Obviously the king was informed of this and any competent ruler would have checked into the charges carefully, if only to have the means to defend himself. There is now incontestable evidence that organized atrocities occurred on a frightful scale for at least fifteen years, and one must conclude that the King of Belgium deliberately and coldly killed millions of people for his personal profit. The Congo, at the beginning of his reign, had about twenty million inhabitants. There are now a few more than twelve million living there, seventy-five years later.

When rumours about the misgovernment of the Congo began to spread, missionary groups, both Protestant and Catholic, jumped to defend Leopold. He may have foreseen that they would prefer to spread the error themselves to facing the truth. It was certainly sinful that these normally warring factions of the Christian Church missed such a perfect chance for disagreement.

Their odious concord persisted until 1903, though appalling reports had been coming into the Home Executives of the societies for years. In those early days only one religious man, braving imprisonment, dared to confront Leopold's agents in the Congo and Leopold himself. He was a Swede named Sjöblom, and his courage and high spirit adorn his sect, which was American Baptist.

As the Protestants had less stake in the Congo than the Catholics, it is not surprising that they were the first to turn on Leopold, though their protest came so late that it did them little honour. The Catholics continued to support the king until 1905, when the report of a Belgian Commission of Inquiry was published and proved beyond all doubt that the charges were true. When one remembers that many Catholic missionaries had been sending in regular reports of these horrors for years, Roman timidity appears truly shameful.

Part of Leopold's success in perverting the Catholic Church in the Congo for so long was due to his insistence that priests sent there be Belgian. These were more subject to his control, as were their home societies. When, in 1903, the British Protestants began to reveal some of the things that were happening, Leopold suggested to the Roman Church that this was simply a religious attack on *them*. And so, at last, the Christian factions fell out just at the moment they should have been falling in.

Leopold also charged that Britain was preparing to take over the Congo. This may have been true. Surely it was so in 1908 and 1909. But the British were not the only ones spreading these reports, though the king managed to keep most of the others suppressed. French, Americans, Swiss, Danes and Germans had been saying the same things.

Even the Italians, a nation devoted neither to disinterested philanthropy nor to Great Britain, had begun to make semi-official protests. Of all the Europeans stationed in the Congo—Leopold had hired army officers of other nations for his own service—the Italians probably acted with the greatest personal bravery and sense of honour. Captain Baccari, a navy surgeon and royal Italian envoy to the Congo said that Italian officers in Leopold's private army were persecuted because they couldn't stomach what was going on. 'We have all the ghastly scenes of the slave trade,' he wrote, 'the collar, the lash, and press-gang.'

A young Italian lieutenant, who joined the king's army without knowing the nature of his work, wrote:

The caravan road between Kasongo and Tanganyika is strewn with corpses of carriers, exactly as in the time of the Arab slave trade. The carriers, weakened, ill, insufficiently fed, fall literally by hundreds; and in the evening, when there happens to be a little wind, the odour of bodies in decomposition is everywhere noticeable, to such an extent, indeed, that the Italian officers have given it a name—'Maniema perfume.'

The protests of these officers grew so strong that the Italian Government was at last moved to forbid all further recruitment, even among officers on the retired list. This should have refuted Leopold's habitual defence, that all attacks against him were made by sentimental grandmothers. No grandmothers on earth can be so mordantly unsentimental as the Italian ones.

Stanley, who for a while worked devotedly for Leopold as a sort of exalted publicist, called him a 'dreamer of dreams,' without ever mentioning what else he might dream. Leopold had big plans. For one thing, he wanted to conquer the Sudan, a land almost as vast as the Congo. He was nearly successful in this and was only stopped by the mutiny of one of his armies. He had little hope of keeping the Sudan, but he might have presided over its division between France and England and wrung concessions from both.

His real work was the Congo. A secret decree, dated 21 September 1891, was the turning-point of his policy. It laid down, as the paramount duty of the officials of the Free State, the collection of revenue. That wasn't exactly the way to start a philanthropic enterprise and this violation of his mandate as Head of State bore the seeds of the trouble to follow. The decree was followed by a series of regulations forbidding the natives to sell ivory and rubber to free European merchants and threatening the latter with prosecution if they bought them.

With the market sewed up, the king's agents were instructed to buy as cheaply as possible. A letter to Governor General Wahis, dated 20 June 1892, coming from Leopold's Secretary of State, offered up to fifty per cent bonus on the price of rubber, gum, copal and ivory if government agents could persuade natives to sell their goods at half-price. There was also a sliding scale given, with the bonus growing smaller as the cost of these articles went up. This was a direct incitement to robbery and violence, especially as the salaries of the agents were kept deliberately low.

But, so far, this was merely vicious commercial practice and a great many people in the last few years of the nineteenth century were doing the same.

Real trouble began when the Government's policies had the opposite effect to what was intended. Coercive methods produced indifferent and even rebellious workers. This was particularly true with rubber collections. Natives reacted to the lowered prices by adulterating the latex they brought in or by openly resisting requisitions. There was simultaneously a slump on the world rubber-market, and the Government, seeing revenues fall, demanded still more rubber at lower prices.

The pressure naturally increased as it descended the chain of command. A letter from the Governor General to Commandant Verstraeten in charge of the Rubi Welle zone read:

I close by advising you that the Government firmly hopes . . . you will exhibit a fresh proof of your activity and devotion, by making the district you command produce the maximum of resources which can be drawn from it.

Commandant Verstraeten, who knew perfectly well what was required of him, wrote to his subordinates:

I have the honour to inform you that from 1 Jan., 1899, you must succeed in furnishing 4,000 kilos of rubber every month. To this effect I give you *carte blanche*. You have, therefore, two months in which to work your people. Employ gentleness first, and if they persist in not accepting the imposition of the State employ force of arms.

At still a lower level of command this became a licence to murder. Armed bands of native troops were sent out to punish rebellious tribes. The Government was, as usual, methodical about this. They suspected, probably with reason, that the African troops were going into the forest, firing off cartridges, or, better yet, selling them, and coming back with tales of their own valour. Most stations therefore established the policy that expended bullets had to be accounted for by some part of the body of the victim, usually the right hand.

The logic was faultless except that less and less rubber came in and still greater pressure had to be applied as districts began to lose their population. Also, *hands* began to grow scarce and the troops turned on the women and small children. Roger Casement, the British Consul whose report rocked Leopold's empire at the end of 1903, collected photographs of little hands and feet in the lake district just below the present site of Coquilhatville.

These trophies were presumably taken from corpses, adults and children, but many people survived handless. From the *Domaine de la Couronne*, Leopold's private fief within his own state, Joseph Clark, an American, wrote in 1895:

The scenes I have witnessed while unable to help the oppressed have been almost enough to make me wish I were dead. The soldiers

are themselves savages, some even cannibals, trained to use rifles
... Imagine them returning from fighting some rebels (?) see on
the bow of the canoe is a pole, and a bundle of something on it.
These are the hands (right hands) of sixteen warriors they have
slain. 'Warriors!' Don't you see among them the hands of little
children and girls? I have seen them. I have seen where the trophy
has been cut off, while the poor heart beat strongly enough to
shoot the blood from the cut arteries at a distance of fully four feet.

At last, whole districts were almost deserted. In spite of the
fact that it had been made a crime to run away, death put the
workers out of the State's reach. Villages which once had
thousands of inhabitants were left with a pitiful few hundred
who were nevertheless expected to collect the rubber quota
assigned on the basis of the original population. The policy of
taking hostages was also established, so that a man could buy
back his wife or child only by collecting a specified amount of
rubber. These hostages were kept at Government stations in
miserable conditions and a great percentage of them died.

Mr E. J. Glave, a friend of Stanley's, published the following
account in the *Century* magazine in 1896:

In stations in charge of white men, Government officers, one sees
strings of poor, emaciated old women, some of them mere skeletons,
working from ten to six tramping about in gangs with a rope around
their necks and connected by a rope one and a half yards apart.
They are 'prisoners of war' . . . War has been waged all through the
district of the Equator, and thousands of people have been killed
and twenty-one heads were brought to Stanley Falls, and have been
used by Captain Rom as a decoration round a flower-bed in front of
his house.

Sjöblom, the Swedish missionary, wrote:

If the rubber does not reach the full amount required the sentries
attack the natives. They kill some and bring the hands to the
Commissioner. That was about the time I saw the native killed

before my own eyes. The soldier said, "Don't take this to heart so much. They kill us if we don't bring the rubber. The Commissioner has promised us if we have plenty of hands he will shorten our service." [These were often smoked to preserve them until they could be shown to the European officer.]

The Government stations wanted food for themselves as well as rubber and would lay a tax on the district's remaining inhabitants for it. So many chickens every week, so many kilos of manioc flour, vegetables, etc. The State soldiers had already despoiled the districts, however, and there was frequently no food of any kind to be had. This was not accepted as an excuse and the natives had to go many miles to buy articles, much more luxurious than they would think of eating themselves, to bring back to the stations. The demand naturally sent the prices up, and frequently they could only pay by selling members of their families into slavery, in order to save the rest.

There can be no doubt at all that the European officers were aware of what was going on and that *their* superiors were also aware. By 1905, when the official Commission of Inquiry confirmed the atrocities, a great many reports had come back to Europe and were pressed on people of influence in Brussels, who were urged to get to the king.

The generous assumption was that he knew nothing of what was going on. But even after the report of the Commission of Inquiry was issued—greatly abridged—the horrors continued and even increased and Leopold worked with more diligence to supress all reports from the Congo except those made by his own agents. In the words of Sir Harry Johnston, an explorer and advocate of colonial ventures in East Africa, he seemed, "indurated against the terror of an immortality of bad renown."

In 1905 an American named Kirby wrote:

The further away from publicity the greater the atrocities. I have heard much. I could tell much, but you know enough. A white officer forcing a native to drink from the water closet; shooting down handcuffed men; the employment of fierce cannibal soldiers that terrorise the people; shooting down twenty men to pay for a lost dog.

Some of these white officers were in as much of a trap as the natives. A man wasn't allowed to quit until his service was up and, as an Italian Officer said, "If he insists, and leaves his station, he can be prosecuted for desertion, and, in any case, will probably never get out of the country alive, for the routes of communication, victualling stations, etc., are in the hands of the Administration, and escape in a native canoe is out of the question—every native canoe, if its destination be not known and its movements chronicled in advance from post to post, is at once liable to be stopped, for the natives are not allowed to move freely about the controlled water-ways."

Nevertheless, human courage is, by definition, ready to rise to occasions that demand it. A number of officers in Leopold's army would not consent to follow the orders they were given. Among these was Commandant Scardino who mulishly insisted on running the district of Upoto in a business-like manner, keeping taxes down to the point where people could pay them and even lowering some in depressed areas. He also refused to terrorize the population and displayed his incompetence to serve the State in many other refreshing ways. Standing with him in spirit are a Belgian captain, a Danish Lieutenant and a man called Dooms, who appears to have been killed by a hippopotamus.

Since 1900 Leopold had been defending himself from the growing number of attacks, especially in England, by pointing out that before the Congo had started to be profitable no one had said anything about atrocities and that people were trying cynically to take his prize from him. It is even possible that his indignation at other people's cynicism was genuine. He may have begun to believe the stories his own press bureau was spreading.

As in most controversies, the clamour of battle often obscured the events. Only gradually did the facts come clear, or nearly so. A number of people before 1905—some of them obviously disinterested—were ready to swear (and to have their statements circulated by the king's press bureau) that nothing at all unusual was happening in the Congo. One would probably have to discount pronouncements by the king himself and his Governor General, Baron Wahis. There was also a captain in Leopold's army named Guy Burrows whose intrepid defence of his employer might easily have been in the line of duty. Even Henry Stanley, though perfectly incorruptible, is only muddling the issue when he comes to Leopold's aid by saying that if these charges had any foundation his majesty would have done something about them.

But there is other testimony less easy to discount—that of Mr Mohun, the American consul, Sir Harry Johnston (though he had changed sides by 1903), Mr Grey, an English engineer in Katanga, and the Reverend Verner, of the American Presbyterian Congo Mission. Mr Grey, for instance, said in the *Morning Post* in January 1903:[1]

For myself, I am convinced that during these last two years, at least in the Katanga districts, the European agents treated Central African natives justly and kindly, whenever possible.

The Reverend Verner said, in January 1899, also in the *Morning Post*:

I believe that the Congo administration is in general as well-intentioned and active as the means at the disposition of the govern-

[1] This, however, is a rough translation from the French, itself a translation from English. I have taken this quotation in defence of the Congo Free State Administration, and the other two which follow from a pro-Leopold book published in Brussels in 1903 by J. Lebègue & Cie. Bringing out such a work at that time was a little like praising Caesar in Rome and it is difficult to see why the author should have signed himself, timidly, 'a Belgian.'

ment permit. There have evidently been some isolated cases of reprehensible conduct and unpardonable methods used by government officers . . . but I do not believe that the central administration at Boma or at Brussels was the instigator of these acts.

And, most impressive of all, a certain Belgian Captain Lemaire, a man whose support was claimed by both pro- and anti-Leopold forces, says in *The Times* in 1901:

I am sceptical that there have been frequent and continual atrocities in the Congo . . . Strict orders have been given to responsible agents to inflict severe punishment for mistreatment of the natives and these orders are regularly carried out, but who can restrain the excesses of brute nature? All of the contracts with the natives, whether Congolese or of other tribes, are subjected to minute examination and often Europeans complain that the law shows more solicitude for the natives than for the whites.

By 1905 the Commission of Inquiry had confirmed many of the charges against Leopold, and the Belgian Parliament was asking very embarrassing questions of its constitutional sovereign. But the really damning report was made in 1903 by Roger Casement, the British Consul. In a sense, he was an ideal person to undertake an investigation of a subject which so deeply concerned the British. He was an ardent Irish nationalist, and probably no other high official has identified himself less with the government he represented. If his report served British acquisitive interests it is only because it also served the interests of humanity. Thirteen years later he proved his lack of partiality for the British by opposing them in Ireland so vigorously that he was hanged.

In view of Roger Casement's end, therefore, it would be extremely difficult to throw any doubt on his Congo report, which he presented to the government in London on 11 December 1903. Furthermore, his observations are confirmed in his diaries which were long unavailable because they contained such detailed revelations of his mauve love-life. These reinforce his report, first because they were obviously never intended to be published, and second because a man who can invent his politics still cannot invent his sexual habits and the two, in his diaries, are intertwined.

Unlike most other visitors to the Congo, Casement had a great deal of previous experience there, going back as early as 1884. He had also worked for a while for the Free State and had spent most of his subsequent life in Africa. He chose to investigate the Equator District, near present-day Coquilhatville, because it was the most productive and because he had visited the area in 1887.

One of the first things he noticed was the enormous population decrease. Tribes which had numbered forty or fifty thousand had shrunk to seven or eight thousand; villages which had formerly held six thousand people were reduced to a few hundred.

Casement took long statements from the natives wherever he went. When one reads them now the voices blend, and it is impossible to doubt that they are telling the truth.

"I ran away and left my mother and went with two old people who were running away, but we were caught, and the old people were killed, and the soldiers made me carry the baskets with the things these dead people had and the hands they cut off . . . They got my little sister and killed her and threw her into a house and set fire to the house . . ." Signed R. R.

After she had been a little while in the house with her little brother and sister she heard the firing of guns. When she heard that she took up her little sister and a big basket with a lot of native money in it, but she could not manage both, so she left the basket behind . . . the little boy ran away by himself. S. S. was . . . trying to make her sister walk, as she was very tired, but the little sister could not run away through weakness. While they were standing outside the soldiers came upon them and took them both. One of the soldiers said: "We might keep them both. The little one is not bad looking," but the others said: "No, we are not going to carry her all the way, we must kill the younger girl." So they put a knife through the child's stomach, and left the body lying there where they had killed it . . . At this town she found that they had caught three people, and among them was a very old woman, and the cannibal soldiers asked C. D. to give them the old woman to eat and C. D. told them to take her. Those soldiers took the woman and cut her throat, and they divided her and ate her. S. S. saw all this done . . . They cut the hands off those they had killed, and brought them to C. D.; they spread out the hands in a row for C. D. to see . . . The hands they had cut off they left lying, because the white man had seen them . . . S. S.'s mother was killed by soldiers, and her father died of starvation, or rather he refused to eat because he was bereaved of his wife and all the children. Signed S. S.

"Then my eldest sister called me: 'U. U., come here.' I went. She said: 'Let us run away because we have not anyone to take care of us . . .' When we were going on the way they killed ten children, because they were very small; they killed them in the water. Then they killed a lot of people, and they cut off their hands and put them into baskets and took them to the white man. He counted out the hands—200 in all; they left the hands lying. The white man's name was C. D. . . . On our way, when we were coming to P . . ., the soldiers saw a little child, and when they went to kill it, the child laughed, so the soldier took the butt of a gun and struck the child with it, and then cut off its head. One day they killed my half-sister and cut off her head, hands and feet because she had on rings. Her name was Q. Q. Q." Signed U. U.

In trying to check these stories Casement interviewed the chiefs of a great many villages, though the people often ran away at his approach. The consul himself found a young man, both of whose hands had been beaten off with the butt ends of rifles against a tree and another boy of eleven or twelve whose right hand was cut off at the wrist. Mutilation of hands had never been a custom in the country and was surely imported by the Europeans. The boy who lost his hand had been

237

wounded in a fight and said that while lying on the ground he had been

perfectly sensible of the severing of his wrist, but lay still fearing that if he moved he would be killed. In both these cases the Government soldiers had been accompanied by white officers whose names were given to me.

Though these atrocities are all very similar, the repetition of them adds a sickening dimension. There was a deliberate plan behind it all.

The soldiers took prisoner all the men left in the town, and tied them up. Their hands were tied very tight with native rope, and they were tied up outside in the open; and as it was raining very hard and they were in the rain all the time and all the night, their hands swelled, because the thongs contracted. V. V.'s hands had swollen terribly in the morning, and the thongs had cut into the bone . . . The soldiers seeing this, and that the thongs had cut into the bone, beat his hands against a tree with their rifles, and he was released. The white man, T. U. . . . . was drinking palm wine while the soldiers beat his hands with their rifle butts against the tree. His hands subsequently fell off . . .

This old woman (whose name was V. W.) had fled with her son, when he fell shot dead, and she herself fell down beside him—she supposed she fainted. She then felt her hand being cut off, but made no sign. . . . Of the fact of this mutilation and the causes inducing it there can be no shadow of doubt. It was not a native custom [before] . . . it was the deliberate act of the soldiers of a European administration, and these men themselves never made any concealment that in committing these acts they were but obeying the positive orders of their superiors.

This was nearly the first appearance in the world of a social institution we have come to know as forced-labour. It is to the twentieth century what slavery was to the nineteenth, and one of the most interesting things about it was this psychotic preoccupation with hands, which are the labourer's basic tool.

What is more, the hands were lifted without regard to sex or age—matters of great importance during the era of slavery. They were just working hands.

Policy in the Congo was made by Leopold and his governors, never by the Belgian Government or by the Belgian people. Since 1909 the administration of this land by the elected government has been as exemplary as it was once infamous. Opinion is nearly unanimous—and anyone there can see for himself—that the Belgians run the country with great skill, energy, and forbearance. They appear to be doing everything possible to wipe out the memory of the Free State. It is surprising, therefore, to see decent Belgians even today defend a king who was himself of another nationality (he was a German, related to both Queen Victoria and Prince Albert), and had very little contact with this democratic, industrious little country except to use it as a bank.

When Leopold got his twenty-five million francs from the Belgian Government he probably never intended to fulfil his part of the bargain and will the Congo to them. Soon after this, for instance, he established the *Domaine de la Couronne*, an area five times the size of Belgium, in the centre of the Congo; and after long denying that it existed he sought to have his rights there recognized as inalienable.

The king also divided the rest of the Congo into sections, for the purpose of classifying revenue. One part he set aside to pay administrative expenses, construct public works, etc. This was called the *Domaine Privé*. Other parts—vast tracts of land to the south, the north and the far-east—he leased to eight Congo companies, or trusts, which had been floated on the Belgian stock exchange and in which he had fifty per cent of the shares.

Of these companies, three were gigantic. In six years his

239

income from the ABIR Trust was estimated at nearly ten million francs. In another company his shares alone were worth thirty-two million francs. In still another, twelve and a half million; and in this company he also took fifteen per cent of the profits after they had reached a fixed point.

But Leopold's greatest financial innovation was forced-labour itself. This is essentially a method of levying taxes on people who have nothing, and it has come about in our century whenever large, undeveloped areas have been forced to bear immediate fruit, or when retarded economies have been brought suddenly into world competition. As the king philanthropically put it, '*Il leur faut soumettre les populations à des lois nouvelles dont la plus impérieuse comme la plus salutaire est assurement celle du travail.*'

This forced-labour was most profitable when it was used to cut rubber and it was therefore the rubber-producing areas that were hardest hit. The Belgian Commission of Inquiry described the process:

> In the majority of cases he [the native] must, every fortnight, go one or two days' journey, and sometimes more, to reach the place in the forest where he can find in fair abundance the rubber vine. There the gatherer passes some days in a miserable existence. . . He must take his harvest to the station of the Government or the company and it is only after that he returns to his village, where he can barely reside two or three days before a new demand is upon him.

A man had to devote about three hundred days a year paying taxes in this manner.

This system is more efficient in many ways than slavery because it becomes the worker's responsibility to feed and house himself; it abstracts from him only his time and his liberty. One wonders why it wasn't tried before. It depends to a great extent on modern communications and on methods of mass-extermination, and probably our world will see a great deal more of it, now that we have become so proficient at both.

The profits from the Congo were tremendous. In reporting receipts and expenditures, the king confined himself to the *Domaine Privé* and proudly showed, over fifteen years, a loss of about one million seven hundred and fifty thousand francs a year. This allowed him to claim, with royal modesty, 'considerable personal sacrifice.'

That was a lie. Sales estimates on the Antwerp market showed a net profit from the *Domaine Privé* alone of considerably more than fifty million francs during that period. What was more, in one decade the king was known to have taken ninety million francs out of the *Domaine de la Couronne.* When one adds the income from his company shares and the value of the shares themselves plus his indebtedness to the Belgian State, which reached two hundred and ninety-five million francs by 1904 and admittedly yielded by reinvestment another eighty million francs, one begins to have an idea of the size of his fortune. What is more, all these figures were conservative, because nothing else could be proved. He surely became one of the richest men in the world.

Perhaps feeling the weight of this he offered a thousand pounds to the Liverpool School of Tropical Medicine and, in a royal manifesto dated June 1906, a year after the Belgian Commission of Inquiry had made its report, he offered to spend twelve thousand pounds to fight sleeping sickness.

If God gives me that satisfaction [victory over sleeping sickness] I shall be able to present myself before His judgment-seat with the credit of having performed one of the finest acts of the century, and a legion of rescued beings will call down upon me His grace.

It is likely that a legion of beings was calling down on him something a good deal more tangible than grace. Even the Belgians themselves were beginning to be frightened as he invested his profits in *their* land. As one commentator said, when some of his domestic transactions were revealed, it looked "as if King Leopold aimed at using the proceeds of the Congo for turning Belgium into his private estate." At the same time, he was putting money into other promising estates, San Domingo, Bolivia, China and Persia.

Stanley was sincerely and typically dense when he chided a British audience for a latent scepticism and lack of sentiment towards Leopold and his projects. They could not, he told them, "appreciate rightly, because there are no dividends attached to it, this restless, ardent, vivifying and expansive sentiment which seeks to extend civilizing influence among the dark places of sad-browed Africa."

With all the respect one must have for Henry Stanley, it really is a shame that good, kind, unassuming Frank Pocock should have drowned below Stanley Pool while this well-intentioned sentimentalist survived.

CHAPTER NINETEEN

IT was possibly during his journey to the sea from Stanley Pool that the leader of the first expedition to travel the length of the Congo acquired the name *Bula Matari*, which means rock-breaker and, by modern extension, the Government. Along this stretch of water to the sea Stanley showed his usual tenacity and resolve. He knew that he was only a few hundred miles from the coast but the altitude measurement was 1,147 feet. At Nyangwé it has been 2,077 feet, which meant that they had lost only 930 feet since they had taken to the river. It also meant that there must be falls far worse than anything they had yet seen just below them.

The Expedition no longer had to worry about the tribes along their way. These were used to trade, and on the whole they were peaceful. But the great central plateau here drops off through sheer rock to the coastal plain. As the river courses over these terraces it creates a long series of falls, rapids and cataracts, which are completely unnavigable. The Congo itself had now become their bitterest enemy.

They developed a system of leashing their boats with rattan hawsers and holding them back from the rapids as they walked along the shore. This worked well enough on the smallest stretches of rough water but at many points they had to pull the boats out and carry them overland. At one of these cataracts the river fell from one immense trough to another, at times dashing up twenty or thirty feet straight into the air. Stanley described it:

If I looked up or down along this angry scene, every interval of 50 or 100 yards of it was marked by wave-towers—their collapse into foam and spray, the mad clash of watery hills, bounding mounds and heaving billows, while the base of either bank, consisting of a long line of piled boulders of massive size, was buried in the tempestuous surf. The roar was tremendous and deafening. I can only compare it to the thunder of an express train through a rock tunnel. To speak to my neighbour, I had to bawl in his ear.

In one bad piece of river they lost their best canoe, a seventy-five foot dug-out called the *London Town*. The water tore it from the hands of fifty men and swept it away. Along the shore they were often impeded by the rock, and several of them had bad falls, including Stanley, who nearly broke a couple of ribs. They now had seventeen canoes. The river at this point was not more than four hundred and fifty yards wide but even very close to the shore it was one hundred and thirty-eight feet deep. At the falls which came inevitably at the foot of this silent stretch of water eight men were caught by the current and drowned. One of these was Kalulu, the slave boy Stanley had brought to America and, later, put to school in England. He named these falls after him and was very grieved.

On 3 April 1877, a canoe was upset and they lost fifty tusks of ivory and some trading beads. Four men were saved from drowning by Uledi, and Stanley himself was almost carried down-river by the current. They were making progress, however slow, but their supplies were dwindling so fast that they could not expect to reach the sea without starving to death unless every person worked as hard as possible every daylight hour.

Then, on April 12 the Expedition's European boat, the *Lady Alice*, containing most of their wealth and the leader himself, tore loose from its cables and spun through rapids for several miles before it was shunted miraculously into calm water and they were saved. The other members of the party had run after them but for several hours they feared that Stanley was

244

lost. They were overjoyed to find him. These men had been living together for almost three years and many of them were genuinely fond of each other.

They

rushed up one after another with their exuberant welcome to life which gushed out of them in gesture, feature, and voice. And Frank, my amiable and trusty Frank, was neither last nor least in his professions of love and sympathy, and gratitude to Him who had saved us from a watery grave.

On April 13 Uledi the coxwain saved still another man from drowning. He was becoming the most valuable member of the Expedition. By the 21st they were still only thirty-four miles below Stanley Pool, though they had been travelling five weeks. A few days later they came upon a great falls which plunged through a chasm and was absolutely impassable. What was worse, the banks rose steeply on either side and they, too, were impassable. Stanley decided to drag his canoes over a mountain, one thousand two hundred feet high.

Several of their boats were seventy feet long, carved out of teak, so that they weighed over three tons. Stanley needed help for the portage but he could not convince the natives of the neighbourhood that the job *could* be done until he and his men cut a path and hauled some of the smaller boats up themselves. When this was accomplished the chiefs were full of admiration and agreed to lend him six hundred men to help him with the big canoes.

The latter were moved over the mountain at a rate of five hundred to eight hundred yards a day. In the meantime Stanley established a camp below the falls and hollowed out two enormous trees to replace the canoes that had been lost. These craft were called the *Livingstone* and the *Stanley* and were ideal, in calm water, for taking up bold postures in their prows, staring resolutely into the unknown, and imagining the wood-cuts in the book one would write.

They had now come into the territory of the Babwendé, who were most friendly. These people had many guns and plenty of gunpowder. They also had Delft ware, British crockery, galvanized iron spoons, Birmingham cutlery, glassware and European salt. All of this had come from the coast, though no one among these people had ever seen a European. They simply bought what the tribes directly below had for sale. These articles were fairly abundant and even cheap.

Food prices went way up. They could no longer buy a chicken with cloth because the natives had so many trading goods themselves. Frank and Stanley, therefore, had to give up anything resembling European victuals and they lived entirely on the provisions normally consumed by the rest of the caravan. What was worse, for Stanley, was that they had run out of tea. He could hardly bear to do without it and used to dream of three tins he had left behind at Nyangwé.

In the midst of their troubles the leader found time to rebuke his young assistant for frequently appearing in camp barefoot.

I would reprove him for shamelessly exposing his white feet to the vulgar gaze of the aborigines! In Europe this would not be considered indelicate, but in barbarous Africa the feet should be covered as much as the body; for there is a small modicum of superiority shown even in clothing the feet.

Good Frank was indifferent to this modicum, after having lived so long with these men. But Stanley was inadvertently right, as he was so often. From about this time the boy began to develop ulcers on his feet and this was the indirect reason for his death a month later. They were all nearly starving, now, and many of the men were plagued by ulcers, dysentery and fever. They ate mostly dried cassava and peanuts.

Stanley, whose sensual life was primarily digestive, prepared a kind of green porridge of manioc tops, much as Epis's sister had. To this he added crushed nuts, salt and palm wine. The mixture was fried and served on the only Delft plate the beleaguered Expedition had left. Both Frank and Stanley said grace before they ate it.

On May 25, Stanley was standing above a short stretch of rapids,

pondering unspeakable things, as I listened to the moan and plaint of the tortured river, when Frank came down in the *Lady Alice* and nearly wrecked her on a rock. "Ah, Frank! Frank! Frank!" I cried, "my boat, my poor boat, after so many thousands of miles, so many cataracts, to receive such a blow as this, on a contemptible bit of rapids like the Upper Mowa!" I could have wept aloud; but the leader of an Expedition had but little leisure for tears, or sentiment, so I turned to repair her.

Frank Pocock seemed to be going the way of all Stanley's companions. In spite of his formidable resistance he was becoming, at last, a physical, if not a moral wreck. This was especially serious for the boy, who had few other resources; he did not live much in the world of the mind and had probably never pondered an unspeakable thing. He was already confined to the boat; his ulcers had grown so severe that he could walk only with difficulty and his control was slipping fast.

At this time an event occurred which shook Stanley. His Victorian standards were as incomprehensible to the men of the Expedition—except Frank—as though he had come from the moon. Uledi had, by that time, saved thirteen persons from drowning.

He was not a tall man; he was short, and of compact frame; but every ounce of his strength he devoted to my service . . . He was a devotee to his duty, and as such he was ennobled; he was affectionately obedient, as such he was beloved; he had risked his life many times for creatures who would never have risked their own for

247

his, as such he was honoured. Yet—this ennobled, beloved and honoured servant—ah! I regret to speak of him in such terms— *robbed me.*

There was a great fuss about this and a public trial followed at which others put themselves forward to take Uledi's punishment. In the end everyone was forgiven and the entire camp retired, not quite sure what standards were being applied to them but perfectly certain that *some* were and maybe even comforted by that. They were all so near death, anyway, it was good to have something to think about.

In this district the natives once observed Stanley writing in his notebook and became justifiably alarmed. Warriors were immediately called to arms. The leader bravely approached them and asked what was the matter. One of the chiefs said, "Our people saw you yesterday make marks on some tara-tara [paper]. This is very bad. Our country will waste, our goats will die, our bananas will rot and our women will dry up. What have we done to you that you should wish to kill us?"

This was very prophetic; the people naturally demanded that Stanley burn his notebook. If he did not, they said, they would fight him. The leader thought quickly and went back to his tent, where he found a copy of Shakespeare (Chandos edition), brought it back and offered it up to the fire. To anyone who has ever read *Through the Dark Continent,* or *The Sources of the Nile Around The Great Lakes of Equatorial Africa and Down the Livingstone River to the Atlantic Ocean,* this will seem one of the most unfair acts of barter ever practised by a European on gullible aborigines.

On the night of June 2, Frank came to Stanley's tent, as was his custom. He was now almost completely crippled by his ulcers and could do no other work than sewing up bead-bags and patching tents. He maintained his cheerful attitude, possibly because it was the only one he had. While at work, his fine voice broke out into song, or some hymn such as he was accustomed to sing in Rochester Church. Joyous and light-hearted as a linnet, Frank indulged forever in song, and this night the crippled man sang his best, raising his sweet voice in melody, lightening my heart, and for the time dispelling my anxieties.

The next day he drowned.

Frank died because he had been left behind as a cripple, to be carried overland past a set of rapids in a hammock. This affront to his manliness was more than his stout heart could bear and, after Stanley had gone on ahead, he insisted on travelling the dangerous stretch of water with Uledi and several of the other men. He was, as Stanley said, 'a capital swimmer' besides being an English boatman of good character. Obviously a fellow who could handle the Medway or Thames wouldn't let the Congo scare him. So he ordered the boat on, over the rapids and to his death, though Uledi and most of the others escaped.

He had probably become unhinged. Frank had very few hinges anyway, and one of these was his robust health. He didn't know how to be a cripple and his life was so simple that it was also immutable. Eagle scouts are in this sense like angels. They cannot be devious or sly; they cannot, in the end, be anything but eagle scouts or angels. So poor Frank was drowned in a sea of his own virtue, which was appropriately called Pocock Basin. His body was found some days later and Stanley was grief-stricken.

"Shall you see him again?" one of the head men of a local tribe asked Stanley.

"I hope to."

"Where?"

"Above, I hope."

Frank's loss was not only a blow to Stanley but to all the

other men. They were not just being sentimental—they had got to depend on the two Europeans and didn't want to do without them, at least until they reached the coast. Now that the boy was drowned they felt that much closer to death themselves. It took Stanley almost two weeks to get them started again.

He, too, was greatly depressed; he had been deeply fond of Frank. But the more they lingered here the greater was the danger for all of them. Supplies were rapidly giving out. When he tried to push his people forward they threatened mutiny. Once, when he saw a group of them moving about languidly he asked what was the matter.

One fellow, remarkable for nothing but his great size and strength, turned round and said, sharply, "We are tired, and that's what's the matter."

Thirty-one of the party deserted, but Stanley put so many obstacles in their path—instructing chiefs not to give them food, etc.—that they returned in a few days and went back to work, having really no alternative. At this point the chief carpenter, Salaam Allah, was swept over another falls in one of the new canoes and the whole camp was thrown into deep gloom, sensing the approach of death.

At the end of June, at another stretch of rapids, Stanley's boat again broke loose and was spun downstream out of sight. The men of the Expedition were sure that he was lost this time and they didn't much care, believing that they were all bound to follow him anyway. But when he came back along the shore, some of them argued that God *was* watching over this aggressive little man after all, and that they might just make it if they stuck with him. Stanley won most of his battles with such perseverance. It may even be that God, in His wisdom, had intended him to go the way of poor Frank Pocock; the leader simply outwaited Him.

By July 7 they were in truly desperate circumstances. The men had been stealing in the villages along the way, and when they were caught the Expedition had to ransom them or they would be sold into slavery. At last their supplies were so reduced that Stanley announced that anyone else caught stealing would be abandoned. Two people died at this time, one of suppurating ulcers and the other of dysentery, a disease that was beginning to attack large numbers of them.

They met some people whose complexions and features were faintly European and who were probably mixed with the Portuguese who had been on this coast since the latter part of the fifteenth century. These people, having a genetical knowledge of the matter, did not welcome a white man in their country. They said that they had never known a place that wasn't injured by the presence of people with light skins.

On July 20 and 24 two more of the party were caught stealing and now the expedition had to abandon them because they did not have supplies enough for ransom. Also, the next day, one of the men went insane and ran off into the forest, but Stanley could not stop even a day to search for him because they were all in immediate danger of starvation. On the 28th three more men were caught stealing food and were abandoned. One of these men, Ali Koboga, later escaped and made his way to the coast where he hitched rides all the way around Africa, home to Zanzibar.

At the end of July they decided to abandon the boats and strike out overland for the port of Embomma, where there were Portuguese traders. Stanley divided up his remaining stores among the men so that they could purchase food, but they got very little for their money because the prices were so inflated near the coast. Only rum and guns were considered valuable, and in another few days they were so weak from lack

251

of food that it seemed that they would never reach the sea, though help was now only a few miles away.

Finally Stanley persuaded a chief to carry a letter forward. After a dinner of three fried bananas, twenty roasted peanuts and a cup of muddy water, he wrote the following letter by the light of a lamp made of rotted sheeting dipped in palm-butter:

Village of Nsanda, August 4, 1877

To any Gentleman who speaks English at Embomma

Dear Sir,

I have arrived at this place from Zanzibar with 115 souls, men, women, and children. We are now in a state of imminent starvation. We can buy nothing from the natives, for they laugh at our kinds of cloth, beads, and wire. There are no provisions in the country that may be purchased, except on market days, and starving people cannot afford to wait for these markets . . . I am told there is an Englishman at Embomma, and as you are a Christian and a gentleman, I beg you not to disregard my request . . . [I want] fifteen man-loads of rice or grain to fill their pinched bellies immediately . . . The supplies must arrive within two days, or I may have a fearful time of it among the dying. Of course I hold myself responsible for any expense you may incur in this business . . . For myself, if you have such little luxuries as tea, coffee, sugar, and biscuits by you, such as one man can easily carry, I beg you on my own behalf that you will send a small supply . . . I beg you to believe me,

Yours sincerely,
H. M. Stanley,
Commanding Anglo-American
Expedition for Exploration
of Africa.

P.S. You may not know me by name; therefore I add, I am the person that discovered Livingstone in 1871, H.M.S.

On August 6 a reply came back.

6:30 A.M.,

Boma, 6th August 1877

Embomma,

English Factory.

H. M. Stanley, Esq.

Dear Sir,

Your welcome letter came to hand yesterday at 7 P.M. As soon as its contents were understood, we immediately arranged to despatch to you such articles as you requested . . . The carriers are all paid, so that you need not trouble yourself about them. That is all we need say about business. We are exceedingly sorry to hear that you have arrived in such piteous condition, but we send our warmest congratulations to you, and hope that you will soon arrive in Boma (this place is called Boma by us, though on the map it is Em-bomma). Again hoping that you will soon arrive, and that you are not suffering in health,

> Believe us to remain,
> Your sincere friends,
> Hatton & Cookson.
> A. Da Motta Veiga.
> J. W. Harrison.

That was about all. When Stanley approached Boma he was greeted by Mr A. da Motta Veiga, Senhores Luiz Pinto Marco, João Chaves, Henrique Germano Faro, and Mr J. F. Muller. These gentlemen persuaded him to ride the last bit in a hammock, which the Leader at first declined to do, until he was assured that it was a Portuguese custom. He arrived in the town on August 9 and reached the Atlantic ocean on the 12th.

Here Stanley turned back and looked at the mighty river

on whose brown bosom we had endured so greatly . . . I felt my heart suffused with purest gratitude to Him whose hand had protected us, and who had enabled us to pierce the Dark Continent from east to west, and to trace its mightiest River to its Ocean bourne.

The one hundred and fifteen persons, including thirteen

women, who had survived with him were just looking forward, unable to believe their good luck. But of course they were not planning to write a best-selling book about their experiences one thousand and eighty-eight pages long.

CHAPTER TWENTY

THE business quarter of Leopoldville, capital of the Belgian Congo, is a big, insipid, glass-fronted, many-storied European city. All the stores along the main avenue look like airline offices and many are. Their murals and receptionists seem cut from the same sheet of plastic. Native handicraft is exhibited with self-conscious taste and the furniture is designed to meet the standards of a century which expects to be the world's last. Everything lacks weight and yet manages to be terribly heavy. Nothing is light though it looks as if it were about to slide off into space. It is like every other city built in the last quarter-century, practically anywhere on this planet, and it really wouldn't be fair to blame it all on the Belgians.

Outside of the business quarter there are masses of Africans, drifting. They stand further from their origins and are not so simple as their countrymen in Stanleyville or Albertville. Even the tribes they claim to represent, in anarchic nostalgia for order, were strangers to Stanley Pool until recently. In Stanley's time this site was dotted with villages of the Bateke. The present inhabitants claim descent from the Bakongo and the Bangala tribes and war among themselves when they are not demonstrating against the Europeans. To make matters more confused a number of recent manifestos urging independence were probably written or largely inspired by a group of Belgian Catholic professors at the University of Lovanium, near Leopoldville. In short, one finds the fascinating confusion endemic to all large cities.

But this great pack of cement is not yet perfectly at ease here on the south bank of Stanley Pool. Squalls of rain still come

255

down from the hills and race over the water, streaking the air silver and purple. The sun still dies a pink death over French Africa in the west, and snow-white birds glide a few feet above the water with their black-fringed tails trailing downward like fans, as they did thousands of years before the motor launches came to frighten the fish. The battle isn't won yet and the jungle may have some surprises. All one can ask is that Nature hold out long enough until we do a little better. Here particularly, there is always a hope—a faint hope—that the Africans will find a way, and that when they put down a pavement from Lake Chad to Katanga it will be worthy of the land they tear up, and of themselves.

The morning after we arrived I saw Epis's daughter. I had gone directly to the post office. It wasn't yet open and I had coffee in a bakery, where I met Ann—twenty years from now. She was a large, quiet, voluptuous girl who did light dusting and occasionally handled the cash with soft sensuality. She was very fat and moved like a fully freighted ship bound for some leisurely port. I think Epis would have been happy to see her, though the figure she cut was less noble than contented.

Epis *had* been noble, and because of that it was a temptation to think that she represented a mass of African men and women; but probably she represented no one but herself. Few people can do much more, or even much less. Of course, she was passionately engaged in her fight for freedom—in her own way and for her particular ends—and surely a great many in her land have the same feeling, but this is no more revealing than to say that she was breathing. Apparently none of us is typical except when we are seen from a great distance. That complicates matters hopelessly, but at least one finally knows what Africans are *really* like. They are variations of oneself. That hardly simplifies, of course, but it makes questions more familiar and puts the answers to hand. When I took my change from the young woman in the bakery I smiled and Ann smiled back, languidly.

I sent a telegram from the post office, as I had promised. It reached Epis safely, I learned from a letter she wrote later.[1] Stanleyville already seemed very far away and I could only faintly hear the clang of electric guitars.

Late that night, walking back to the hotel, I saw the rear yard of a house brilliantly lit on an otherwise dark street. Going part way up the drive to the house one could see to the back. I did this because it had seemed from a distance that a number of naked men were prancing around before a few fully dressed women seated in wicker chairs.

When I came closer the men proved to have on little flesh-coloured tights. They were flexing their muscles with great ostentation and occasionally they picked up large weights and raised them above their heads. The women said little and seemed very bored. I supposed it was ladies' night in some sort of male health club. All the men were luminously white.

Then another pedestrian appeared at my side. He was an African, well-dressed but without a tie, as it was very hot. He, too, watched the muscular men for a while then said, half under his breath:

"*Formidable!*"

"*Oui.*"

"*On fait le Tarzan, n'est-ce pas?*"

"*Oui.*"

---

[1] Dear Thomas
How are you on this many days that I do not see you   I my self   I am very well thanks   How do you do?   Thanks so very much for your telegram from Leo   I was very glad to see telegram from you   Happy xmas and new years   Good Bye I have a Belgian bicycle   Epis

He turned to me and nodded, just slightly.

"*Bon soir, m'sieu.*"

"*Bon soir.*"

He went down the street, talking to himself.

THOMAS STERLING

Born in Colorado in 1921, Thomas Sterling spent the greater part of his childhood in Nebraska. When he was thirteen, he moved with his mother to New York City, where they made their home. He has lived in Rome for the past nine years with his wife Claire (who is Mediterranean correspondent for the *Reporter* magazine) and two children, next to their neighboring continent of Africa, where he says he feels "very much at home." His fascination with that continent began in 1956, when as a tourist he traveled through the Sudan. After his next trip, into Central Africa, he began writing the first part of *Stanley's Way*. Mr. Sterling has published five books, including *Silent Siren, The Evil of the Day* and *Strangers and Afraid*.